When You Don't Know Where to Turn

When You Don't Know Where to Turn

A Self-Diagnosing Guide to Counseling and Therapy

Steven J. Bartlett, Ph.D.

CONTEMPORARY
BOOKS, INC.
CHICAGO ■ NEW YORK

Library of Congress Cataloging-in-Publication Data

Bartlett, Steven J.
   When you don't know where to turn.

   Bibliography: p.
   1. Psychotherapy.   2. Counseling.   3. Consumer
education.   I. Title.
RC460.B28   1987   616.89'14   87-20045
ISBN 0-8092-4829-8

Published by Contemporary Books, Inc.
180 North Michigan Avenue, Chicago, Illinois 60601
Manufactured in the United States of America
Library of Congress Catalog Card Number: 87-20045
International Standard Book Number: 0-8092-4829-8

Published simultaneously in Canada by Beaverbooks, Ltd.
195 Allstate Parkway, Valleywood Business Park
Markham, Ontario L3R 4T8 Canada

This book is dedicated to Karen,
my love, wife, and friend.

CONTENTS

BEFORE WE BEGIN . . .

- A recent study by the National Institute of Mental Health shows that one American in five suffers from some type of psychiatric disorder: 50.5 million Americans have one or another of eight serious psychiatric disorders, ranging from anxiety disorders and phobias to depression and schizophrenia.
- Of these, only one person in five seeks professional help. More than 40,400,000 severely troubled people do not receive any treatment.
- An unknown number of healthy, emotionally untroubled Americans enter therapy for reasons of self-development.
- More than 130 distinguishable therapies now exist.
- These therapies are offered by a variety of health care professionals, including social work counselors, clinical and counseling psychologists, psychiatrists, biofeedback therapists, and others. Their backgrounds, training, fees, and durations of treatment vary considerably.
- These professionals practice in a number of different settings: in private practice, group sessions, public and private agencies, hospitals, newly established nonhospital

inpatient facilities, and in the context of educational programs.

- Most people who enter therapy do not know what alternative approaches to therapy exist or how to choose among them. They usually locate a therapist in a more or less random way.

- Most people fear the idea of entering counseling or psychotherapy. They do not have a clear conception of what to expect: they do not know in advance what the *experience* of therapy is like.

- For a variety of reasons, many people who think of going to a therapist are concerned about whether their relationship with the therapist will really be confidential. If you are especially concerned about privacy, you should be aware of several ways that confidentiality may be broken, what the laws concerning confidentiality are, and, in particular (what few people realize), how insurance claims for psychological care can invade an individual's privacy.

- Counselors and therapists tend to specialize in one or a small number of alternative approaches to therapy. Some approaches to therapy are most appropriate for treating certain problems or responding to certain personal interests; others are better suited to providing help with other problems and concerns. Choosing a therapist with an orientation that is right for *you* can be extremely helpful and can help you save much time, money, and energy.

These facts highlight the situation in counseling and psychotherapy that anyone faces who enters therapy today.

From them, you can see that there is a bewildering array of counseling professions, of distinct approaches to therapy, and of settings in which help is offered. This guide's intention and hope is to help you understand the alternatives, and to help you form your own judgment how it may be best to proceed.

The book hopes to give you real assistance so you may make a good choice—thereby saving you emotional investment, time, money, and the potential discouragement of avoidable false starts with therapies that may not help because they are not relevant to your goals, values, and personality.

Be patient. Take the time to think about yourself, your life, and your hopes for a better life. This book was written for you, to help you to improve your life, your self-esteem, and your relationships with others. They are worthy goals.

Nothing in this world can mean as much.

May you have the energy, courage, and perseverance to achieve them!

ACKNOWLEDGMENTS

I would like to express my gratitude to Dr. William Altus, then Professor of Psychology at the University of California, Santa Barbara, who went out of his way to encourage my first interests in psychotherapy when I was a graduate student there twenty years ago. To Professor Paul Ricoeur, I would like to express my admiration for his original contributions to Freud scholarship and my enduring gratitude for his willingness to direct my doctoral research at the Université de Paris.

I am indebted to Dr. Raphael Becvar, Professor, Marriage and Family Therapy, Saint Louis University, both for making it possible for a faculty colleague to learn from him in several of his excellent seminars and for his later comradeship. To my good friend, Dr. Thomas Maloney, clinical psychologist in Clayton, Missouri, I want to extend my warmest appreciation for his personal guidance and voluntary supervision of my first efforts in counseling. If ever the qualities of compassion, depth of understanding, humor, and genuine care are to be found in one person, they are in him. I would also like to thank Professor Lillian Weger, George Warren Brown School of Social Work, Washington University, St. Louis, for generously welcoming me into her fine seminar in psychodynamic models.

I especially thank Dr. Renate Tesch and Professor Hallock Hoffman, of the Psychology Faculty of the Fielding Institute in Santa Barbara, for making possible a writer's retreat in the California desert: the loan of their home in Sky Valley made writing the last group of chapters a special and memorable pleasure. One is fortunate to have such friends.

If this book became more readable after its first draft, it was due in great part to the conscientious energy of my wife, Karen, in spotting the weeds of obfuscation that seem to grow effortlessly in an academic's garden. I want to thank her for her patience, with both me and the book.

I would also like to take this opportunity to thank Miss Libby McGreevy, Assistant Editor, Contemporary Books, Inc., for her helpful suggestions and for her regular doses of encouragement that made writing this book a happy experience.

When You
Don't Know
Where
to Turn

THE PURPOSE OF
THIS BOOK

I would like to introduce this book by telling you what happened to a real and likable person who ran into some very difficult times and as a result entered therapy.

Frank is a large man, a former college football player, powerfully built. He has always prided himself on his strength and determination. He used to be friendly and outgoing. He had a pleasant smile, complemented by his clear blue eyes.

Frank had worked for eleven years for a manufacturer of tools. Not long ago, he was promoted to the position of managing the company's sales division in a large midwestern city. Soon after Frank and his wife moved, his wife became pregnant with their third child. Frank had a well-paying job, excellent benefits, a pleasant home they had just bought, and a contented relationship with his wife. But in spite of these things, he became severely depressed. And he began to feel terribly frightened: he had to leave his desk several times each morning and again in the afternoon. He would go to the men's room, lock the door, turn on the water faucets, and cry.

Frank lost fifteen pounds in three months. He had a poor appetite, slept badly, and was very anxious around his co-workers. He couldn't understand what had happened to him, and he was unwilling to let others know how unhappy he felt. He was ashamed of what he took to be a weakness in himself: like many men, he was raised to believe that men shouldn't cry, and his crying bouts shook his sense of identity and stability. His marriage began to suffer. Frank and his wife seldom made love. Frank was irritable and impatient with his wife and his children. Frank's wife knew he was very troubled, but he refused to talk to her about it.

For several months, Frank fought against his depression. (If only he had been aware of the *strength* that he mustered to do this!) Then he reached a crisis and could not force himself to go to work. He stayed home with a bad cold, slept as much as he could, and was very short-tempered. He was crying a good deal.

Frank's wife persuaded him to see a doctor. The doctor referred him to a psychiatrist. The psychiatrist saw Frank twice a week for two-and-a-half months, but Frank was troubled by side effects from the antidepressant medication he took under the psychiatrist's supervision. He resisted the idea of "taking drugs," so he decided to see a psychotherapist who, in cooperation with the psychiatrist, monitored Frank's condition as he gradually went off the antidepressants.

However, after five months, Frank did not feel he was making any real progress. He changed to another therapist who, his wife had heard, specialized in the treatment of depression.

Together, Frank and his new therapist came, over a period of months, to recognize that Frank's depression had resulted from two conflicts: Frank had hated his job but had refused to admit this to himself, and now his wife was pregnant again, and because of this added financial responsibility he felt forced to stay with his present job, where he had seniority, good salary, and benefits.

Once the basis for his depression was made clear, it was possible to begin to treat Frank's problem. His wife was very willing to encourage him to plan for a change of jobs, even though this would mean a temporary reduction in his income. Frank saw a vocational therapist and received guidance that led him to take some evening classes and then to become a computer programmer for a rapidly growing local company. His depression faded away, and he now seems genuinely to be content.

WHAT YOU CAN EXPECT FROM THIS BOOK

I knew Frank personally, as his therapist in a group. (His name, like all others in this book, has been changed, along with certain details about his situation.) With professional help, Frank was able to improve his life—his sense of self-esteem, his marriage, and his family life. It was a long and painful process, as much self-change can be. But perhaps Frank's experience might have been *less* painful, perhaps Frank might have felt less devastating isolation, and perhaps his path to a resolution of his difficulties could have been shortened if a practical guide to counseling and therapy had been available to him when he first decided to find help.

MAKING INTELLIGENT CHOICES

This book is about how you can get the most appropriate kind of help for your problems, goals, and personality. Specifically, *When You Don't Know Where to Turn* sets out to help you become adequately informed about the range of therapists and therapies—*as these relate to your own assessment of your goals and interests*—so that you will be able to make intelligent decisions about these issues:

- the *kind of professional* to seek out
- the *type of therapy* most likely to help you with a certain complaint or set of interests and values
- how to locate the form of therapy that seems most promising to you at *a price you can afford* and with *an expected duration* you can live with
- what *setting* to look for in which the help you would like is offered

This book uses two approaches, both presented here for the first time and both based on common sense and intelligent advance planning.

First, you will be able, through a series of carefully organized questions and easily followed instructions in Part I, to pinpoint one or more approaches to therapy that may be most promising given your initial objectives, problems, or interests. For the first time, a *self-diagnosing map* to the major approaches to therapy is made available.

Second, you will have the opportunity to glimpse what typically happens during the sessions of counselors, psychologists, and psychiatrists as they treat clients or patients using the different main approaches to therapy. You will come to see what the *experience* of therapy is like in these different approaches.

In other words, the self-diagnosing map will point you in the direction of one, and sometimes more than one, approach to therapy that may be most promising for you to begin the process of self-change, and you will then be able to gain an insider's perspective on that approach so that you can judge how well suited to you the approach is and how it compares to the other main approaches to therapy.

If this guide helps you choose a path to the kind of therapy that will be appropriate and useful to you, it will have done something worthwhile. A guide to counseling and psychotherapy should, however, do more than this.

OVERCOMING ISOLATION AND GETTING STARTED

People who are troubled tend to try to hide it. They frequently isolate themselves when they are distressed, so overcoming the desire to withdraw is the first order of business if they are to improve their lives and feelings.

One of the things this book sets out to do is to help you see that very likely the problems you are facing are not one of a kind. You have a lot of company; the difficulties you are having are probably very familiar to counselors and therapists. Realize that there *are* ways of resolving most problems and that doing so often is easier with the sympathy, empathy, moral support, friendship, or direction of a counselor or therapist than by yourself.

CAN YOU HELP YOURSELF?

However, sometimes it *is* possible to help yourself a great deal through your own initiative. This book will describe ways that you can be your own source of help and will pay particular attention to *when* it may be appropriate and safe to rely upon inner resources.

CLEARING THE CONFUSING JUNGLE

Most people are not familiar with the differences among the main kinds of "psychosocial" helping professionals — the various types of counselors, clinical psychologists, psychiatrists, psychotherapists, psychoanalysts, social workers, etc. Another purpose of this book is to clarify these labels, to describe how the approaches used by their practitioners are distinct and how they are similar, and to give an idea of how their fees and durations of treatment vary.

Individual chapters in Part II are devoted to describing the main varieties of therapy available today: psychoanalysis; psychotherapies; behavior-changing therapies; marriage and family therapy; group therapies; exercise, biofeedback, relaxation, hypnosis, and meditation; and drug therapy. Each approach will be described in the context of experiencing professional help *and* in terms of how and when it may be possible to apply the approach on your own. These chapters will help you understand what in general to expect if you choose a particular kind of treatment, how the course of treatment may go, and what point of view is shared by professionals who use it.

FINDING SOMEONE TO HELP

Part III of this book will describe how you can go about locating good professional care, whether from a family therapist, an analyst, a social worker, a psychiatrist, a clinical psychologist, or another kind of therapist. You will learn how you can find a reputable professional with a particular specialization, and you will be encouraged to ask him or her some useful questions before beginning treatment.

As we will see in detail later on, there are numerous settings in which counselors and therapists work. Many are in private practice, but many also work for a variety of agencies, both public and private, for hospitals and newly established nonhospital residential facilities, and even for educational institutions. We will discuss each of these settings in Part III so that you will have a clear idea both of the alternatives that exist and of important factors to consider when deciding among them.

SHOULD YOU BE HOSPITALIZED?

"Should I consent to hospitalization?" "What will I encounter if I accept hospitalization?" "Is it necessary, is it desirable?" Another chapter in Part III is devoted to answering these and related questions.

IS YOUR PRIVACY PROTECTED?

In many ways it will be, and in other ways it may not be. Confidentiality as it relates to the treatment of emotional or psychological difficulties is a thorny issue, one that worries many people. In Part III, a chapter is devoted to a discussion of this potentially important area of personal concern.

DOES THERAPY WORK?

You may, of course, feel a certain amount of skepticism about the real utility and effectiveness of any one of the many therapies that now exist. This is, in my judgment, a healthy skepticism. A chapter in Part III will review what you may be able to expect, and perhaps should not expect, in the light of recent evaluations of the effectiveness of the main therapies. To complement these as yet incomplete scientific findings, I will emphasize a measure of ordinary common sense as we go along.

LIFE AFTER THERAPY

The last chapter in this book deals with what to expect *after* therapy. Recurrences, future crises—they often come with the package: life! Relapses—reexperiencing feelings of distress— have received too little attention. Often, old habits and feelings remain with us and reappear during times of stress. Too, we know that as life goes on, we need to be able to tackle new problems and new situations and sometimes must handle unexpected crises. Chapter 21 tells you how the experience of therapy will help you cope with possible setbacks and the uncertainties of the future.

PART I
GETTING STARTED

1
PRISONS WE MAKE
FOR OURSELVES

Which of us is not forever a stranger and alone?
> Thomas Wolfe,
> *Look Homeward, Angel*

What other dungeon is so dark as one's own heart! What jailer so inexorable as one's self!
> Nathaniel Hawthorne,
> *The House of the Seven Gables*

When you have shut your doors, and darkened your room, remember never to say you are alone, for you are not alone, but God is within, and your genius is within.
> Epictetus, *Discourses*

When people are in pain and most need others, many wall themselves in. This very human tendency is illustrated by a famous story.

In 1934, Admiral Richard Byrd led an expedition to Antarctica, where he established a base on the edge of the Ross Ice Barrier, 700 miles north of the South Pole. Byrd then decided to set up a small weather observation post closer to the pole, which he chose to man alone. He would stay in a one-room cabin, a *box*

9

that measured nine feet by thirteen feet, lowered into a rectangular hole cut into the ice to protect the cabin from gale-force winds during the coming winter months.

Byrd was committing himself to a degree of personal isolation few men have ever taken on. What happened to him in the months ahead reveals something important to psychologists that all of us should bear in mind.

Byrd's men left him in his tiny station and returned across the ice to the main base 123 miles to the north. Winter blizzard conditions soon surrounded Byrd. He knew he was in for a long period of solitary confinement, with no hope of returning to the base, even if a medical emergency demanded this. He could never make the return trip to the base on his own, and it would be too dangerous for a team of men to try to get to him in the winter darkness across the miles of ice.

After several months of isolation, Byrd became very ill. He was distressed and confused about his condition—nausea, vomiting, terrible headaches, blurred vision, great weakness. Days would go by, and he would cling to life by a thread, his mind wandering, drifting in and out of the dizzying incoherence of frequent comas. He would, by sheer force of will, gather his reserve of fading energy and stagger across the tiny room to light the stove and open a can of food, which he soon lost from his stomach. Gradually, he came to realize that the fumes from his kerosene stove and from the gasoline-powered generator for the telegraph were poisoning him. But if he turned off the stove, he would freeze to death, and the telegraph was his only contact with others.

He knew his life was in real danger, yet he refused to let his men know of his desperate situation. Nor could he *admit to himself* that he was in trouble.

Listen to his own words, written half a century ago, in his snow-buried room with the air heavy with fumes and the inside walls encrusted with glistening ice:

> It is painful for me to dwell on the details of my collapse. . . . The subject is one that does not easily bear discussion, if only because a man's hurt, like his love, is most seemly when concealed. From my youth I have believed that sickness was somehow humiliating, something to be kept hidden. . . .
>
> To some men sickness brings a desire to be left alone; animal-like, their instinct is to crawl into a hole and lick the hurt. . . .

There were aspects of this situation which I would rather not mention at all, since they involve that queer business called self-respect. . . .

For a reason I can't wholly explain, except in terms of pride, I concealed from [my] men, as best I could, the true extent of my weakness. I never mentioned and, therefore, never acknowledged it. . . . I wanted no one to be able to look over the wall. . . .*

In spite of his efforts to keep his condition to himself, Byrd's radio operator at the main base seems to have intuited that Byrd was in danger. A rescue party was sent as the winter weather became less harsh, and Byrd was brought back to the base, probably just in time, before the fumes killed or permanently injured him.

In many ways, Byrd's Antarctic experience parallels that of many of us who, because of our own pain and hardship, isolate ourselves from others. Our lives become cold, desolate, despairing. Our suffering is real, but for one reason or another we cannot or will not reach out to others.

WALLING YOURSELF OFF FROM OTHERS

Most of us are aware of a need for human company and companionship. But when we are in pain or are severely troubled, we often forget what has been recognized for a long time:

Frederick II, the thirteenth-century ruler of Sicily, believed that all children were born with a knowledge of an ancient language. When they were taught the language of their parents, however, he believed, their knowledge of the older language was overridden and blotted out. King Frederick hypothesized that if children were raised without being taught a language, they would, in time, spontaneously begin to speak in some ancient tongue.

He therefore appointed a group of foster mothers, had newborn infants taken from their natural mothers, and ordered the foster mothers to raise the children in silence.

The upshot of this early experiment—as the legend goes—was

---

*Richard E. Byrd, *Alone* (New York: G. P. Putnam's Sons, 1938), pp. 166, viii, 294-295.

that Frederick never found out whether his theory was true. All of the babies died. They could not live without affection, touching, and loving words. Apparently, the foster mothers withdrew all human warmth when they sought to obey the king's order.

Today, we are aware of a baby's vital need for affection, for human contact—and even so, in our adult lives, when human contact is equally essential, we sometimes cut ourselves off from others.

THE MYTH OF SELF-SUFFICIENCY

As adults, we tend to emphasize self-control. We think of ourselves as *responsible*—to ourselves, our parents, our employers, our children. All this responsibility can sometimes be a heavy load! During periods of illness or emotional crisis, the emphasis on *control* can be excessive. It can create the bars of a prison, a grillwork of defenses that stands between us and others who are able to offer encouragement, warmth, understanding, and direction.

There is no lonelier person than someone who has decided to take his or her own life. The decision is the ultimate form of self-isolation. It is the ultimate admission that one's imprisonment is final and that there is no escape.

Fortunately, the decision to take one's life is reversible, if the person is helped in time. The help may come from within or from without, but it always involves the *recognition of hope* that the self-imprisonment may not be final, that there are others who would help, that, even for someone who is terminally ill, there may be periods of satisfaction and joy that make living worthwhile.

Western European, American, and Japanese societies are very control-oriented. There is much evidence that when members of these societies are emotionally troubled they often perceive a fault within themselves. They see their troubles as springing from a loss of self-control: "Just pull yourself together!" "It's just a matter of self-discipline, of *will*!"

The greater our sense of responsibility—the more we emphasize personal control over our inner and outer affairs, the more we see ourselves as individualists whose individualism is based on strength of will, discipline, guts—the more we are *trapped by the myth of self-sufficiency.*

People who as children were forced to become independent too early, who lacked a long enough period of closeness to their mothers, whose parents were immature and self-absorbed frequently develop what is called *pseudo-self-sufficiency* or *premature ego development*. Such a person is the neurotically extreme form of the "do-it-yourselfer." He or she refuses to relinquish control, whether to the car mechanic, the sewer cleaner, or a lover. There is an urgent and obsessive need to maintain control, never to be "out of control."

For such people, anxiety, depression, and loneliness can be especially devastating because they have walled themselves in to such an extent that emotional growth and change are blocked.

Yet most of us share, to some extent, this belief in self-sufficiency. It is one of the most tenacious forms of self-imprisonment that we have available to us, literally at our own disposal. It is a prison we can take great pride in. Pride, control, and self-sufficiency are usually close friends. They keep us from having *real* friends and stand in the way of our being good friends to ourselves.

THE FEAR OF BEING LABELED EMOTIONALLY DISTURBED

It is woven into the fabric of our society that we should conform. A young teenager from Australia now in a California high school tries as quickly as possible to lose the accent that differentiates her, that makes her the object of laughter. The same pressures motivate the stutterer to keep quiet, speaking only when absolutely necessary. The National Merit Scholar says "ain't" among his school friends to be one of them.

Children are especially sensitive to covert expectations, the implicit *shoulds* that are handed down from the adult world and are frequently refashioned to fit the stages children move through.

At each stage, the implicit maxims are *dress alike, talk alike, think alike*. Be "in." Especially, have the same feelings, values, and hopes. Most of us are raised to fear being different because we might come to be a lonely minority of one.

But when we become ill, especially if we are emotionally troubled, the rules change radically. Animals, from the aquarium angelfish to the household dog or cat, seem to have an instinct to seek isolation when ill. This tendency probably has evolved because it contributes to survival: the sick animal can more easily rally its energy for self-healing in quiet, undisturbed by others of its kind. And going off to be alone reduces the chance that the animal will spread any disease it has.

Added to an animal's self-isolating tendency is the tendency to hide the very *signs* of illness or injury. An animal that shows signs of injury or illness is immediately a target for predators who look for the weaker members of the species.

We human beings also tend to choose solitude and to hide the revealing symptoms of sickness or injury. Admiral Byrd admitted to these defenses only in his loneliness. But it is important to realize that hiding our feelings and isolating ourselves frequently are not in our best interests.

Animals do not practice medicine, though many species are capable of offering moral support and even a certain amount of physical assistance, as in the case of a sick whale who may be supported by its fellows in the water in order to breathe. But only we have developed medicine, and we have more recently begun to develop ways to treat problems that affect our emotions, attitudes, and behavior. When individuals, perhaps instinctively, distance themselves from others and bottle up their malaise, they turn their backs on the educated assistance and goodwill that are available.

Sometimes we do so out of fear of treatment coupled with fear of admitting that we are not as self-sufficient as we want to believe. But more often in the case of problems that directly affect our moods—i.e., "psychological problems"—we feel ashamed and afraid of the stigma, the disgrace, that our society attaches to those who admit they have unhappy or confused feelings.

There can be little doubt that society is imbalanced in legitimating physical sickness while reacting with alarm and repugnance to problems of a psychological nature. Think of the discrimination *against* psychological disorders, in favor of physical complaints, practiced openly by nearly all health insurance companies. Psychological pain does not hurt any less because it is emotionally based. Even so, emotional distress is held suspect, and insurance coverage for it, if not ruled out completely, is frequently only partial. It was, after all, not more than a century ago that our mental hospitals were run with an inhumanity that still can send shivers down one's spine. Unhappily, it is clear that we have not entirely left this phase of our development: the film *One Flew over the Cuckoo's Nest*, for example, points to continuing inhumanity in some psychiatric hospitals. And there is the alleged case of a Ukrainian woman who was involuntarily committed and held for some thirty years in a mental hospital. She was thought to be insane because, unfortunately, no one involved in her case recognized her "gibberish" as Ukrainian!

Emotional and mental illness is still not accepted by many. There is a fear of the unknown and a skepticism that psychological problems are nothing more than signs that a person is malingering, simply does not want to *try* to get better. And there is a gut-level anxiety when confronted by someone who, we worry, "may be close to going over the edge."

TEARING DOWN PRISON WALLS

What undue hardship this causes! As wonderful as the body is, we accept its imperfections, its susceptibility to disease and injury. But our brains, our minds, our spiritual dimension—how less well we understand these in their greater complexity! Is it so strange and unacceptable that they should be prone to their own problems, that they, too, may bring suffering?

Because society does not legitimate emotional pain, many people are not able to see their own pain as legitimate. So they deny it, to themselves and to others. But pain is usually a *healthy* signal; it tells you that something is wrong: Withdraw your hand from the fire! Move your cramping legs! Do something about your abusive, alcoholic husband! Get help for your depression!

Every one of these pains is a warning. To ignore all except those that are physical would be like saying that we are only bodies, without feelings, without humanity.

When you are in pain, whatever its source and kind, pay attention to it! Pain is often what points to a better life.

It is surely better to cope with a label applied in ignorance by some members of society, if this must be, than to live an unsatisfying and painful life. You must not manage your life just to avoid the potentially critical judgment of people who are ignorant of, or who refuse to acknowledge, the realities of human psychology. You can feel sure that among well-informed people, if you have had to deal with alcoholism, drug abuse, a difficult marriage, job depression, or any other "psychological" problem, you will be thought to be just as "respectable" as if you had coped with major surgery after an automobile accident. In fact, since overcoming a psychological difficulty demands a great deal *more* of your own voluntary effort, coming up a winner will increase your own self-respect and the respect, and even admiration, of those whose judgment is meaningful.

The first step to freedom from pain is to become aware of the walls of the prison that shut you in. Only then can you begin to tear them down.

2
PATHS TO HELP

To wrench anything out of its accustomed course takes energy, effort and pain. It does great violence to the existing pattern. Many people want change, both in the external world and in their own internal world, but they are unwilling to undergo the severe pain that must precede it.

Rivers in extremely cold climates freeze over in winter. In the spring, when they thaw, the sound of ice cracking is an incredibly violent sound. The more extensive and severe the freeze, the more thunderous the thaw. Yet, at the end of the cracking, breaking, violent period, the river is open, life-giving, life-carrying. No one says, "Let's not suffer the thaw; let's keep the freeze; everything is quiet now."

Mary E. Mebane, Mary, Wayfarer

If you decide to enter therapy, your therapist will probably ask you to think about two interrelated questions (they may be expressed in a variety of ways): "Where are you now?" and "Where do you want to go?" Your therapist or counselor will, as he comes to know you, often be able to help you to answer these by sharing his perceptions of you. One of the main tasks of the counseling process is to help a person gain improved self-understanding that embraces both present problems and future goals.

Yet if you can gain a certain measure of self-understanding and self-direction *before* entering counseling or therapy, it will be easier for you to choose an approach to counseling or therapy that more closely fits your problems, values, objectives, available time, and even your financial needs. You should find in this book a basis for preliminary *self*-counseling that will give you a sense of how and where best to begin therapy.

It is important to recognize that none of us ever reaches a final state of self-knowledge: as long as we live, our self-understanding is capable of growing. What we really understand about ourselves and what we believe ourselves to need and want are never more than provisional, tentative. Additional experience, just the fact of living longer, very likely will lead you to perceive yourself differently and motivate you to modify your priorities and change your goals.

WHERE ARE YOU NOW?

Late in 1984, the National Institute of Mental Health released the first published results of the largest mental health survey ever conducted. The results are startling and are an unhappy commentary on our society and world.

The report shows that 20 percent of Americans suffer from psychiatric disorders. Yet only one in five of these seeks help. The others live with their suffering.

The most common problems are these:

Psychiatric Name of Condition	*Millions of Americans with This Disorder*
Anxiety disorders	13.1
Phobias	11.1
Substance abuse (alcohol, drugs, etc.)	10.0
Affective disorders (including depression and manic depression)	9.4
Obsessive-compulsive disorders	2.4
Cognitive impairment	1.6
Schizophrenia	1.5
Antisocial personality	1.4

The NIMH study also shows that women are twice as likely to seek help as men. Two interrelated inferences are commonly made from this previously known fact: women are often more accepting of their emotional state (men in our society are taught to disregard their feelings, part of *machismo*), and women are less willing to allow pride to stand in their way of getting help (women are less affected by the myth of self-sufficiency).

The NIMH report indicates, too, that the incidence of psychological problems drops by approximately half after the age of forty-five. The below-forty-five years are usually those of highest stress. Above forty-five, individuals tend to become psychologically better integrated. This probably reflects increased maturity and a more accepting, calmer attitude toward life. The lowest rate of emotional disturbance appears to be in people over sixty-five. Yet there are many thousands of individuals over forty-five, and indeed over sixty-five, for whom life remains a difficult inner struggle.

The statistics from the NIMH study reveal how very widespread personal psychological difficulties are. Given the degree of complexity of our mental, emotional, and spiritual makeup, this should be understandable, especially when we take into account twentieth-century stresses that wear us down. Caught up as most of us are in our jobs, families, and daily worries, we are unaware that, in a very real sense, mental and emotional health problems have assumed epidemic proportions. If you bear in mind how fearful our society encourages us to be of admitting such difficulties, you can perhaps imagine how substantial the "iceberg" of psychological suffering is: most of it lies below the waterline of public consciousness.

The NIMH study results should encourage you, if you suffer from personal emotional difficulties, to realize that you are not alone in the problems you face. Knowing that there are many good and fine individuals with very likely similar problems may urge you to take an honest look at where you are now and then to try to decide what changes may be helpful to you: where you want to go from here.

If you are fortunate, you may already be aware of the main things in you and in your life that bring you distress. If so, you are one step closer to being able to do something about them. Many of us, however, have become so clever and effective in denying what we really feel that we have lost touch with our true selves.

Desires to repair an unhappy marriage are shelved while the children are growing up; the unrewarding nature of a job is ignored because priority is given to financial security; you may be unable or unwilling to face the pain you bring to yourself and others as a result of a drug- or alcohol-abuse habit.

In most cases, it is not possible to gain the motivation and means to solve a problem until you are willing to accept that there *is* a problem that needs to be solved.

Because of the blinding nature of the habits you may have established, and because of your defensive desires to disregard what disturbs the equilibrium of habit, it may be hard to acquire a clear picture of where you stand right now. Sometimes it can be useful to check with others: how do they see you?

A close friend of mine, after years in her profession, began rather suddenly to feel how unrewarding her job was, and she began to suspect that she may have hidden these feelings for a long time. She had maintained a regular, almost once-a-week exchange of letters with her mother for twelve years. She knew that her mother kept her letters, so she went to visit her and asked if she might skim through them, paying attention to comments she had made over the years about her work. It quickly became clear to her that, consistently, she had had only very negative things to say about her job. After skimming through dozens of letters written over a period of years, she became convinced of her real and enduring feelings and changed her line of work.

Such self-knowledge does not usually come this easily. We may pride ourselves on honesty, but there are few of us who permit ourselves self-honesty to any real degree. Existential-humanistic psychologists have paid much attention to these ways that we live "in bad faith"—each of us trying to be a person he or she really is not and denying the person he or she really is.

We live in a society that emphasizes conformity, "being somebody," gaining status and wealth and a good position—yet these values may not coincide with being true to ourselves. Parental influences can be strong, as can expectations from our spouses. We internalize many of these values so that it becomes difficult to see who we really are and what we really want from life and from our efforts.

There are no easy routes to self-realization. We must all do a certain amount of hunting in the dark—or, as a colleague of mine likes to say, "scrabbling about"—for a sense of real identity.

Recognizing that your self-understanding is probably always imperfect does not mean that it is of little value. It is, in the end, all any of us has to go on.

It may be useful to ask people close to you what they perceive about you. Reading through a group of old letters, keeping a journal, or simply setting aside a few minutes for self-appraisal at the end of each day or week may also be enlightening. If you do this self-examination, gradually where you are and what you feel will become clearer, and then it will be natural and appropriate to ask what the next step is.

WHERE DO YOU WANT TO GO? WHAT KIND OF PERSON DO YOU WANT TO BECOME?

Influences from society, your parents, your spouse, or your close friends make it difficult for you to know yourself. Defensive habits and fear of change also stand in the way. These are significant blocks to self-understanding.

When you turn your attention to the future, to what kind of person you want to become, you will encounter more blocks to overcome. Life is like that! It seems that few things come without effort and perseverance.

There are two major obstacles to designing the model of the person you would like to become. Because they can be so important, I want to introduce them early in this book. They are blame and guilt, and they are like the two ends of a seesaw.

When we appraise what we have done in our lives, we usually find reasons to blame others, or perhaps to blame limited educational opportunities, or social pressures, or discrimination—in short, our past environment: all the factors that limited our lives, interfered with the attainment of our hopes, and were not under our control.

On the other end of the seesaw sits guilt. And guilt is really blame turned inward.

If we try to pinpoint the factors that have been responsible for our lives not having turned out better, we tend to blame environmental limitations, or else we feel guilt for what we see as our own failings. Usually, we locate responsibility in both areas.

Most of us, however, have unbalanced seesaws. We usually

blame things *outside ourselves* for our disappointments. Doing so is a habit that allows us to avoid responsibility for ourselves and, in turn, limits our future development.

On the other hand, some of us blame ourselves much too readily: we carry an exaggerated burden of responsibility, which weighs us down and also limits our growth as individuals.

Ideally, psychotherapy would like us to let go of so-called "past negative conditioning"—blame as well as guilt—so that we are free to choose what we are and will become. Even though this is certainly a desirable attitude, most of us cannot really forget and let go. We are all inheritors of a tenacious past: the influences of past events have a certain power over us, and we must either resign ourselves to being controlled by the past or fight its influence. The *attitude* we take toward the past will usually affect how we meet the future, often diminishing our freedom to change old habits and undermining our hope and faith in ourselves.

For example, if Jeff blames his limitations today on his parents, on the ways they influenced him, he may set goals for himself that are far from being freely chosen. Jeff may choose them *in reaction to* domination by his parents years ago. His parents may have tried to influence him to be a gentle, courteous person with artistic interests. But as a result of other past influences—for example, because of frequent moves of the family and repeatedly being bullied as the "new kid" at different schools—Jeff may feel hostile toward others, so (in reaction to his parents' influence and because of pent-up hostility) he decides to go into science (rather than art, for which he perhaps has a talent) and rejects gentle, courteous qualities in himself.

It is difficult to choose freely. Some psychologists do not believe it actually is possible. And yet, whether we are ever truly free or not, we still try to plan our lives, and we believe our plans (and frequently the lack of them) have something to do with what we make of living.

Most people who enter counseling or psychotherapy want to improve some aspect of their living. Individuals whose seesaw is weighted on the side of blaming outside influences too often come to feel it is too much work and quit therapy because they cannot accept the need to make choices and decisions *in spite of* past influences. On the other hand, people who blame themselves may be so guilt-ridden that they are impaired in their openness to the future and feel unable to initiate fundamental changes in their lives.

When you ask yourself, "What kind of person do I want to become?," try to be aware of the extent that your answer may be weighed down by feelings of blame and guilt. All too often we continue to perpetuate, unknowingly, the same old unsatisfying patterns because we are trapped by our habits of blaming others or ourselves.

If you feel bogged down by feelings of guilt or burdened by the limitations of an unfair past, it may be difficult for you to develop a freely chosen sense of direction. But perhaps you will be able to acknowledge that the guilt or blame you feel is an obstacle to be overcome. If so, you have defined an objective that you may use to decide what type of counseling or therapy may be a most promising first step.

What I am suggesting is that an obstacle that makes it hard for you to gain a sense of direction can *itself* point you in a direction. If there are blocks, it can be helpful to meet them head-on. In therapy, the phrase *working through a problem* often means exactly this.

Choosing what kind of person you wish to be is a *process*, not an event. It is not something that happens and then is over. Choice is something implicit in each day of your life; sometimes it is quite conscious, but it is often dulled by the unconsciousness of habit. Your personal goals may undergo gradual or abrupt change. Psychological growth is your response to these changes in outlook.

WHAT DOES THERAPY TRY TO DO?

Individual therapy or counseling (therapy for groups and families will be discussed in detail later) is really an attempt to build a bridge between answers to these two now familiar questions: "Where are you now, or what kind of person are you now?" and "Where do you want to go, or what kind of person do you want to become?" Think of therapy as an attempt to build a bridge so that you can pass from a present situation to a desired way of being.

Carl Rogers defines therapy as "a relationship in which at least one of the parties has the intent of promoting the growth, development, maturity, improved functioning, improved coping with life of the other."*

Psychiatrist Allen Wheelis takes this definition further:

> Therapy may offer insights into bewildering experience, help with the making of connections, give comfort and encouragement, assist in the always slippery decision of whether to hang on and try harder or to look for a different way to try. . . .
>
> The place of insight is to illumine: to ascertain where one is, how one got there, how now to proceed, and to what end. It is a blueprint, as in building a house, and may be essential, but no one achieves a house by blueprints alone, no matter how accurate or detailed. A time comes when one must take up hammer and nails. . . .**

Therapy involves a three-fold relationship among a helping professional, the approach to therapy used by him or her, and, what is most important, the outlook of the individual client. In this book we will examine each of these three dimensions of therapy in some detail, but here we will concentrate on the one therapists generally agree is the most important: *you*—the kind of person you are, what your attitudes and outlook are, and, of course, how much you really want to develop or change. Your attitudes will determine, probably more than anything else, what variety of therapy you will most benefit from.

Therapists, like teachers (which they really are), find that their clients or patients can be divided into two groups: active and passive learners. When you go to a doctor with a broken arm, your relationship to your doctor is a *passive* one: you need only to cooperate as he examines your arm, perhaps administers an anesthetic, and sets the break. You may take medication for pain, and then you simply *wait* until, thanks to the body's automatic healing processes, the break is fused. The public's conception of medicine is predominately a passive one. To be a "patient" is for the most part to be a passive bystander: the physician is the active agent who brings about healing. There are occasional

---

*Carl Rogers, *On Becoming a Person: A Therapist's View of Psychotherapy* (New York: Houghton Mifflin, 1961), pp. 39-40.
**Allen Wheelis, *How People Change* (New York: Harper and Row, 1973), pp. 101, 107.

exceptions—for example, physical therapy and rehabilitation therapy after a serious injury or illness, when the patient must become more active and accept more responsibility.

As we will see, a few approaches to counseling and psychotherapy preserve, to some extent, the traditionally passive role of the patient. Most of them, however, require a good deal of initiative and just plain hard work on the part of the patient or client.

> In building the house of one's life or in its remodeling, one may delegate nothing; for the task can be done, if at all, only in the workshop of one's own mind and heart, in the most intimate rooms of thinking and feeling where none but one's self has freedom of movement or competence or authority. The responsibility lies with him who suffers, originates with him, remains with him to the end. It will be no less his if he enlists the aid of a therapist; we are no more the product of our therapist than of our genes; we create ourselves. The sequence is suffering, insight, will, action, change. The one who suffers, who wants to change, must bear responsibility all the way. "Must" because so soon as responsibility is ascribed [outside oneself] the forces resisting change occupy the whole of one's being, and the process of change comes to a halt. A psychiatrist may help, perhaps crucially, but his best help will be of no avail if he is required to provide a degree of insight which will of itself achieve change.*

WHY IS IT SO COMPLICATED?

For better or for worse, human nature is a many-splendored thing. It doesn't take an advanced degree in psychotherapy to know that people can have many different kinds of personal problems. This fact, if we appreciate it fully, makes more understandable why there are so many alternative approaches to helping people with their difficulties.

In the world of theory, a *model* is a simplified representation of reality. Your checking account record is a model, in just this sense, of how many real dollars and cents you have in the bank.

Here is a much simplified model that represents five main psychological, emotion-laden dimensions of a person:

---

*Wheelis, *How People Change*, pp. 101-102.

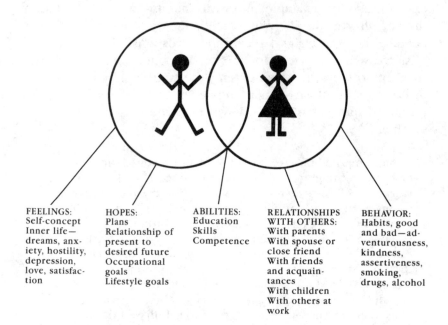

| FEELINGS:
Self-concept
Inner life—
dreams, anx-
iety, hostility,
depression,
love, satisfac-
tion | HOPES:
Plans
Relationship of
present to
desired future
Occupational
goals
Lifestyle goals | ABILITIES:
Education
Skills
Competence | RELATIONSHIPS
WITH OTHERS:
With parents
With spouse or
close friend
With friends
and acquain-
tances
With children
With others at
work | BEHAVIOR:
Habits, good
and bad—ad-
venturousness,
kindness,
assertiveness,
smoking,
drugs, alcohol |

We see right away that, for the same reasons that there are specialties in medicine—e.g., orthopedy for bones, neurology for nerves, dentistry for teeth—there should be special approaches that focus on different psychological dimensions of the person.

Something else you may see is that the five dimensions in the model are not isolated from one another. They interrelate and overlap a good deal. Just as a dentist must know about the orthopedy of the jaw and skull and the neurology of the teeth, a neurologist and an orthopedist are expected to know something, though not in great detail, about dentition. Each of us is a unity of what all the medical and psychological specialties study in different ways, plus a good deal more, as artists, writers, theologians, and musicians make evident.

That more than 130 distinguishable therapies have now been developed may perhaps strike us, even so, as excessive. But efforts are being made to unify many of these approaches, and this book is one of them. Rather than talking about 130 different approaches, we will center our attention on the main categories into which the many approaches can be sorted.

One of the interesting and hopeful things that can be said

about the multiplicity of approaches to therapy and counseling is that treatment by any one of them can often be of some help. For example, Helen may wish to stop drinking (a habit in the behavior category), and she may be helped by means of behavior modification. She may then find that, as a direct result, her self-concept (feeling category) has grown stronger, while her marriage (relationship category) has also improved. Or, Ralph may go to a vocational counselor who helps him define a direction (hope category) in keeping with his interests and aptitudes. Ralph goes back to school and develops a background (abilities category) that reflects these aptitudes and interests. The sense of direction he has gained helps Ralph stop using drugs (behavior), reduces his hostility and anxiety (feelings), and improves his relationships with others. In other words, a helpful change in one direction can often lead to noticeable changes in others.

However, there also are risks that we should not ignore: Sue goes to an analyst and learns over a period of months that her marriage to Fred was based on a sense of inadequacy Sue learned during her childhood. Her father was so highly controlling and critical of her that she was never able to develop a sense of her own value. Her husband, Fred, is also domineering and authoritarian, and he abuses Sue frequently, usually mistreating her through criticism, but he has sometimes also beaten her physically. Sue has accepted this without question for a long time, but due to the emotional support received from her analyst, she is beginning to develop a sense of self-esteem. As her self-esteem grows, she comes to realize that her marriage is a self-destructive relationship and decides to divorce Fred. Her therapy has been helpful to Sue, but it has, indirectly, resulted in a breakdown of her admittedly unhappy marriage. A change in one dimension can sometimes lead to an initially unintended change in another area.

IF IT HURTS, DON'T PROCRASTINATE!

One of the marvelous things about human nature is the ability to feel pain. This may seem like an odd thing to say, but reflect for a moment. Pain is frequently what spurs us on from an unsatisfying and even destructive situation to a better future. Pain tells you to jerk your hand away from a hot stove. A different kind of pain tells you it is time to get on with living, time to initiate some positive changes. Anxiety, sleeplessness, irritability, resentment, depression—they all can be painful inner feelings that tell us that all is not well in our inner selves.

It is well known to counselors and therapists that, in general, the longer these signs of need are ignored, the longer it may take to help a person resolve the difficulties that have been pressing for attention. Distress is not easily buried. When suppressed, it tends to pop up again later, sometimes with increased severity.

We can, ironically, choose to be "strong" and ignore these messages from within, or we can listen to our feelings, pay attention to our hopes, develop needed abilities, seek to improve our relationships with others, and work to change some ways we behave that block our happiness.

Problems that concern your inner well-being and the health of your relationships with others who are important to you are better resolved than buried, and the earlier they are given the attention they deserve, the easier your path through change to a better life will be.

3
BRIDGES FROM HERE TO THERE

AN OVERVIEW OF THE FIELD OF THERAPY

THE HELPING PROFESSIONAL

Professionals in the fields of counseling and psychotherapy have a wide range of different backgrounds and perspectives. They can be broken down into these categories:

Social work counselors: counselors for individuals; marriage and family counselors; group counselors; and vocational guidance counselors
Psychologists: clinical psychologists; counseling psychologists; and psychometrists
Psychiatrists
Other therapists: religious counselors; biofeedback therapists; hypnotherapists; relaxation and meditation instructors; holistic therapists such as bioenergetics therapists, yoga instructors, and exercise therapists; etc.

The education, supervised training, and outlooks of these professionals vary greatly, as do their fees and the average length of time therapy can be expected to last. We will look more closely at these differences later on.

THE RANGE OF APPROACHES TO THERAPY

Because of their differences in training and personal or theoretical preference, the distinct classes of therapists represent a diversity of approaches to therapy. There are numerous schools of psychoanalysis, psychotherapy, behavioral therapy, group therapy, and marriage and family therapy, and a range of approaches to personal adjustment, including exercise therapies, relaxation techniques, forms of meditation, and drug and nutrition therapies.

From any one of these, a multitude of schools of thought branches out. For example, psychoanalysis has, since Freud, developed along a number of different lines: each major psychoanalyst has formulated his or her own approach to analysis that distinguishes itself from Freud's. Psychotherapy, to take another example, is not a single approach to therapy, but rather makes up an entire field. It is the largest and most rapidly growing area relating to mental health. In it are included distinct approaches, such as client-centered therapy, Gestalt therapy, transactional analysis, rational-emotive therapy, existential-humanistic therapy, reality therapy, logotherapy, Adlerian therapy, emotional flooding therapies, and direct decision therapy.

In later chapters, we will look at these approaches to psychotherapy more closely. The goal throughout this book will be to enable you to understand enough about each of the major therapies to make an informed decision in choosing an approach (and there may be more than one) that will be most useful in relation to your own understanding of your objectives, whether they are long-range or focused on the need to eliminate immediate obstacles to growth.

THE DIFFERENCE BETWEEN
COUNSELING AND PSYCHOTHERAPY

Counseling and psychotherapy have developed a great deal in recent years—so much so that their boundaries have often overlapped. Clear-cut distinctions between the two fields are increasingly hard to draw. Nevertheless, some professionals prefer to call themselves by one name and some by the other.

In general terms, *counseling* tends to be a short-term process, the purpose of which is to help the client, couple, or family overcome specific problems and eliminate blocks to growth. Counseling gives individuals a chance to resolve personal problems and concerns. Most counselors attempt to help their clients become aware of a widened range of possibilities of choice; from this perspective, counseling tries to free clients from rigid patterns of habit.

Habits can be useful, but they can also interfere with life. The technical habits of a pianist, for example, are essential in performance. Similarly, only when language skills become habitual does a speaker of a foreign language achieve command of it.

On the other hand, fears can also become habitual, and they may come to interfere with everyday activities. Anxiety over public speaking may become habitual. There are many personally destructive habits—alcoholism, smoking, over- or undereating, abusive behavior, shyness and social withdrawal—and all can become self-perpetuating patterns. Counseling can help people break out of these habits, often in part by helping clients become aware of unrecognized alternatives.

Psychotherapy tends to be more concerned than counseling with fundamental personality-structure changes. Frequently, psychotherapy is a longer-term process. Frequently, too, the problems treated in psychotherapy are hard to pin down and are less specific. They include chronic depression, pervasive ("free-floating") anxiety, generalized lack of self-esteem, and so on. Such difficulties are not well defined; their causes may be vague or uncertain, and often much time must be spent to get at their basis. Psychotherapy seeks to bring about an intensive self-awareness of the *inner dynamics*—the internal forces and the principles that govern them—that are involved in chronic forms of personal distress. Sometimes, as in analytical psychotherapy or psychoanalysis, attention is focused on the role of unconscious processes in inner conflicts; treatment attempts to resolve these conflicts by understanding the unconscious forces involved.

The term *psychotherapy* is often used to imply more advanced professional training, whereas counseling is something individuals with more modest academic credentials may practice. Whether a professional is called a counselor or a therapist has to do with his or her level of training, with the setting in which services are offered, and, to a certain degree, with that person's theoretical orientation.

In practice, these differences in outlook frequently amount to differences in *emphasis* rather than approach. In this book, I will speak of counseling and psychotherapy interchangeably unless there is a need to be especially restrictive.

THERAPY: THE ART OF CHANGE

HOW WE ARE ABLE TO CHANGE

We are what we do . . . and may do what we choose.
           Allen Wheelis, *How People Change*

Freud identified five causes of personality development:

• growth and maturation
• frustration
• conflict
• inadequacy
• anxiety

By the time we become adults, most of us have developed sets of defenses to enable us to cope with everyday problems *in spite of* feelings of frustration, conflict, inadequacy, and anxiety. But as these feelings become more pronounced, when we encounter situations that intensify these feelings, we must put more and more energy into our defenses. They allow us to continue living and acting in habitual ways, usually by hiding, by denying, and sometimes by distorting our perceptions of reality.

Facing the inadequacies of a marriage, the unrewarding nature of a job, the extent of conflicts with a child, or difficulties relating to friends can cause intense anxiety. So, to avoid this anxiety, we frequently "defend against" these realizations: we try to uphold the belief that our marriages are just fine, that things are OK between us and our children, that our jobs are at least tolerable—that, in spite of some problems "here and there," we can get along all right. We do, in short, try to see our lives through rose-tinted glasses.

We continue to do this until our negative feelings become too strong, until we have expended so much energy to maintain our defenses that we are *emotionally exhausted.* If we reach such a state of real depletion, and our defenses can no longer hold against the building pressure of our feelings, the result is *nervous breakdown*. This is the layman's name for a variety of psychological conditions that develop due to *a burned-out emotional fuse*.

A fuse is a protective device that prevents an overload of electricity. Our defense mechanisms are analogous devices that protect us against emotional overload. When an emotional fuse burns out, it is often because we have maintained defenses too long in the face of increasing inner frustration and pain. The result may involve severe depression, incapacitating anxiety, or serious withdrawal.

Now, when you decide to change in some psychologically fundamental way, you must push against the rigid framework of certain of these protective defenses. When you do this, you will feel anxiety. You are forcing your emotional fuses to adjust to a different pattern of behavior and feelings.

Your sense of personal identity is made up of a network of ways you have come to perceive yourself, your loved ones, your work, and your world. Any attempt—even if it is your own, entered into through your own choosing—to change patterns that are psychologically basic to your sense of identity will threaten that established identity and produce a measure of anxiety.

The longer these habitual patterns of behavior and feeling have been in force, the more deeply rooted they become in your sense of identity, and the more unsettling and anxiety-producing an attempt to change them will be.

Although your defenses protect against emotional overload, they also stand in your way of change. They are fundamentally *conservative* mechanisms: established habits of thought, feeling, and behavior are *familiar*, and familiarity reduces the anxiety brought about by uncertainty. If you are considering making significant changes in your life, your defenses will rally to protect the equilibrium of habits you have formed in the past. If you push yourself to change, you will face a predictable degree of anxiety. Fortunately, there are, as we shall see, many ways of coping with the anxiety brought about by change; therapy offers some of these, and some are available to us all if we draw on inner resources.

As long as you are alive it is possible to change. Ultimately, the decision to change is an expression of your choice and will. When change *is* achieved, it usually comes after long and arduous trying. We are all aware of the heroic efforts some people can and do make to overcome a physical handicap. Overcoming deeply entrenched emotional habits can require similar tenacity and commitment. If you want to bring about some basic changes in yourself or in your relationships with others, your inner strength and resolve will be essential.

Frequently, individuals expect a therapist to accomplish change *for* them: they are willing to come for an hour's consultation once or twice a week, and they will be very cooperative during each visit, but they seem unwilling or unable to develop the initiative to carry on efforts begun in the therapist's office.

Some clients, in spite of what they say, do not really *want* to change. Their habits are deeply ingrained, serving purposes they may be only dimly aware of at the beginning of therapy. Sometimes it becomes necessary in therapy to reappraise the goals that have been set. The decision to pursue a certain course of change may result in so much anxiety and upset that both therapist and client must pause to reconsider. Some changes may turn out to be too difficult, too taxing; some clients may be unwilling to put in the work required to bring about a certain change.

Most changes of the kind I am referring to—fundamental changes in outlook, in daily thoughts and feelings, in behavior— can be made only gradually. Since any move in the direction of change will threaten your existing defenses, resistance and protest are likely to well up from within you. New ways of *being* will feel intimidating, unpleasant, or just plain *unnatural*. And this is understandable, is it not? You must confront and do battle against habits that may have been with you for a long time. *The longer that undesirable patterns have been in force, the more control they acquire over you, and the more your defenses become committed to preserving them.* Change is made steadily more difficult.

Always remember, however, that change *can* be brought about. You need to be patient with yourself; it will not come overnight. Long-standing habits take time to be replaced. You must have patience, and you must feel hope and encouragement. If you are depressed now, if maintaining your defenses has exhausted you, then it will be difficult to feel the measure of hope that you need to begin the process of therapy.

This, perhaps more than anything else, is the most immediate and perceptible benefit of therapy: a good therapist is a source for hope and encouragement when you cannot sustain these yourself. Therapists are trained to help people who want to change, to bring it about.

THE RESULTS OF THERAPY

In the past twenty to thirty years, there has been a gradual shift away from a medical, illness-based orientation in therapy to one that focuses on personal growth. By no means everyone enters therapy because of emotional pain. Increasingly, therapists are seeing clients who enjoy psychological and emotional good health but believe that therapy can help them lead fuller, richer, more satisfying lives. As a consequence, the objectives of many current approaches to therapy involve more than only the resolution of personal difficulties and crises.

There are many potential benefits of therapy. To varying degrees, all the therapies we will discuss in this book claim to assist you in achieving the following goals.

Resilience and Tolerance to Stress

As a consequence of therapy, you come to be less frustrated by stress, able to recover from stressful experiences more quickly. You become less defensive and more accepting of others and yourself, able to adjust more easily to unexpected demands in living. You have a decreased tendency to hold rigid expectations of the world, so you feel less disappointment and frustration.

Congruence

You come to be more unified in the present moment, aware of your feelings, and less disposed to ignore, deny, or distort your perceptions out of defensive needs. Congruence means a close match between what you feel and how you think and act. Congruent people are well integrated, no longer in need of "masks." When we admire a person's sense of "integrity," we often feel that the person not only behaves in ways that show self-respect, but that he or she is self-accepting, is genuine, and appears to be comparatively free of inner conflict. Such individuals are, in short, able to be themselves. People who no longer are engaged in a battle against themselves and against others will tend to show congruence.

Self-Esteem

People with high self-esteem can allow themselves to feel modest and to behave with modesty. High self-esteem does not imply pride or arrogance. Self-esteem and self-acceptance (and hence congruence) are interrelated. Individuals with strong self-esteem no longer need to *prove* themselves. They value the kind of people they are and are not inclined to be self-undermining through perfectionistic self-criticism.

Openness and Love

Ideally, if you undergo therapy, you become less defensive and less uptight about yourself; you will therefore have less need for self-absorption, so you will be able to develop an increased capacity to feel warmth for others. You may become more giving, and less hooked on the need to recover for what you do give, tit for tat. There are fewer "shoulds" to stand in your way, to use to blame yourself, or to use to criticize others. You can let go of these requirements and accept others for what they are, for what they can do, and for what they may feel. You feel less disappointment and resentment about your relationships and more of a sense of ease and peace.

Freedom

Since you are less hooked by the expectations and values of others, and you have reduced the list of requirements that others must fulfill in order to be acceptable, you gain a great measure of personal freedom. The habitual process of sizing others up and comparing them with yourself, which many of us expend so much time and energy doing, is no longer needed. You can more freely set your life goals. You will probably feel more real, meaningful satisfaction with your life, since you are no longer imprisoned by uptight standards of judgment. You are able to be much more relaxed because you are able to feel more accepting toward others and toward yourself.

Displacing the Negative with the Positive

These are among the major potential positive benefits of therapy. They make up one way of describing the *ideal outcomes* of therapy. They are one side of the coin; the other side consists of the many negative feelings and ways of behaving that are eliminated when they are *displaced* by these positive personality qualities. The negatives that make up such a familiar part of "normal" life include these:

- fears that stand in the way of desired goals
- anxiety and depression that cripple normal living
- low self-esteem, resentment, and hostility that poison the formation and development of satisfying relationships
- incapacity to deal with stress, and dependence on alcohol, drugs, or other means to reduce anxiety
- inability to accept yourself, your family, or your present place in the world—which often leads to bitterness, withdrawal, and even the cultivation of fantasies that further isolate
- confusion, disorientation, and perhaps even physical signs of poor health, as a result of emotions that have assumed a magnitude that can no longer be held in check by tired defenses

We tend to think of these as the usual reasons for entering therapy. But, again, the positive qualities we have described are attracting clients increasingly to therapy. Whether you need to eliminate emotional pain or are fortunate to be comparatively untroubled but are searching for certain positive qualities of perspective and character that you believe will bring increased satisfaction to your living, therapy may offer what you are seeking.

WHAT MAKES A GOOD THERAPIST?

According to several studies, certain qualities in therapists are associated with effective therapy. The kind of person who is able to help others bring about important life changes has these qualities:

- the ability to understand the client's feelings and life world
- heightened sensitivity to the client's feelings and attitudes so that the therapist frequently is able to uncover significant aspects of the client's outlook and personality of which the client would probably remain unaware

- warmth of interest in the client's well-being, without emotional overinvolvement
- psychological maturity, characterized by self-acceptance, genuineness, and congruence
- a sense of acceptance toward the client: a nonjudgmental, noncritical, positive regard for the client, his separateness, and individuality
- an attitude, conveyed by the therapist's behavior and approach, that encourages positive change, independence, and freely made choices and decisions, and implicitly discourages the formation of long-term dependence of the client on the therapist

These studies also identified several attitudes that clients, regardless of the orientation of their therapists, felt were especially *counterproductive* in some therapists:

- lack of interest
- remoteness or distance
- excessive sympathy

In general, clients whose evaluations of therapy have been studied appear to be in agreement that the personal character, attitudes, and feelings of therapists are more important than a therapist's technique, procedures, and theoretical orientation. Therapy is an intrinsically human process, one that is especially sensitive to the human dimensions of therapists. Later we will look at objective evaluations of the effectiveness of various approaches to therapy and weigh them against the emphasis that clients place on the personal qualities of therapists.

4

THE THERAPEUTIC JUNGLE, PART I

Social Workers, Psychologists, and Psychiatrists

> I have reluctantly come to concede the possibility that the process, direction, and end points of therapy may differ in different therapeutic orientations.
>
> Carl Rogers, *On Becoming a Person*

Fifty years ago, people with personal or marital problems had a choice between two main kinds of assistance: psychoanalysis and religion. Freud's approach to psychiatry had gained popularity among physicians, psychoanalytic training was being made available to clinical psychologists, and the ideas of Freudian analysis had come to dominate the public's conception of therapy. And, sometimes overlooked in this context, the church—the world's faithful and oldest psychiatrist—continued to offer spiritual and personal guidance.

These two basic choices have expanded into an impressive—and confusing—array of different therapies. The more than one hundred varieties of counseling, even when they are grouped together, cannot be reduced to fewer than perhaps twenty families of therapies.

Different counseling professions have evolved that now range from social work to psychotherapy to psychiatry; religious counseling is still offered; and there are the newer therapies of relaxation training, biofeedback, bioenergetics, etc., as well as a renaissance of older approaches such as meditation, yoga, and holistic practice. The choices of fifty years ago seem modest, limited, and certainly less perplexing. However, the recent proliferation of therapies has brought with it increased sensitivity, sophistication, and effectiveness.

In spite of this growth of therapeutic options, most people who decide to enter therapy are unaware of the choices open to them and so cannot intelligently weigh their alternatives. This and the next chapter will help you to see clearly what alternatives exist. As the book helps you to clarify your personal objectives, you will be able to home in on one or more approaches to therapy that may be especially promising for you, your temperament, interests, and goals. You will be encouraged to follow a "map" that will guide you to several approaches to therapy, to help you find the shortest and most effective route to where you want to go.

SOCIAL WORK COUNSELORS

As we have seen, the four main categories of social work counselors are counselors for individuals, marriage and family counselors, group counselors, and vocational guidance counselors.

ORIENTATION AND TRAINING

The main purpose of social work is to help people cope with stress from interpersonal or social problems. The focus of the social worker may therefore be on individuals, families, or groups or on their social and work environments, their organizations, and their communities.

Social workers are trained to deal with developmental problems, life crises, and emotional problems that arise in a variety of social situations.

Graduate schools of social work require varying periods of supervised internship; they usually offer specializations within the field—e.g., drug and alcohol abuse, developmental disabilities, child welfare, correctional approaches, family services, care of the aged, and others. It is now possible to find social workers whose training is quite specialized.

In some states, social workers may practice with a bachelor's degree; in many states, a master's degree is required. In addition, counselors are usually required to put in a substantial number of hours of counseling under the supervision of a licensed counselor.

FEES

Social workers in private practice normally charge on an hourly basis for their services, with sessions lasting thirty to fifty minutes. Rates vary considerably, in direct relation to other health care costs. Rates are higher in larger metropolitan areas and also higher in New England and California than in the South and Midwest. An approximate range of $35 to $65 per counseling session is normal at the time of this writing.

Costs for marriage and family counseling and for vocational guidance counseling are similar to rates for individual counseling.

The charge for group therapy is frequently made for a block of sessions. The group therapist may, for example, recommend that a group meet for ten sessions. The resulting per-session cost is normally significantly lower than is individual counseling. (However, the goals of individual and group therapy are in general different, as we will see; neither can automatically be substituted for the other.)

Many social workers offer their services through a counseling agency. Some of these are privately run; others are funded by the county or state. Frequently, agencies charge for counseling services based on a sliding scale, which takes into account the financial situation of clients. Sliding scale rates can be very economical for lower-income individuals. Bills for services in some county and state agencies are made on a monthly basis; individual counseling may cost only a few dollars per session for individuals with restricted budgets.

There are many opportunities for clients to obtain economical care, especially in metropolitan areas where counseling services are widespread.

DURATION OF TREATMENT

It is impossible to give any hard and fast rules as to how long counseling will take. Obviously, much has to do with an individual's objectives, the severity of the problem, and, frequently, how long the problem has been neglected or ignored. On the other hand, much also has to do with the counselor's own orientation.

Today, many counselors receive training that emphasizes "brief" therapy. Specific goals of therapy are set, and it is frequently possible to reach those goals within a matter of a few months. On the other hand, some counselors prefer, or have been trained, to offer long-term individual psychotherapy. Some counselors have been influenced by the psychoanalytic approach, which is usually of long duration, frequently requiring one to several years.

There is no reason you, as a prospective client, should not ask a counselor what kind of approach he or she uses and approximately how long therapy can be expected to last. You should not hesitate to ask a counselor questions that reflect your concerns. As you read further, this book will provide you with a frame of reference so that you may evaluate more fully the answers a counselor gives you.

PSYCHOLOGISTS

As mentioned in the last chapter, there are three kinds of psychologists who are involved in different aspects of therapy: clinical psychologists, counseling psychologists, and psychometrists.

ORIENTATION AND TRAINING

Clinical psychology emphasizes the understanding, diagnosis, and treatment of individuals in psychological distress. Clinical psychology is historically based on laboratory work that stressed experimental and statistical analysis.

Clinical psychologists generally have a Ph.D. and complete a lengthy internship in a clinical setting. Most clinical psychologists develop competence in both diagnostics and intervention. The area of diagnostics includes individual interviews, psychological testing, and personality assessment (psychological evaluation to determine what a client's difficulties are). Intervention (the actual approach used to help a person) includes individual psychotherapy, group therapy, and marriage and family therapy.

The objective of *counseling psychology* is to encourage growth in the three major life areas of family, work, and education and to prevent excessive psychological stress in them. Like clinical psychologists, counseling psychologists receive training in individual, group, and marriage and family counseling as well as in vocational counseling, assessment, and rehabilitation.

Often, you will find clinical psychologists in private practice, while many counseling psychologists hold positions in organizations, schools, and social service agencies. Counseling psychologists generally have a master's degree or Ph.D. and also are required to complete internships in supervised counseling.

Psychometrists are specifically trained to give and to evaluate psychological tests. They are, so to speak, the "radiologists" of the fields of counseling and psychotherapy. Clients may be referred to a psychometrist in order to take one or more psychological tests; the psychometrist's interpretation of the results is then forwarded to the client's therapist or counselor. Increasingly, psychologists are being trained to do much of this work themselves, so it has become less common to refer clients to psychometrists unless an extensive amount of testing is desired.

If you are advised to take one or more psychological tests, you may be interested in knowing what to expect. Most psychological tests are multiple-choice. You are given a printed list of questions and an answer sheet. There are no "right" answers. You answer such questions as "Would you rather go to a party or stay home and read a good book?" Tests like this attempt to provide insight into a client's outlook, personality, concerns, values, and interests. Some tests help to assess concentration, coordination, and problem-solving ability. Results of psychological tests can be helpful to a counselor in deciding how best to treat a client's problems. Testing can be a great time- and money-saver in therapy: the results of a twenty-minute test can give a counselor information about a client that might otherwise be gained only through a number of sessions.

FEES

Because of their more advanced training, clinical psychologists can be expected to charge fees that are somewhat higher than what social workers in private practice receive. Charges for the services of a clinical psychologist are made on an hourly basis; counseling sessions usually last forty-five to fifty minutes, although some psychologists will see clients for shorter periods.

Rates vary considerably according to geographical area. An approximate range of $50 to $80 per private session is normal at this time. Group session rates tend to be significantly lower.

If you consult a clinical or counseling psychologist who works through an agency, you will often find that a sliding scale is used to determine charges, as in social work. If you have limited or no health insurance, and financial concerns are a problem, you can telephone counseling agencies in your area to ask whether a sliding scale is used and, if so, what charges correspond to your monthly income. Later, we will look at how to locate counseling agencies, as well as professionals in private practice.

Fees for psychological testing, whether through a psychologist or a psychometrist, are usually billed on the basis of the tests administered. To give some idea, many tests cost $15 to $20 for a psychologist to administer. This charge is passed on to the client. The test results are frequently reviewed during a counseling session so that no additional charge may be made for the evaluation of the results.

DURATION OF TREATMENT

Duration of treatment under a clinical or counseling psychologist is similar to that of a social work counselor. The best way to proceed is to ask prospective therapists how long they believe it will be necessary to see them. Most professionals will be open and candid; if the client's goals are specific and lend themselves to "brief" therapy, a psychologist will make this clear. And, as we have already observed, much depends on the type of therapy practiced by the psychologist. Behavioral therapies tend to be of shorter duration; psychoanalysis is longer-term. In between these there are, as we will see, many therapies that have different emphases, methods, and goals.

PSYCHIATRISTS

ORIENTATION AND TRAINING

Before they specialize in psychiatry, psychiatrists receive the training required of any physician. After this, there is specialized course work followed by a period of psychiatric internship. The educational background of psychiatrists enables them sometimes to identify physical bases for emotional difficulties. A later chapter discusses this growing area of awareness.

Until fairly recently, the therapeutic training of psychiatrists emphasized almost exclusively the approach of psychoanalysis. Psychoanalysis developed within a medical context: Freud was a physician, and his outlook was influenced by his medical orientation. His approach was therefore felt to be the special province of psychiatric medicine. Eventually, as we have already noticed, the methods of psychoanalysis came to be used by psychologists and some social workers. But for a long period, analysis was the primary and exclusive focus of medical psychiatry.

The psychoanalytical orientation still dominates much psychiatry, and many psychiatrists in private practice use psychoanalysis as their therapy of choice. However, there has been a general broadening of the perspective of psychiatrists. Other approaches to psychotherapy are increasingly being used by psychiatrists. Cognitive therapy is important among these; we will discuss its purpose and methods later.

Psychiatrists are the only therapists who may prescribe medication, and some of the most important recent advances in psychiatry have come in this area. Many emotional problems appear to have a biochemical basis. Many forms of anxiety, panic disorders, and depression respond well to the growing family of psychopharmaceutical drugs. Other emotional difficulties, including alcohol and drug abuse, can be moderated by pharmaceutical therapy.

Psychiatrists, then, can be especially helpful in these ways:

* to provide a medical evaluation for complaints that sometimes have a physical basis
* to give assistance especially by means of psychoanalysis and by means of an increasing number of alternative therapies
* to help patients with medication to acquire a degree of emotional equilibrium that will allow them to begin to solve personal problems so that, in time, they may no longer require medication

Although any M.D. may call himself a psychiatrist, most psychiatrists have had specialized advanced training in psychiatry. Full qualifications involve completion of a residency in psychiatry, full membership in the American Psychiatric Association, completion of a program of study at an institute of psychotherapy, and board certification. Many psychiatrists who practice are *eligible* for board certification but simply have not yet taken the national examinations that are required in order to be certified by a national examining board. Although apparently many of us need to be reassured of this, you need not feel that there is anything wrong or embarrassing about asking a prospective psychiatrist, or his or her secretary, to describe the doctor's background and training.

FEES

The fees of psychiatrists in private practice range approximately from $75 up to $100 and occasionally more per session. Private psychiatric assistance is therefore largely reserved for the fairly well-to-do or for those who have health insurance with substantial psychiatric benefits.

Fortunately, psychiatric care is available through many agencies; those that are run by counties and states normally have sliding scales (some private agencies will also take an individual's finances into account when setting fees). Rates for consultation with a psychiatrist at a public agency can be very reasonable (as little as a few dollars per visit, depending on the patient's income). This makes the services of psychiatrists available to those with modest or low incomes.

DURATION OF TREATMENT

If a psychiatrist finds that an emotional problem has a physical basis, or that it is due to biochemical depletion or imbalance in the body, successful treatment may be relatively short, sometimes a matter of a few months.

If you choose to enter psychoanalysis, then the duration of treatment generally will be longer, often lasting a year and more; during this time, psychoanalysts normally expect you to come for two or three sessions each week.

Shorter-term therapies, such as cognitive therapy, are—in part because of the normal long duration required by psychoanalysis—increasingly advocated by psychiatrists. Biofeedback and relaxation training (see Chapter 5) are also among these shorter-term approaches. They are often effective within a period of several months.

In this chapter, we have discussed the professions that make up the mainstream of professional practice in counseling and psychotherapy. However, beyond the established and more closely regulated professions of social worker, psychologist, and psychiatrist, there are a number of other kinds of therapists who offer services that are sufficiently different in nature that they deserve to be treated in a separate chapter. The next chapter describes their contributions to therapy.

5
THE THERAPEUTIC JUNGLE, PART II
Outside the Mainstream

Outside of any profession's frame of reference that defines what problems it will handle and how, we usually find a group of approaches that do not completely fit the established mold. They often can contribute creative and innovative ideas, and yet they often lead to abuses in the name of novelty and experimentation. And sometimes an older approach that fails to fit the newer frame of reference is left behind, to keep company with more radical approaches.

Just these things have happened in the practice of counseling and psychotherapy, as we will see.

RELIGIOUS COUNSELORS

The world's first professional counselors were religious. Guidance from priests, rabbis, and pastors has a long tradition. The tradition is such an old one, in fact, that going to talk to a religious counselor has a respectability that the public has not yet extended to other forms of counseling.

Many people with problems, even people with a religious attitude or upbringing, tend to ignore the kind of help religious counselors may be able to give. This probably stems from the

48

belief that social workers, psychologists, psychiatrists, and some other certified therapists whom we will discuss in a moment have received special training in helping people with personal, emotional problems, whereas religious advisors have not.

However, this is not universally true. Many professional religious representatives now *do* receive training in contemporary therapies. Increasingly, Catholic, Protestant, and Jewish educational institutions are incorporating course work and workshops in modern counseling methods into programs of study for priests, pastors, and rabbis. Individuals who have been trained in this way are easily located within a religious organization; a telephone call to the organization should give you leads to follow.

In spite of the widespread attempt many religious institutions are making to remain up to date on contemporary approaches to counseling, there is probably something also to be said for traditional guidance. All religious views seek to fulfill the needs of men and women to find meaning in everday life and to cope effectively with life's hardships. Contemporary approaches to psychotherapy and counseling can offer much; their history, however, is comparatively brief, extending over just the last century. For many people—depending on their inclinations, values, and sympathies—traditional religious guidance may provide much that is as yet not to be found in the more scientific and systematic schools of contemporary therapy.

If you decide to go to a religious professional for counseling, you will probably find the process relatively informal and friendly. Also, religious professionals generally expect that their private counseling services will not be remunerated; contributions to the supporting religious organization are of course hoped for but are not usually required in exchange for guidance.

In contrast to the authorized community of social workers, psychologists, and psychiatrists, it can be more difficult to locate a religious professional who *specializes* in a particular approach to counseling. The background in modern approaches to counseling that religious professionals tend to receive is "eclectic." They normally receive training in a variety of approaches; their programs of study are based on the belief that flexibility in counseling is essential, that nothing works well for everyone. This openness can be of value to many people. But, as you read this book, you may decide to locate a therapist who has a certain specific orientation. He or she may be a religious counselor, a psychologist, or another qualified professional. In general, if you have a specific form of therapy in mind, you will have to ask a prospective therapist whether he or she has the training to give you the kind of help you are looking for. This is especially true of religious counselors.

BIOFEEDBACK THERAPISTS

Biofeedback is a newcomer to the therapeutic world that has grown tremendously in popularity in the last ten years or so. Biofeedback therapy gradually enables individuals to become aware of certain physical changes in their bodies. These physical changes are detected by means of sensitive measuring instruments that give information back to clients so they can learn to control a particular physical response.

Biofeedback is used by therapists who have been specially trained in its use, as well as by some licensed psychologists, psychiatrists, social workers, physical therapists, speech pathologists, and even some dentists. Some psychiatrists now work jointly with a biofeedback therapist: the psychiatrist can prescribe medication and provide psychotherapy or analysis, while the associated biofeedback therapist can teach patients how to lessen pain- and stress-related problems.

The Biofeedback Society of America is an interdisciplinary group of health care professionals; it is presently developing training standards and guidelines for certification of biofeedback practitioners.

RELAXATION, HYPNOSIS, AND MEDITATION THERAPISTS

Relaxation training, hypnosis, and meditation all seek to bring about a deep sense of relaxation in a person. We will examine each in detail later.

RELAXATION TRAINING

Relaxation training involves exercises that enable a person to learn to induce *at will* a state of physical and mental calm. Relaxation training is a practical skill—it can be very effective and useful in coping with stressful situations. Like any learned skill, control comes only with practice, usually over a period of several months. Many social workers and psychologists teach clients relaxation techniques. Certification standards specifically for relaxation training have not been established.

HYPNOSIS

Hypnosis involves two stages: (1) progressive, deep relaxation to a point at which an individual is in a peaceful, trancelike state, still self-aware but profoundly relaxed; and (2) suggestion, which persuades the person to adopt certain future attitudes, thoughts, or behavior.

Hypnosis, like relaxation training, can be learned. Most people treated by means of hypnosis steadily improve in their ability to be hypnotized so that they can more effectively allow themselves to be influenced by means of carefully planned suggestions. Many psychologists and psychiatrists make use of hypnosis in the context of therapy; some practitioners treat patients exclusively by means of hypnosis.

The certification of therapists trained in hypnosis is still unsettled in many states, where anyone can hang out a shingle. Since many licensed psychologists and psychiatrists and some certified social workers *do* receive professional training in hypnosis, these are the professions to which it is most reliable to go for hypnotherapy.

MEDITATION

Meditation is still a "fringe" therapy. Techniques of meditation are seldom taught to clients in psychotherapy, although there is a growing body of evidence that meditation is able to bring about great resistance to stress, an increased sense of inner calm, and even actual changes in brain-wave patterns associated with deep relaxation. These effects of meditation are now being studied, with encouraging results.

The practice of meditation is, in the author's view, at present best learned on one's own, although some commercial organizations provide instruction. A later chapter discusses approaches to meditation and suggests some of the ways meditation can be of value.

HOLISTIC THERAPIES:
BIOENERGETICS, YOGA, AND EXERCISE

Holism views man as a unity of body and mind. The established approaches to therapy and counseling, represented by social workers, psychologists, psychiatrists, and to a certain extent by some religious professionals, all focus attention on our mental-psychological dimension. Similarly, biofeedback, hypnosis, and meditation emphasize the central role of *mental* control.

Holistic approaches, on the other hand, attempt to bring about positive change by means of emphasis on physical factors that are believed to have a close connection to mental processes. Although holism sees human beings as integral organisms, holistic approaches are inclined to have this physical focus.

Holistic therapies, like meditation, are "fringe" therapies. They are not generally employed by members of the "authorized" community of health practitioners, for two reasons: First, a kind of professional respectability and elitism have come to be associated with the psychological approach; social work, psychology, and psychiatry have an accepted place in institutions of higher learning, whereas fringe therapies do not. Second, since physicians treat the body, there is an institutionalized prejudice against nonmedical treatment that has the same focus.

Chiropractic has encountered this problem, as have other forms of holism, such as bioenergetics, yoga, diet therapy, and rolfing.

Although much of value may be offered by these fringe therapies, they have also resulted in abuse to consumers. Because of a general absence of licensing standards and of scientific credibility, people frequently are drawn in by the sometimes extravagant promises of unscrupulous or overly enthusiastic fringe therapists. In this area, as in all others that affect the consumer, the proper attitude is one of healthy skepticism and restraint.

BIOENERGETICS

Of these holistic therapies, bioenergetics is perhaps considered the most respectable because it *is* used by some psychologists. Bioenergetics attempts to diminish an individual's psychological defenses by means of sequences of specially designed physical exercises that, in a controlled and deliberate way, stress the person physically. Practitioners of bioenergetics believe that physical exercises of this kind rapidly put a person in touch with buried (repressed) feelings and speed up the process of inner integration that all holistic practices, as well as traditional therapy, wish to achieve.

YOGA

Yoga exists in various forms. The two main varieties are hatha yoga and raja yoga. Hatha yoga emphasizes physical flexibility; raja yoga teaches breathing techniques and meditation. Hatha yoga, because of its focus on the body, belongs to the family of approaches we are considering here.

Hatha yoga practitioners believe that the physical flexibility and control that are acquired through an extended period of physical training in yoga exercise tend to influence your mental orientation. You become, in this view, more flexible, less rigid, less defensive, less subject to stress, more open, responsive, alert, and capable of warmth in human relationships.

EXERCISE THERAPY

Counselors and therapists are starting to take very seriously the idea that exercise brings emotional benefits. Exercise therapy, more so than other physically based approaches discussed in this chapter, has been tested in various ways. Many emotional conditions—for example, anxiety and depression—seem to be significantly reduced thanks to periods of sustained vigorous exercise. Tolerance to stress and to pain appears to be increased. Physical exercise can be an outlet for pent-up hostility and aggression that, according to many theorists, may be turned inward, then fester, and eventually take the form of a variety of psychological disorders. Furthermore, vigorous, sustained aerobic exercise—like running or swimming—appears to have a calming effect as a result of certain chemical compounds that are released into the bloodstream. We will look at some of the interesting recent studies of the therapeutic value of exercise later on.

6
WHERE YOU CAN FIND HELP

PRIVATE PRACTICE

As we have seen, social work counselors, psychologists, psychiatrists, biofeedback therapists, hypnotherapists, and other therapists may all offer their services through private practice. In general, there can be definite advantages to counseling in the setting of a therapist's private practice. You are given a degree of personal care that, as an individual paying customer, you are less likely to receive in counseling provided by agencies. You become part of a therapist's own practice, so it is natural for him or her to devote special attention to you. Therapists are likely to be more personally involved in their private practice and in the quality of care they try to give their private clients than it is possible or even personally desirable for them to be when they work by the hour for an agency.

On the other hand, private sessions with a therapist tend to be considerably more expensive than counseling can be through many agencies. You ought not to take too seriously general comparisons between therapy as you may encounter it privately and therapy in the setting of an agency. You can often find a counselor who is congenial, interested, attentive, and skilled; whose services will be easier for you to bear financially; and who offers his or her services through an agency. If finances are restrictive for you, you should look into agency-sponsored counseling.

Many social work counselors, psychologists, and some psychiatrists who maintain private practices intended mainly for individual therapy also offer group therapy. Often, a therapist will observe that a number of individual clients share certain problems and experiences, and he or she will suggest that these people meet together as a group. The per-session price can be expected to be a good deal lower than for individual sessions; the rate usually reflects the number of people who meet in the group and the length of time the group is expected to continue.

Some social workers and some psychologists *specialize* in group therapy. Groups are formed periodically, run a set number of weeks, and may or may not bring together individuals with common problems. Some group therapists believe that diversity in a counseling group is valuable: in such a group, you might find one person combating alcoholism, another trying to cope with loneliness and grief after the death of a spouse, someone trying to break out of the confines of shyness, a person suffering from public speaking anxiety, someone wanting to change careers but who is blocked by fear, and others. An exchange of views among participants with diverse backgrounds can frequently encourage growth in the group members.

Most counseling agencies also offer group therapy, as do many hospitals and schools. We will take a look at each of these settings in turn.

COUNTY, STATE, AND PRIVATE AGENCIES

Individual, marriage and family, and group counseling are all offered by most counseling agencies.

County and state agencies receive public funding and usually have sliding scales for the rates they charge. Often, one or more psychiatrists work in association with counselors, who may be social workers or psychologists. If you go to a county or state agency, you will probably be interviewed initially by a receptionist or nurse. You will be asked questions about your financial situation and health insurance coverage, if you have any, and you will be asked to agree to a proposed rate for the services of the agency. Some county and state agencies make a monthly charge for their services; you may consult regularly with members of the staff, counselors and/or psychiatrists, in accordance with your individual needs.

Private counseling agencies function in a similar way. Their services tend to be more expensive because they do not receive public financial support, as do county and state agencies.

Normally, health insurance that provides psychological benefits can be used to pay for the services of a private or a public counseling agency.

HOSPITALS AND
OTHER INPATIENT SERVICES

Individuals with severe problems who need complete care can enter private, county, or state hospitals that offer psychiatric services. A separate chapter discusses pros and cons of the sometimes frightening alternative of hospitalization.

Again, publically funded hospitals tend to charge on the basis of a sliding scale, which takes a person's financial situation into account. Where financial concerns are not pressing, private hospitals in general tend to offer a greater degree of individual attention and higher quality of care and physical facilities.

In addition to hospital facilities, many metropolitan areas have established organizations to provide counseling services on an inpatient basis. Some are private; some are public. They offer an alternative to hospitalization. They tend to be more informal and open and are managed by their own staffs of professional counselors and psychiatrists. These residential care facilities usually are intended for stays of from one to several weeks. They have a variety of counseling programs, ranging from individual therapy to group counseling and vocational guidance.

One way to locate such an inpatient organization is to telephone a crisis intervention (sometimes called *suicide prevention*) number likely to be listed at the beginning of your telephone directory. A volunteer probably will answer your call and should be able to direct you to inpatient facilities available in your area.

ACADEMIC SOURCES OF COUNSELING

Counseling is one of the services available to full- and part-time students who are enrolled in junior or four-year colleges and graduate schools. Many educational institutions offer individual counseling, normally by counseling psychologists, and all colleges offer academic advising in the context of a certain amount of vocational guidance.

Colleges with programs in counseling and psychology usually also offer certain classes with a practical, problem-solving focus. Although they may not be specifically intended to help individual students with life problems, this is in fact what they frequently end up doing. It is inevitable for students in a practically oriented counseling class to apply much that they learn to their own problems. Many class meetings of this kind tend to be almost indistinguishable from group therapy sessions: students receive guidance from a professionally trained instructor, exchange views, and express personal concerns. You might think of college classes with a practical, psychological emphasis especially if you are drawn to therapy as an opportunity for general personal growth.

Classes of this kind may be offered in a college's regular programs, which are sometimes open only to students working toward a degree. Other similar opportunities, however, are available through many continuing education, or adult education, programs. Many secondary school districts offer practical, psychologically focused classes for adults who do not choose to enter a degree program. This is also true of community, state, and many private colleges.

Colleges and private professionals offer intensive workshops with a variety of counseling emphases. Two-day weekend workshops have become especially popular. Topics range from alcoholism, drug abuse, child-rearing problems, and separation and divorce to illness and chronic pain, marital concerns, depression, stress control, and so on. Newspapers announce counseling workshops; you will often find notices about them posted in public and college libraries.

SOME REFLECTIONS ON WHERE YOU GO FOR COUNSELING

You should bear in mind that where you go for counseling or therapy is nothing more than an address. What *is* important is what happens in your relationship with your counselor or therapist. If you have found a therapist whom you respect and feel motivated to work with, it makes little difference, as far as the benefits you obtain from therapy are concerned, whether your therapist works in private practice or offers his or her services through an agency, school, hospital, or residential facility.

On the other hand, where you go for counseling *will* greatly determine the price you will pay for services and frequently whether health insurance will cover your expenses. To some extent, where you go can sometimes, as we have noted, influence the quality of care and individual attention you receive. But this *is* a generalization; you frequently will be able to locate excellent care through less expensive facilities. This will depend to some extent on luck, but more on the amount of effort you put into locating the kind of help you may need.

Since you are reading this book, you already have initiative like this: you have the ability to influence what kind and quality of therapy you will receive. For you, it will be less a matter of pure luck than it is for people who choose a therapy and therapist arbitrarily.

7
SELF-DIAGNOSIS
Mapping Your Way to a Therapy

This chapter is central to your use of this book as a guide. There are two main ways to use this book to help you to choose a therapy:

1. You can familiarize yourself with all of the major approaches to therapy, weigh their advantages and disadvantages in relation to your needs, and then make a choice. Twenty-six approaches to therapy are discussed and evaluated in this book, so keeping your judgments of their pros and cons clearly in mind can be challenging. Although comprehensive understanding has a value of its own, it may not be essential to you.

2. You may prefer to go through three simple steps to narrow the alternatives down to a small number of therapies that have been most successful for specific goals, problems, and personal attributes that most closely approximate your own. This is a less time-consuming process, and it will take into account professional evaluations of the different therapies.

In either case, your informed judgment will be the basis for your eventual choice. This chapter is intended to help you if you prefer the second route—to narrow down the alternatives in a clear and logical way. If you prefer, however, to become acquainted with all of the major therapies discussed in this book, you might skim through sections of this chapter to give you a framework for more efficient understanding.

The information in this chapter relates to many different sets of goals, problems, and kinds of people. Not all of this information will be relevant to you, so you will find instructions to direct you to specific recommendations that take into account your own needs and interests.

This chapter is where practical and prudent planning can begin. In fact, this book represents the first attempt to match you, your personal qualities, and your goals with the most effective therapy or therapies available to you.

Even though nearly all of the main approaches to counseling and therapy are creations of the past century, it may seem surprising that no unified effort has been made to identify what specific kinds of problems each approach is especially useful for treating and for what types of clients. In this respect, the field of medicine is much better developed. The discipline of medical diagnostics is now on the verge of becoming scientific, and it is now possible to identify for many conditions and in individual cases very concrete and well-defined treatment procedures that are likely to be effective. This has not been true in the field of psychology: most research efforts have so far gone into formulating definitions of the various mental and emotional disorders. But the important work, from the prospective client's point of view, had yet to be done: to make it possible for him to know— in relation to his individual problems, goals, interests, abilities, and temperament—which approaches to therapy are likely to help him the most.

If you are in serious emotional pain, waiting until all of the research results are in is just not possible; you need help *now*. In spite of incomplete knowledge in psychotherapy, a large body of information has come from studies of the effectiveness of therapies for different problems and for different kinds of people. But until now this information existed only in fragmented form and was accessible only to professional psychologists. Enough data are in to begin to draw reasonable guidelines for individuals who seek psychological help.

The mapping process described in this chapter is the result of assembling and then organizing large quantities of data from many sources. It was then necessary to design an easily followed step-by-step approach to enable you to narrow down the many therapeutic alternatives to a small number that, through your efforts and the assistance of a therapist, can be of help to you. Guidelines of this kind are never static; they will change to some extent as time and knowledge advance.

OBSTACLES TO FINDING A THERAPY THAT FITS YOU

There are real obstacles to efficient treatment in psychotherapy. They cost people much time, energy, hope, and money as they try to find appropriate help. Psychotherapy is not yet a systematic field.

There are three main reasons why it is so difficult to find approaches to therapy that will fit individual clients and their needs:

- Emotional and mental difficulties vary tremendously. Psychologists and psychiatrists are still in the process of classifying the kinds of emotional and mental problems people have.
- People are individuals. Their personalities, likes and dislikes, and motivations for entering therapy differ greatly.
- Therapists, too, are individuals. Their personalities, interests, values, and motivations for *offering* therapy differ greatly. Their professional training and preferences in favor of one or several approaches to therapy also vary significantly.

As a result, what works for one patient will not necessarily work for another. *What* helps and *who* helps in one person's situation may not help in another's. Yet all three of the factors on which effective treatment depends—a patient's goals and problems, his or her personality traits, and the approach of the therapist—in many cases *can* be matched intelligently. You, as a prospective client, know a great deal about yourself; it doesn't make sense to choose arbitrarily among the many therapies. It takes very little time to map your way: in the process, you will learn more about yourself, what to anticipate in therapy, and in what direction to start.

REALISM: A GOOD BEGINNING

In order to identify one or more therapies that may be most promising in relation to *your* goals, *your* problems, and *the kind of person you understand yourself to be*, you must begin your search with a good measure of realism.

SETTING GOALS

It can be very difficult for anyone who is seriously troubled to think clearly and use good judgment. You may find it hard, perhaps impossible, at this time to identify your goals. You may feel confused, anxious, depressed, and not know why you feel that way. Even so, you will find as you read on that you *can* set important goals for yourself.

If you are at a loss and have no sense of purpose, *that* fact gives you a goal to work toward in therapy: to develop clearly thought-out goals. Though you may not know what precipitated your feelings of confusion, anxiety, or depression, you at least *know* that you feel confused, anxious, or depressed, and you will find recommendations in this chapter on how to find appropriate help for your suffering. Do not judge yourself harshly if you lack a sense of direction or if you are troubled but do not know why. Just keep reading.

OPENING YOURSELF TO CHANGE

There is a second thing you should be realistic about when you *do* know what you want and what your problems are. Our experiences and what we learn about ourselves *change* us. If you enter therapy based on your present perceptions of yourself, it is likely that these are going to change to some extent as a result of your experiences in therapy. Does that mean that you cannot plan or select a therapy intelligently? Clearly, it doesn't. *Everyone has to start where he or she is.* There is no other choice. But you should try to persuade yourself to be open to changes in your views and feelings. If you feel rigid about your own perceptions of yourself, it is just possible that your rigidity may be contributing to the problems you want to resolve. As in any attempt to learn or to change, it is important periodically to reevaluate your needs, values, and the results you may have achieved so far. If you select a therapy using the structured approach in this chapter, you may decide to retrace your footsteps a few months in the future. You may find that you would take a different path in the light of what you then see.

BEING HONEST ABOUT YOURSELF

There is a third piece of realism that I would like you to consider, and this is *very* hard for anyone to take to heart. If you can, you are a very unusual person. Answering the following questions honestly takes some real courage. But you must ask yourself: "To what extent do I *need* my present symptoms? Is it useful to me *not* to have a sense of direction? Am I somehow *benefiting* from feeling depressed? Is my anxiety *helpful* to me in some way?"

You may think these suggestions are no more than contrived and unkind psychologizing. After all, who *chooses* to suffer? Does anyone *want* to wake up at 4:00 A.M. shaking and crying? Yet, again and again, therapists who care very much about their patients find that many of them "cling to their symptoms with the desperation of a drowning man hanging onto a raft."[*]

For diverse reasons, many people—even people who are suffering greatly—do not *want* to change. Their unhappiness, pain, and confusion can serve numerous functions. You may not believe this right now, but from time to time as you read this book, and later in your life, this question may occur to you, if only for a moment: "How may this unresolved problem benefit me?"

The plain truth is that even suffering can confer benefits on us. This is at the root of much of the tragedy of emotional problems that prove to be resistant to treatment. The distressed, despondent, overwrought, and trembling person seated before the therapist may have found a way to gain the attention he was unable to get otherwise. Or perhaps his suffering is a way to lighten a burden of guilt that eventually caused an inner collapse. There are many "benefits," many very good reasons to want *not* to change but to try *anyway*.

So, before you begin to seek a specific type of therapy, try to be realistic and keep these thoughts in mind:

---

[*]Lewis R. Wolberg, *Hypnosis* (New York: Harcourt Brace Jovanovich, 1972), p. 238. (In this guide, see Chapter 15, on hypnosis.)

1. Specifying clear-cut goals and understanding why you feel troubled are not essential now. Certainly it will be helpful if you can translate vague complaints into concrete problems, to help both your own understanding and eventually your therapist's. The more specific you can be about what is troubling you, what situations especially distress you, and what has motivated you to come to therapy, the easier it will be for you to find help and for the therapist you choose to help you. But in times of crisis, clarity can be very hard to gain, so be patient.

2. If you *do* have clear-cut goals and a good understanding of yourself now, use these to plan how to proceed, remembering that openness to change will profit you and that, in all likelihood, your initial perceptions of yourself will change as you become involved in therapy.

3. You may, at least now, *need* your symptoms, however painful they may be. How successful therapy will be for you may have a great deal to do with your willingness to let go of the benefits of being troubled, in pain, or disabled.

4. Resist digging ruts for yourself. Try to refrain from locking into a particular course of action until you have given yourself time to consider alternatives. Once you have chosen a direction, if after a reasonable time the therapy and the therapist you have selected do not seem to be helping you, it is essential to try another approach. This is especially difficult once you have invested your time, energy, and money and perhaps have developed a good relationship with your therapist. You may *like* him or her, feel comfortable and comforted, but if you are not gaining what you want, you have to stop and try again.

5. Finally, have a thorough physical examination before entering therapy, if you have not had one recently. Be truthful and open with your physician. Some emotional and mental problems are produced by underlying physical conditions, many of which can be treated effectively (see Chapter 8).

HOW TO MAP YOUR WAY TO A THERAPY

The remainder of this chapter presents a three-step process

for choosing an approach to therapy that is potentially best suited to your personal needs and personality.

In the first step, you become familiar with the main kinds of goals and problems that motivate people to enter therapy. You check those that seem to be most relevant to you and then try to confirm the accuracy of your choices. This will point you in the direction of one or more promising therapies.

In the second step, you consider a list of the main personality traits that are relevant to your choice of therapy. Again, you check those that seem most to apply to you and then confirm your self-understanding. Step 2 will also direct you to one or more therapies.

In the third step, you use your results from Step 1 and Step 2 to select an approach to therapy that most closely matches your needs, interests, and personality.

Let's begin.

STEP 1. DIAGNOSING YOUR PROBLEMS AND SETTING YOUR GOALS: IDENTIFYING APPROPRIATE THERAPIES

a. Read through Table 1 (pages 67-69).

b. Check the goals or problems most applicable to you. If you are in doubt, refer to the numbered short descriptions in the section following Table 1.

c. Choose one or two goals or problems that are the most important to you.

d. Confirm your choices: Refer to the section following Table 1. Read the short descriptions of the one or two goals or problems you checked and ask yourself whether, in fact, these accurately apply to you.

e. If, after doing this, you continue to believe that the goals or problems you checked relate to you, make a record of the therapy letter codes given at the end of each description. You will find that occasionally letter codes are divided into two groups: those judged to be generally more effective (called "primary"), and a set of alternatives ("secondary"). Now go directly to Step 2. On the other hand, if you come to feel that the goals or problems you checked really do *not* apply to you, go back to Table 1 and consider other alternatives.

STEP 2. SELF-UNDERSTANDING:
IDENTIFYING APPROPRIATE THERAPIES

a. Read through Table 2 (page 79).
b. Check the personal qualities that seem best to describe you.
c. Choose one or two of these that are the most significant to you.
d. Confirm your self-understanding: Refer to the section following Table 2. Read the short descriptions of the one or two personal qualities you checked and respond to the questions you will find there.
e. If, after doing this, you believe that the personal qualities you checked do, in fact, describe you accurately, make a record of the therapy letter codes given at the end of the questions. Now go directly to Step 3. If, on the other hand, judging from your responses to the questions you answered, you do *not* feel that the personal qualities you checked are true of you, return to Table 2 and consider other alternatives.

STEP 3. CHOOSING A THERAPY

a. Compare the two sets of letter codes you recorded as a result of Steps 1 and 2. If one or more letter codes are common to both sets, make a special note of the common code(s); otherwise, group the letter codes together.
b. Refer to Table 3 (pages 86-87), which summarizes the letter codes of all the therapies discussed in this guide. Check the code(s) you just listed.
c. If you feel that you have taken your time, have been thoughtful about yourself, and now feel reasonably confident about the tentative conclusions you have reached, turn to the chapter(s) in this book that discuss the approaches to therapy you checked. As you read these, try to imagine yourself as a client in each of the therapy situations described. Which approach seems most appropriate given your goals or problems? Do you feel that *you* have the personal traits that the therapy is most suited for? If so, give that approach to therapy a reasonable trial period. If not, consider other alternatives you checked.

AN EXAMPLE OF FOLLOWING STEPS 1, 2, AND 3

Suppose you check §3.1, shyness/passivity, in Table 1. You refer to the section following Table 1, relating to personality trait problems. You feel that shyness *is* something that interferes significantly with your life, interests, and desires, and you want to do something to overcome it. Therapies Q, C, N, and D are recommended to you as potentially useful. Then, on Table 2, you check §7. You refer to §7 following Table 2, and you decide that you especially need to work on pent-up feelings in need of release. Therapies C and J are suggested there as potentially appropriate for you.

You now have two sets of therapy letter codes to consider: Q, C, N, and D; and C and J.

Therapy C is common to both recommended groups of therapies, but you are interested in comparing the other therapies with C. In addition to reading about C, you decide to read the discussions of therapies D, J, N, and Q. From Table 3, the five letter codes C, D, J, N, and Q denote Gestalt therapy, transactional analysis, bioenergetics, counter-conditioning, and group therapy, respectively. After reading about these therapies, you come to feel that Gestalt therapy probably would challenge you in especially needed ways, so you decide to locate a therapist with training in Gestalt therapy. (For information on locating a therapist, see Chapter 17.)

TABLE 1:
AN OVERVIEW OF PRINCIPAL GOALS AND MAIN EMOTIONAL AND MENTAL DISORDERS THAT LEAD PEOPLE TO ENTER THERAPY

§1 **Personal development goals**
☐ §1.1 **developing new skills and personal traits: education leading to growth**
☐ §1.2 **eliminating self-destructive habits or undesirable personality traits: reeducation leading to change (see §3 below)**

S
T
E
P

1

S
T
E
P
1

§2   **Disorders usually first noticed in childhood or adolescence**
☐ §2.1 **mental retardation**
☐ §2.2 **autism**
☐ §2.3 **emotional disturbances: separation anxiety, sleep terror and sleepwalking disorders, etc.**
☐ §2.4 **suffering from childhood pain, neglect, or abuse; traumatic experiences from childhood, unmet childhood needs**
☐ §2.5 **behavior problems: hyperactivity, antisocial behavior, movement disorders (see §10 below)**
☐ §2.6 **delinquency and criminal behavior**
☐ §2.7 **eating disorders: obesity, bulimia, anorexia nervosa**

§3   **Personality trait problems**
☐ §3.1 **shyness/passivity**
☐ §3.2 **loneliness/emptiness**
☐ §3.3 **hostility/overbearing personality**
☐ §3.4 **fear of withdrawal of affection and of abandonment**
☐ §3.5 **general interpersonal problems**
☐ §3.6 **need to improve effectiveness of communication skills**
☐ §3.7 **difficulties in coping with persons in authority**
☐ §3.8 **loss of faith in oneself or in others, or in life's purpose or end**
☐ §3.9 **low self-worth, desire for a success-identity (self-esteem resulting from a sense of achievement)**
☐ §3.10 **deep discouragement with life (see §5 below)**

§4   **Neuroses**
☐ §4.1 **anxiety disorders, panic disorders, post-traumatic stress disorders, etc.**
☐ §4.2 **phobias**
☐ §4.3 **compulsions**
☐ §4.4 **noögenic neuroses (resulting from serious conflicts between opposing values)**
☐ §4.5 **psychosomatic disorders, hypochondria**
☐ §4.6 **sexual disorders**
☐ §4.7 **impulse control disorders: e.g., pathological gambling, kleptomania, pyromania**

§5   **Mood disturbances (affective disorders)**
□ §5.1 **depression**
□ §5.2 **mania**
□ §5.3 **manic depression**

§6   **Adjustment problems**
□ §6.1 **in relation to a new environment or an already familiar one; work inhibitions**
□ §6.2 **in persons with counterculture attitudes and values**
□ §6.3 **emotional difficulties arising from poverty and from the deprivations suffered by minority groups**
□ §6.4 **inability to accept realities that limit life: e.g., financial limitations, restricted opportunities, aging and death (see §9 below), jobs with "no future," responsibilities that stand in the way of personal development**

□ §7   **Marital problems**

□ §8   **Family problems**

§9   **Problems related to aging**
□ §9.1 **emotional problems in facing old age**
□ §9.2 **problems facing the recently widowed**
□ §9.3 **coping with physical pain and disability**

§10   **Involuntary behaviors**
□ §10.1 **stuttering**
□ §10.2 **shaking or motor tic disorders**
□ §10.3 **insomnia**

□ §11   **Crisis intervention: a need for *prompt* relief from severe symptoms**

□ §12   **Psychoses: schizophrenia, manic and paranoid psychoses, hysterical psychoses, etc.**

§13   **Organic disorders**
□ §13.1 **senescence, Alzheimer's disease**
□ §13.2 **Parkinsonism/Huntington's chorea**
□ §13.3 **substance-induced: alcoholism, drug addiction, smoking**
□ §13.4 **organic brain dysfunctions: epilepsy, narcolepsy, amnesia, dementia, delirium**

S T E P 1

S
T
E
P

1

MATCHING YOUR GOALS AND PROBLEMS WITH MOST PROMISING THERAPIES

§1 Personal Development Goals

These may involve either (§1.1) *adding* new skills or qualities or (§1.2) *subtracting* habits or undesirable traits.

§1.1. There are basically two different approaches to achieving the first goal:

- You identify a specific skill or personality trait you would like to develop—see Table 1, §3. For example, you may want to develop a stronger success-identity (§3.9), improve your communication skills (§3.6), gain a stronger sense of life's purpose (§3.8), or become more assertive (i.e., overcome a degree of shyness, §3.1). For references to recommended therapies for these goals, see §3 below. For vocational counseling and therapy: ♦H, I, M.
- Alternatively, you decide to approach self-development with a desire for *broad-spectrum* improvements. Therapies with this orientation are not especially concerned with highly specific behaviors or problems but attempt to treat the whole person so that self-esteem is gradually increased, as are a sense of satisfaction in daily living, enjoyment of others, and a feeling of being at ease with them.

  Primary therapy (judged to be generally more effective) ♦A, B.
  Secondary therapy (somewhat less effective) ♦J.

§1.2. Refer to §3 below.

§2 Disorders Usually First Noticed in Childhood or Adolescence

§2.1. Mental retardation ♦O.

§2.2. Autism: self-injuring behavior, withdrawal from reality ♦O, Y.

§2.3. Emotional disturbances in children ♦S, W.

§2.4. Suffering from childhood pain, neglect, or abuse: traumatic experiences from childhood, unmet childhood needs (see §3.4) ♦A, K.

§2.5. Behavior problems in children   ▶O, C.

Hyperkinetic behavior:

    Primary   ▶Y, O.

    Secondary   ▶Z.

§2.6. Delinquency and criminal behavior   ▶O, E, H, I.

§2.7. Eating disorders: obesity, bulimia, anorexia nervosa   ▶O, W.

§3 Personality Trait Problems

§3.1. Shyness/passivity   ▶Q, C, N, D.

§3.2. Loneliness/emptiness   ▶F, Q, D.

Sense of estrangement, alienation from others   ▶G.

§3.3. Hostility/overbearing personality   ▶E, D, N, Q.

§3.4. Fear of withdrawal of affection and of abandonment (also see §3.2 above)   ▶R or S, D, A.

§3.5. General interpersonal problems:

    If you are willing to work on these within a wider focus   ▶A.

    Involved in relating to others on an individual basis   ▶E, P, W.

§3.6. Need to improve effectiveness of communication skills   ▶D.

In groups of people   ▶Q.

§3.7. Difficulties in coping with persons in authority   ▶C, D.

§3.8. Loss of faith in yourself or in others or in life's purpose or end   ▶F, G, X.

§3.9. Low self-worth   ▶B.

Desire for a success-identity   ▶H, M.

§3.10. Deep discouragement with life (see §5 below)   ▶I.

§4 Neuroses

A person is said to suffer from a neurosis if he or she has exaggerated emotional responses or ideas of reality that blow things out of proportion. Individuals with neuroses are able to communicate normally or with mild emotional interference. Their emotional problems interfere with normal living but do not impair them so that their lives are clearly out of control (as in psychoses, alcoholism, drug addiction, etc.).

§4.1. Anxiety disorders, panic disorders, post-traumatic stress disorders, etc.:

STEP 1

S
T
E
P

1

Anxiety and panic attacks are characterized by feelings of fear, dread, and tension. You may have a sense of imminent disaster or death, a feeling of helplessness often followed by depression. (These are also symptoms of *chronic anxiety*.) Other symptoms of anxiety and panic attacks include dizziness, dry mouth, sweating, headaches, heart palpitations, increased blood pressure, rapid breathing, weakness, insomnia, increased urination, a feeling of unreality, diminished concentration, memory difficulties, indecision, obsessive thinking about anxiety symptoms, second-order anxiety (anxiety that you are or will be anxious), and desperation to obtain relief.

Primary   ♦Y, E, P, V, T, W, X.
Secondary   ♦H, K, U.

Post-traumatic stress disorders are frequently misdiagnosed as anxiety disorders. Patients suffering from post-traumatic stress have been exposed to situations of great stress—e.g., battlefront conditions, rape, imprisonment in a concentration camp. These situations are perceived as inescapable, and they leave long-lasting emotional scars. Symptoms include reactions delayed until days or months have passed since the trauma situation, emotional numbing, chronic anxiety, restlessness, irritability, recurrent nightmares, increased startle responses, impulsive behavior, and depression.

♦Y, in conjunction with therapies recommended for anxiety and panic attacks.

§4.2. Phobias: Phobias are fears that are disproportionate to the threat of a situation. They are involuntary and cannot be reasoned away. They lead to avoidance of the feared situation.

Primary   ♦N, L, Y W, V.
Secondary   ♦U, A, K, D.
For fears of public speaking, especially   ♦E.

§4.3. Compulsions: People with neurotic compulsions engage in repetitive rituals that give them temporary relief from anxiety. Compulsive behaviors are often motivated by a desire for exactness and perfection—for example, compulsive hygiene, washing, counting, praying, reflecting about yourself, repetitive isolated thoughts, preoccupation with trifling details, etc.

Primary   ♦E, M, O, A.
Secondary   ♦Y, T, K.

Compulsions that arise, or may be resolved, in relation to your family   ♦S.

§4.4. Noögenic neuroses: A person can be emotionally disabled by serious conflicts between opposing personal, ethical, or
religious values. This problem has not gained widespread recognition among psychiatrists and therapists. It is a focus of logotherapy (see Chapter 11).   ▶G.

§4.5. Psychosomatic disorders, hypochondria: Physical disorders caused by emotional problems are psychosomatic. Examples include some cases of colitis, stomach cramps, diarrhea,
constipation, ulcers, cardiac arrhythmias, impotence, back and
neck spasms, and migraines. Hypochondria involves an exaggerated concern over potential and imagined symptoms of disease.
     ▶Physical examination followed by P, C, N, W, X.

§4.6. Sexual disorders: These include impotence, frigidity,
vaginismus (vaginal muscle spasm), premature ejaculation, and
sexual role disturbances when accompanied by emotional disorders or poor social functioning (some cases of homosexuality,
transsexualism).   ▶P, E, O, N, W; sometimes with Y.
If you are willing to work on this within a wider focus   ▶A.

§4.7. Impulse control disorders: e.g., pathological gambling,
kleptomania, pyromania   ▶O, M, E, Q.

§5 Mood Disturbances (Affective Disorders)

There are three primary mood disorders: depression, mania,
and manic depression. They may be neurotic, or they may be
psychotic, in which you experience hallucinations, delusions,
and withdrawal from reality. Each disorder may be situational or
nonsituational, depending on the role of precipitating events,
such as the death of a loved one, loss of a job, diagnosis of
terminal illness, etc. Situational mood disorders usually disappear with time. All three disorders may appear as isolated
episodes, or they may be recurrent.

§5.1. Depression: Clinical depression is not simple sadness or
grief. Severely depressed people speak slowly, laboriously. It is
difficult for you to maintain attention and concentration. You
may have feelings of hopelessness, despair, heaviness, self-blame,
heightened self-criticism, great pessimism about the future,
inability to make decisions, tendencies to think of suicide and
sometimes to commit it. Dependence on loved ones increases as
you feel helpless. Interests diminish in work, hobbies, and
friends. You may cry frequently; you may be irritable and

S
T
E
P

1

inclined to have angry outbursts. You probably sleep poorly and awaken frequently, particularly in early morning. Anxiety is common in about 50 percent of patients. There is frequently little appetite for food or for sex.   ♦Y, E, P, U, T, W, X.

As a sense of deep discouragement with life   ♦I.

Depressed as a result of a conflict in personal values   ♦G.

If you are willing to work on your problems within a wider focus (also see §1.1)   ♦A.

§5.2. Mania: You tend to have exaggerated beliefs in your capabilities; you tend to be euphoric and may fall in love easily and repeatedly. You suffer from impulsiveness, poor judgment, racing thoughts, sometimes explosive anger. Milder degrees of mania are often welcomed by you, family, and friends, who admire your enormous energy and your many "irons in the fire." Only when family and friends become aware of your poor judgment in buying sprees, delusions of grandeur, or sexual excesses do they try to encourage you to seek treatment, usually against your own wishes.

♦Y (especially lithium therapy), E, P, T, W, X.

§5.3. Manic depression: You are trapped on an emotional roller coaster: at times you are depressed (see §5.1), and at other times you experience the highs of mania (see §5.2).

♦Y (especially lithium therapy), and therapies listed under §5.1.

§6 Adjustment Problems

Some critics of psychotherapy have argued that its main purpose is to serve the interests and values of society: a person is judged to be "abnormal" if he does not want, or refuses, for example, to work from nine to five all but two weeks of the year; if he does not accept the responsibilities society claims he should respond to as an adult, a citizen, a husband, or a father. These social demands—so critics of therapy have argued—have been internalized by most therapists so that therapies often do not really serve the individual's needs but rather the prevailing belief-system of society. Whatever validity the critics' argument may have, it relates particularly to this area of emotional suffering that falls under the heading of adjustment disorders.

Some adjustment disorders clearly lie outside the boundaries of this criticism. For example, a woman faces the loss of her husband and resulting poverty. She becomes anxious and de-

pressed, and these feelings do not go away with time. Or, a man
agrees to a job transfer, wants to succeed at his new position, but
is overwhelmed by anxiety in his new environment. His anxiety
doesn't go away.

§6.1. In relation to a new environment or an already familiar
one; work inhibitions ♦H, M, E, P, N.

§6.2. In persons with counterculture attitudes and
values ♦H, D.

§6.3. Emotional difficulties arising from poverty and from the
deprivations suffered by minority groups ♦C.

§6.4. Inability to accept realities that limit life: e.g., financial
limitations, restricted opportunities, aging and death (see §9
below), jobs with "no future," responsibilities that stand in the
way of personal development ♦F, H.

§7 *Marital Problems*

It may be worth mentioning that after a period of therapy some
problems turn out to be marital in nature even though both
husband and wife believed them to be an *individual's* emotional
problem—the man's problem, not the wife's, or vice-versa, and
certainly not a "marital problem." Sometimes it is only after
many individual sessions of therapy that the marital basis of a
problem becomes clear. When appropriate, the expressed willingness of a spouse to become involved in his or her partner's
individual therapy can be a real help, providing emotional and
treatment support and also saving time when in fact the marital
relationship itself contributes to the individual's problems.

General marriage therapy: Primary ♦R, D, E, H, I.
Secondary ♦P, N, I.
For communication problems ♦R, D.

§8 *Family Problems*

There is a growing realization among therapists that many
individual problems are produced by families torn by conflict.
Often, family therapy can provide more effective help to a
troubled individual than therapy that treats the individual alone.
This seems to be especially true in many cases of schizophrenia
(see §12 below) and in fears of withdrawal of affection and of
abandonment (see §3.4 above).

General family therapy ♦S, D, C, I, N.

STEP 1

§9 Problems Related to Aging

§9.1. Emotional problems in facing old age   ♦E, G.

§9.2. Problems facing the recently widowed   ♦H, G.

§9.3. Coping with physical pain and disability

♦U, V, W, Y, X.

§10 Involuntary Behaviors (see §13 below)

§10.1. Stuttering   ♦U, G, I, O, W.

§10.2. Shaking or motor tic disorders   ♦U, G, I, Y, W.

§10.3. Insomnia   ♦V, U, W, Y.

§11 Crisis Intervention:
A Need for Prompt Relief from Severe Symptoms

Crisis telephone hotlines are available in most metropolitan areas for immediate counseling and referrals. If such services do not exist in your area, your family physician, minister, local clinic, hospital, and even police can be of assistance.

Primary   ♦usually Y followed by B, C, F, or G.

Secondary   ♦W, N, O, or P.

§12 Psychoses

If you have a psychosis, you behave in response to delusions or hallucinations. Your behavior is seen by others as strange and inappropriate; you are inclined to withdraw from social groups. You are severely impaired, out of touch with reality, often unable to communicate, illogical, rambling, incoherent. Your emotional responses are greatly out of proportion, even inconsistent, with external events.

There are numerous forms of psychosis, including types of schizophrenia, manic and paranoid psychoses, hysterical psychoses, and others. Since self-diagnosis for these conditions is neither appropriate nor likely to be accurate, no detailed discussion of the distinct forms of psychosis will be given here. Any diagnosis of psychosis requires a careful evaluation by a psychiatrist, clinical psychologist, or psychotherapist.

Primary   ♦Y (antipsychotic drugs) in conjuction with M, O, or H.

Secondary   ♦Y with S or A; Y with T.

§13 Organic Disorders

§13.1. Senescence, Alzheimer's disease: Senescence is associated with aging. Three-quarters of persons sixty-five years old and older have a chronic, disabling condition such as emphysema, heart disease, or hypertension. Most elderly individuals are able to cope with these disabilities for the rest of their lives. Some, however, begin to have psychological problems associated with senescence—e.g., confusion, depression, paranoia, and sometimes delirious states.

♦Supportive therapies (e.g., B) and sometimes Y.

In Alzheimer's disease, which is a distinct disease and not simply a sign of aging, you may have numerous physical complaints that cannot be traced to a physical illness. You may be irritable, lack energy, be apprehensive, show increasing forgetfulness and changes of personality. The family may complain that you "are not yourself." Presenile and senile dementia are two forms of Alzheimer's disease; both are progressively degenerative. ♦Y, care by family or by nursing home to provide supportive environment, planning of daily activities, etc.

§13.2. Parkinsonism/Huntington's chorea: Both are movement disorders that can produce psychiatric problems, including depression and schizophrenic disturbances. ♦Y.

§13.3. Substance-induced: alcoholism, drug addiction, smoking.

Alcoholism	♦Y, O, Alcoholics Anonymous.
Drug abuse: Primary	♦Y, Synanon, O.
Secondary	♦M, D, K.
Smoking	♦O, W.

Potentially useful for all of the above as adjunctive treatments ♦T, X.

§13.4. Organic brain dysfunctions: epilepsy, narcolepsy, amnesia, dementia, delirium. There are numerous conditions caused by abnormalities in brain function. They do not lend themselves to self-diagnosis or treatment. The main treatment is ♦Y.

S
T
E
P

1

S
T
E
P

2

TAKING YOUR PERSONALITY INTO ACCOUNT

What is challenging for a therapist is discerning the form of learning that each patient can best utilize and then working to adopt techniques that are best suited for the patient. . . . An important area of research is a way of detecting in a patient his optimal modes of learning. If we can pinpoint these, we can then more precisely determine the best means of therapeutic operation.*

Some people are more amenable to certain approaches to therapy than others; for example, some people like and benefit from group therapy, while others hate it. Sometimes what a person likes or would prefer needs to be overlooked in favor of treatment that is believed to be effective. But the vast majority of people who enter therapy do this of their own volition. If the therapy they enter is unsatisfying or downright distasteful to them, they will soon give it up. We simply tend not to learn and profit from experiences we dislike or that don't fit the kinds of people we are.

For some time now therapists have recognized that a client's personality often tends to incline him or her toward certain approaches and away from others. In the second step in identifying a potentially promising approach to therapy, you are encouraged to take traits of your own personality into consideration. It is not merely the *goal* or *problem* that suggests a particular approach to therapy, but—what is often more important—the nature of the *person*. Too little attention is given to the appropriateness of an individual for a given kind of therapy.

---

*Lewis R. Wolberg, *The Technique of Psychotherapy*, 2 vols. (New York: Grune & Stratton, 1977), vol. I, p. 271.

TABLE 2:
AN OVERVIEW OF MAIN PERSONALITY TRAITS
RELEVANT TO THE CHOICE OF A THERAPY

Choose no more than three of the following that you believe influence most strongly the way you approach day-to-day living:

☐ §1   Self-discipline

☐ §2   Commitment to tasks you set for yourself

☐ §3   Patience

☐ §4   Initiative

☐ §5   Tolerance to frustration

☐ §6   Rigidity

☐ §7   Inhibition

☐ §8   Introversion or extroversion

☐ §9   Motivation and capacity for physical exercise

☐ §10 Need for acceptance, human warmth, and gentle encouragement

☐ §11 Articulateness and analytical attitude

☐ §12 Reflectiveness—thinking about your own feelings, thoughts, and behavior

☐ §13 Imagination

☐ §14 Sensitivity to values

☐ §15 Comfort in a group setting

☐ §16 Severe impairments—learning, communication, or emotional disabilities, including addictions that seriously disrupt your daily life

In the following section, you will find questions relating to the sixteen personal qualities listed in Table 2. For those qualities you check, answer the questions as realistically as you can. If, for the most part, you answer "yes" to a given group of questions, then the approach(es) to therapy identified there may be especially appropriate for the kind of person you are. If you answer "no" to most of the questions in a group, then the listed therapy or therapies may not be especially well suited to you.

MATCHING YOUR PERSONALITY WITH
THE MOST PROMISING THERAPIES

§1 Self-Discipline

Therapies rely on self-discipline in clients in several ways:

Are you able to *stick to* a prescribed routine and do practical assignments on your own outside of therapy sessions to practice attitudes, communication skills, or behaviors?

Will you take *personal responsibility* for coming to regular appointments on time?

Can you *give up* any real payoffs of being emotionally troubled?

When *any* approach to therapy is successful, it is in large measure because a client has strong personal motivation, a strong will. However, some approaches to therapy depend more heavily than others on a client's strength of determination.

◆M, O, E, P, I, N, H, A, X, T.

§2 Commitment to the Process of Therapy

Do you believe you can commit yourself to therapy that spans many months and sometimes several years? If you hope to gain long-lasting benefits from your experience in therapy, you will need to commit yourself to certain practices and ways of thinking *after* formal therapy has ended. Do you feel that you have this kind of *tenacity* and *ability to follow through*?

These are both qualities related to self-discipline, but they have more to do with sustaining a process over a long period of time: in a word, *commitment*.

Do you feel you can develop a strong sense of commitment to long-term therapy?   ◆A.

To a long-range plan for life improvement?   ◆H, M.

§3 *Patience*

If you are suffering from incapacitating anxiety or depression, being patient about the process of therapy can be very demanding. Long-term therapies require more patience, endurance, and tolerance than do short-term therapies.

Are you able to put your trust in a process where results are noticed only very gradually? (If not, you may feel that what is most urgent now is to obtain prompt relief from symptoms—see the "Summary of Main Approaches to Psychotherapy," at the end of this chapter, to get some idea of the average durations of the different therapies.)

Therapies especially requiring patience—with yourself, with the challenge, or with the duration of therapy   ▶A, H, M, X.

§4 *Initiative*

Some approaches to therapy offer very little direction or specific advice from the therapist.

Do you feel that you have the initiative to proceed without explicit direction from the therapist? If so, what you probably need in a therapist is primarily the capacity to understand you well, to accept you as a person, and to encourage you in a warm and positive way to do what *you* think is best.   ▶B.

§5 *Tolerance to Frustration*

Do you have a fairly high threshold of frustration when your beliefs and ideas are challenged? When you do not immediately get what you want, can you tolerate fairly well what may seem like a long route to get where you want to go? (Do you cope well with the frustration of getting lost in your car, for example?) Can you tolerate, without serious irritation, anger, or hurt, being pushed to confront some of the pretenses or distortions or illusions you may have lived by?

Can you accept, with some calmness of mind, having someone point out to you that you have not been as clear about things as you thought, and that sometimes your attitudes are not consistent, that you are, to some extent, confused?   ▶A, C, E, P.

§6 *Rigidity*

Do you often find yourself trying to be, or wishing you were, someone you're not?   ▶C.

S
T
E
P

2

Are you perfectionistic? Upset when you make even fairly minor mistakes? Concerned that "things be in their proper place"? Are you frequently intense and uptight?   ▶C, J.

Are you "overcontrolling"—anxious when you do not feel you have things clearly under control?

Are you depressed (see §5, Table 1) or phobic (see §4.2, Table 1)?

Do you suspect that other people think that you magnify evils, blowing negative things out of proportion? Are you inclined to be moralistic, dogmatic, critical, or judgmental?

Are you an uncompromising person?

Do you feel, deep down, that perhaps your expectations and demands (concerning others, yourself, and the world) may be unrealistic?

Do you think you are often inclined to confuse what you would like with what you *need*?   ▶E, P, H.

§7 *Inhibition*

Do you feel blocked, inhibited, or held in check by an overly critical self?   ▶B.

Do you feel that you have pent-up feelings that are in need of release? Do you feel stultified or oppressed by your relationships with your spouse, friends, or family? Does your life lack emotional intensity? Do you obtain little joy or satisfaction from living?   ▶C, J.

Do you feel that somehow there are blocks *in you* that are standing in the way of your self-realization, of fulfilling your potential?   ▶I.

§8 *Introversion or Extroversion*

Are you inner-directed? Would you rather be alone or with one or two friends than attend a party? Are you impatient, or do you even resent receiving unsolicited suggestions?   ▶A, F.

On the other hand, are you at ease with groups of people? Is it important to your self-image what other people think of you? (Are you perhaps moderately status-oriented?) Do you often find it useful or helpful to receive advice?   ▶Q.

§9 *Motivation and Capacity for Physical Exercise*

Are you free of physical handicaps?

Do you *like* to be physically active, to exercise?

Do you begin to feel restless when a week or more goes by and you have been sedentary?

If you are not physically fit now but are healthy, does it *appeal* to you to work regularly and hard to become physically stronger and to improve your endurance?   ▶T, J, yoga (see U).

§10 Need for Acceptance, Human Warmth, and Gentle Encouragement

Do you feel that perhaps no one has ever taken the time to listen to you, to take a genuine interest in you and in your problems as a person?

Do you feel, perhaps because of circumstances or problems over which you've had no control, that you have received rather little human warmth from others?

Would you prefer encouragement that is patient and warm rather than a forceful push to change your life?   ▶B.

§11 Articulateness and Analytical Attitude

Can you talk openly and clearly about your feelings, about what is troubling you? Can you fairly readily describe examples of situations that may bother you?

If you were asked to describe the *personality* (not his or her physical features and behavior) of someone you talked with last night for half an hour at a party, could you do this without a lot of hesitation and brow-furrowing?

Do you *like* to talk about personal problem solving, about your feelings, past events, and why you have come to feel as you do? Do you feel a *need* to acquire an overall sense of understanding of yourself, your family, and how they have influenced you? ▶A.

§12 Reflectiveness

Do you often find yourself thinking about your feelings, about the purpose of life, and about whether yours has a meaningful direction?

Do you tend to come home from a visit with friends or family and go over in your mind what went on and wonder why people said and did certain things?

Do you have a mental habit of standing apart from what you're doing and judging yourself and your work?

Do you spend much time just "thinking about things," even dwelling on problems that concern you?   ▶A, G. ↓

S
T
E
P
2

§13 Imagination

As a child, did you have an imaginary friend?

When you sit on a rock by a brook in the woods, do you quickly begin to feel a special sense of relaxation? Or, watching the waves breaking on the beach, do you find yourself lulled into a sense of absorption in nature?

Do you enjoy reading? As you read a descriptive novel, do you tend to "see" many of the places and people? Do the events come alive for you? Do you find yourself thinking about the events in the book as though they make up a real world of their own?   ▸W.

§14 Sensitivity to Values

Are personal values very important to you? For example, do you sometimes find yourself thinking that so much of television programming is mediocre, trash, a waste of time? Do you *feel* that there are human values that are more important than how much money you make, what model car you drive, and the luxuriousness of your home?

Are you a religious or spiritual person, whether you attend church or not?

Do you like art, music, or literature?

Do you feel, really feel, a sense of compassion or empathy for people who face poverty and misfortune? Do you sometimes feel guilty because of your own situation, that there always seem to be others who are worse off?

Have you ever faced the opportunity to take advantage of someone or of a situation and simply decided not to (even though you *knew* you could do this without risk) because you simply wanted to feel honest or retain a sense of your own integrity?

Are you in search of a richer meaning in life? Do you wonder whether what you are doing with your life is really right for you?   ▸G.

§15 Comfort in a Group Setting

Do you feel comfortable and safe in groups?

Do you feel friendly when you pass a house where a party is going on?

Do you enjoy parties or social gatherings?

Did you come from a family with several children?   ▸Q, C.

§16 Severe Impairments

Do you have any learning or communication disabilities?

Are you so troubled because of emotional upheaval that you cannot work or maintain your family responsibilities?

Do you have any addictions that are causing grief for you or others close to you?

Do you sometimes have to "let off steam," even though you know you are hurting others, damaging their property, or injuring yourself?

♦O, Y.

S
T
E
P

2

S
T
E
P

3

TABLE 3:
THE APPROACHES TO THERAPY
DISCUSSED IN THIS BOOK

In the left column are the letters used in this chapter to identify each approach to therapy:

Letter Code	*Approach to Therapy*	*Chapter*
☐ A	Psychoanalysis	9
☐ B	Client-centered therapy	10
☐ C	Gestalt therapy	10
☐ D	Transactional analysis	10
☐ E	Rational-emotive therapy	10
☐ F	Existential-humanistic therapy	10
☐ G	Logotherapy	11
☐ H	Reality therapy	11
☐ I	Adlerian therapy	11
☐ J	Bioenergetics ⎫ Emotional	11
☐ K	Primal therapy ⎬ flooding	11
☐ L	Implosive therapy ⎭ therapies	11
☐ M	Direct decision therapy	11
☐ N	Counter-conditioning ⎫	12
☐ O	Behavior modification ⎬ Behavioral psychotherapies	12
☐ P	Cognitive approaches to behavior change ⎭	12
☐ Q	Group therapy	13
☐ R	Marriage therapy	14
☐ S	Family therapy	14
☐ T	Therapeutic exercise	15
☐ U	Biofeedback	15

☐ V	Relaxation training	15
☐ W	Hypnosis	15
☐ X	Meditation	15
☐ Y	Drug therapy	16
☐ Z	Nutrition therapy	16

S
T
E
P

3

HOW TO USE THE INFORMATION YOU NOW HAVE

If you have followed the instructions for Steps 1, 2, and 3, you should have identified a potentially promising therapy, or group of therapies, in relation both to your goals or problems and to your own estimation of certain important traits of your personality or character.

The therapy or approaches to therapy you have identified now need to be tested, first, in your imagination as you read the chapters of this book that will give you an idea of what each major approach to therapy is like, and then, if you decide to proceed, in reality, when you have located a suitable therapist (see Chapter 17).

The need for this testing is a matter of simple realism: you now have a sense of direction, or perhaps several alternative directions, to consider. The approach to self-diagnosis described in this chapter is intended to be useful, but it is not infallible; much depends on the accuracy of your problem diagnosis, the appropriateness of the goals you have set, and your self-understanding. Much also will depend on the therapist you locate and how well you are able to work together.

The recommended therapies listed by letter codes for Steps 1 and 2 reflect evaluations from several sources: (1) Therapists themselves claim that certain approaches favored by them have been shown to be useful for treating certain problems, for realizing certain goals, and for clients with certain personal qualities. (2) Various studies also have attempted to demonstrate for what and sometimes for whom many of the major therapies are most successful (see Chapter 20). (3) Primarily in the *ordering* of letter codes in connection with the specific

S
T
E
P
3

goals, problems, and personal qualities listed in Steps 1 and 2, I have relied on my own experience and judgment. After each arrow, the letter codes *listed first* designate therapies that, in general, are commonly regarded by therapists and psychologists as most useful. At times, when general consensus appeared to be lacking, I used my own evaluation.

The intention in this chapter is to make explicit a simple and reasonable process of choosing a therapy. Many therapies are not mentioned in connection with specific goals, problems, or personality traits. To be sure, some of the therapies that are not mentioned *can* be useful to certain individuals who have a given goal, problem, or trait. But the objective of this book is to improve the *general reliability* of a person's self-diagnosis and self-understanding. The book is a *guide*, not a bible.

COMBINING APPROACHES

There is evidence that combining two therapies for certain problems can frequently be more effective than using either in isolation. Treatment for individuals suffering from severe anxiety or depression often will combine drug therapy, for example, with one of the fourteen approaches to therapy described in Chapters 9-12 and 14 (and listed below, under "A"). Or, individuals who have problems due to excessive stress may, for example, be advised to combine biofeedback, relaxation training, hypnosis, meditation, or exercise therapy with a form of psychotherapy.

Usually, when therapies are combined, one is a formal psychotherapy and the other is an *adjunctive* therapy—that is, a therapy that most often is not relied on exclusively. Some adjunctive therapies lend themselves very well to use by individuals on their own. Combined treatments tend, then, to employ one approach taken from list A and one from list B:

A (Main Therapies)

Psychoanalysis
Client-centered therapy
Gestalt therapy
Transactional analysis
Rational-emotive therapy
Existential-humanistic therapy

Logotherapy
Reality therapy
Adlerian therapy
Direct decision therapy
Behavior modification
Cognitive approaches to behavior change
Marriage and family therapy

B (Adjunctive Therapies)

Drug therapy
Meditation
Hypnosis
Relaxation training
Biofeedback
Therapeutic exercise

Approaches That May Appear Under Either A or B

Bioenergetics
Primal therapy
Implosive therapy
Counter-conditioning
Group therapy

A SUMMARY OF THE MAIN APPROACHES TO PSYCHOTHERAPY

Therapy	Best Suited For: Problems or Goals	Client's Personality (not all traits may apply to a single person)	Average Duration*	Cost**
A. Psychoanalysis	self-development: broad-spectrum improvements; suffering from childhood traumas; fear of withdrawal of affection and of abandonment; interpersonal problems; phobias; compulsions; sexual disorders; depression; mania; manic depression; psychoses	self-disciplined; committed; patient; tolerant to frustration; introverted; articulate; analytical; reflective	3	++ #
B. Client-centered	self-development: broad-spectrum improvements; low self-worth; crisis intervention	inhibited; possessing initiative; needing acceptance, human warmth, and gentle encouragement	2	+ #
C. Gestalt	behavior problems in children; shyness/passivity; coping with persons in authority; psychosomatic disorders; adjustment problems: minorities and the poor; family conflicts; crisis intervention	tolerant to frustration; rigid; inhibited; able to work in a group setting	1-2	+ to 0

			1-2	0 #
D. Transactional analysis	interested in effective communication	shyness/passivity loneliness/emptiness hostility/overbearing personality fear of withdrawal of affection and of abandonment improving effectiveness of communication coping with persons in authority phobias adjustment problems marital problems, especially those involving communication difficulties family conflicts drug abuse		

			2	+
E. Rational-emotive	self-disciplined rigid	hostility/overbearing personality interpersonal problems anxiety disorders post-traumatic stress phobias compulsions sexual disorders impulse control disorders depression mania and manic depression adjustment problems marital problems delinquency and criminal behavior		

* 1 = Brief therapies, frequently 12 weekly sessions or less; 2 = 3-6 months; 3 = long-term therapies, 6 months to several years

** = initially expensive, then $10-25/hr.; ++ = expensive $50-100+/hr.; + = moderate, $25-50/hr.; 0 = inexpensive, $10-25/hr.; # = often available on a sliding scale basis (see Chapter 4) through county clinics, agencies, etc.

Therapy	Best Suited For:		Average Duration*	Cost**
	Problems or Goals	Client's Personality (not all traits may apply to a single person)		
F. Existential-humanistic	loneliness/emptiness loss of faith in yourself, in others, or in life's purpose inability to accept life's limitations crisis intervention	introverted sensitive to existential issues	2	+
G. Logotherapy	estrangement/alienation from others loss of faith in yourself, in others, or in life's purpose noögenic neuroses depression due to value conflicts inability to accept life's limitations emotional problems in facing old age problems of the recently widowed stuttering shaking and motor tic disorders crisis intervention	reflective sensitive to values	2	+
H. Reality	desire for a success-identity anxiety disorders post-traumatic stress adjustment problems marital problems problems of the recently widowed vocational problems delinquency and criminal behavior psychoses	self-disciplined committed patient rigid	1-2	+

I. Adlerian	deep discouragement with life marital problems family conflicts stuttering shaking and motor tic disorders vocational problems delinquency and criminal behavior	self-disciplined inhibited	1-2	+ #
J. Bioenergetics	self-development: broad-spectrum improvements suffering from childhood pain	inhibited motivated and able to undertake physical exercise	1-2	+
K. Primal	anxiety disorders post-traumatic stress phobias compulsions drug abuse	pent-up feelings	1-2	=
L. Implosive	phobias	(nonspecific)	1	+
M. Direct decision	desire for a success-identity compulsions impulse control disorders vocational problems adjustment problems psychoses drug abuse	self-disciplined committed patient	2	+

* 1 = Brief therapies, frequently 12 weekly sessions or less; 2 = 3-6 months; 3 = long-term therapies, 6 months to several years

** = initially expensive, then $10-25/hr.; ++ = expensive $50-100+/hr.; + = moderate, $25-50/hr.; 0 = inexpensive, $10-25/hr.; # = often available on a sliding scale basis (see Chapter 4) through county clinics, agencies, etc.

Therapy	Best Suited For:		Average Duration*	Cost**
	Problems or Goals	Client's Personality (not all traits may apply to a single person)		
N. Counter-conditioning	shyness/passivity hostility/overbearing personality phobias psychosomatic disorders sexual disorders adjustment problems marital problems family conflicts crisis intervention	self-disciplined	1-2	+ #
O. Behavior modification	mental retardation autism behavior problems in children hyperkinetic behavior delinquency and criminal behavior eating disorders compulsions sexual disorders impulse control disorders stuttering crisis intervention psychoses	self-disciplined possibly impaired	1-2	+ #

P. Cognitive approaches to behavior change	interpersonal problems anxiety disorders post-traumatic stress psychosomatic disorders sexual disorders depression mania and manic depression adjustment problems marital problems crisis intervention	self-disciplined rigid	1-2	+ #
Q. Group	shyness/passivity loneliness/emptiness hostility/overbearing personality improving communication effectiveness impulse control disorders	extroverted tolerant to group involvement	1	0 #
R. Marriage	marital problems supportive therapy for individual problems fear of withdrawal of affection and of abandonment	(nonspecific)	1-2	+ #
S. Family	family conflicts supportive therapy for individual problems emotional disturbances in children fear of withdrawal of affection and of abandonment family-based compulsions psychoses	(nonspecific)	1-2	+ #

* 1 = Brief therapies, frequently 12 weekly sessions or less; 2 = 3-6 months; 3 = long-term therapies, 6 months to several years

** = initially expensive, then $10-25/hr.; ++ = expensive $50-100+/hr.; + = moderate, $25-50/hr.; 0 = inexpensive, $10-25/hr.; # = often available on a sliding scale basis (see Chapter 4) through county clinics, agencies, etc.

Therapy	Best Suited For:		Average Duration*	Cost**
	Problems or Goals	Client's Personality (not all traits may apply to a single person)		
T. Therapeutic exercise	depression anxiety disorders post-traumatic stress marital problems alcoholism drug abuse smoking psychoses	self-disciplined motivated and able to undertake physical exercise	2-3	0 or no cost
U. Biofeedback	physical pain and disability shaking and motor tic disorders stuttering insomnia anxiety disorders post-traumatic stress phobias depression	(nonspecific)	1-2	+ #
V. Relaxation training	anxiety disorders post-traumatic stress phobias physical pain and disability insomnia	(nonspecific)	1-2	+ #

			1-2	+
			3	0 or no cost
W. Hypnosis	emotional disturbances in children eating disorders interpersonal problems anxiety disorders post-traumatic stress phobias psychosomatic disorders sexual disorders depression mania and manic depression physical pain and disability stuttering shaking and motor tic disorders	imaginative trusting	1-2	+
X. Meditation	loss of faith in yourself, in others, or in life's purpose anxiety disorders post-traumatic stress depression mania and manic depression physical pain and disability alcoholism drug abuse smoking	self-disciplined patient	3	0 or no cost

* 1 = Brief therapies, frequently 12 weekly sessions or less; 2 = 3-6 months; 3 = long-term therapies, 6 months to several years

** = initially expensive, then $10-25/hr.; ++ = expensive $50-100+/hr.; + = moderate, $25-50/hr.; 0 = inexpensive, $10-25/hr.; # = often available on a sliding scale basis (see Chapter 4) through county clinics, agencies, etc.

Therapy	Best Suited For:		Average Duration*	Cost**
	Problems or Goals	Client's Personality (not all traits may apply to a single person)		
Y. Drug	autism hyperkinetic disturbances anxiety disorders post-traumatic stress phobias compulsions sexual disorders depression mania and manic depression physical pain and disability shaking and motor tic disorders insomnia crisis intervention	possibly impaired	1-3	++#
Z. Nutrition	possibly hyperkinetic behavior as well as other problems (see Chapter 14)	no data available	—	—

* 1 = Brief therapies, frequently 12 weekly sessions or less; 2 = 3-6 months; 3 = long-term therapies, 6 months to several years

** = initially expensive, then $10-25/hr.; ++ = expensive $50-100+/hr.; + = moderate, $25-50/hr.; 0 = inexpensive, $10-25/hr.; # = often available on a sliding scale basis (see Chapter 4) through county clinics, agencies, etc.

8
EMOTIONAL PROBLEMS
THAT MAY HAVE
PHYSICAL CAUSES

This chapter has a single important purpose: to persuade you, if you are in serious emotional distress, to have a comprehensive physical examination *before* beginning psychotherapy. Imagine how disheartened and frustrated you might feel after a period of unsuccessful therapy, only to find out afterward that your problems could be traced to a physical cause. It is essential that you eliminate the possibility of a physical basis for your problems before seeking therapy. In fact, most therapists routinely recommend that you have a complete physical before entering therapy.

Rest assured that doing so will *not* be a waste of time. Richard Rada, Director of College Hospital in Cerritos, California, estimates that between five and ten percent of clients with depression, anxiety, or unusual thoughts and behavior may have underlying physical conditions that are responsible, including gland dysfunction, an epileptic abnormality, heart disease, cancer, and so on. The following facts, too, should convince you that having a comprehensive physical is paramount:

- As many as one patient in every ten who suffer from serious depression has a thyroid disorder.
- One person in every four who are diagnosed as having psychiatric disorders and who are over sixty-five has an underlying physical illness that is responsible.
- An equal number of individuals over sixty-five have emotional problems that are made worse by underlying physical disorders.
- Three percent of people who regularly take prescription medication develop mental symptoms.

Dr. Leonard Small, a specialist in the field of neuropsychodiagnosis, has found that the more severe emotional or mental symptoms are, the more likely it is that therapists (and patients) will overlook the possibility of underlying physical disorders.*

It isn't necessary or possible to give a detailed or comprehensive catalog of physical causes of emotional and mental disturbances here, but it may be helpful to many people to see some of the principal ways in which psychological symptoms can be produced by physical problems. Hopefully, these illustrations will persuade you, if you are emotionally or mentally troubled, of the wisdom of a thorough physical. It is a small price to pay if emotional symptoms can be traced to a physical cause.

It is well known that virtually any serious organic illness or injury can produce emotional suffering, either in the form of physical pain or in the form of anxiety and depression. Chronic pain is a chronic stress and can lead to the same emotional problems as prolonged stress of any variety: anxiety or depression. Similarly, prolonged severe anxiety or depression can cause physical deterioration and make the body more susceptible to disease.

---

*Leonard Small, *Neuropsychodiagnosis in Psychotherapy* (New York: Brunner/ Mazel, 1980), p. vii.

There are, then, two "vicious circles," or feedback loops, that can play a role in causing or aggravating emotional disturbance:

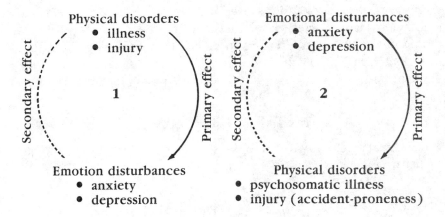

In the first loop, an underlying physical disorder, which may be a disease or a physical injury, leads to emotional symptoms (and very likely to physical symptoms as well, although these may not be as pronounced). However, the emotional reactions that are produced can themselves make the physical disorder worse, and certainly emotional disturbance makes living with and treating the underlying physical disorder more difficult.

In the second loop, emotional disturbances cause certain physical disorders: a peptic ulcer, heart palpitations, ulcerative colitis, backache, hypertension, or high blood pressure, etc., and may predispose certain individuals to arthritis, cancer, or diseases of the immune system. Once a psychosomatic link has been established between a troubled mind and the body, and an organic disorder has come about, the physical disorder, in turn, can produce stronger or more exaggerated emotional reactions. Anxiety or depression may increase because the person is now *both* physically ill and emotionally troubled.

These two so-called positive feedback loops can obviously

lead to a runaway process that becomes worse and worse. Psychosomatic medicine focuses on the second of these; our focus here is on the first: physical origins of emotional disturbance.

Underlying physical disorders of this kind include metabolic diseases, disorders and diseases affecting the brain and nervous system, head injuries, other physical disorders and conditions, infectious diseases, reactions to medication, and drug addiction and alcoholism. Each is discussed in the remainder of this chapter.

METABOLIC DISEASES

Several well-known metabolic diseases can lead to emotional disturbances:

HYPERTHYROIDISM

An overactive thyroid, known as *hyperthyroidism*, is usually caused by the pituitary gland's overproducing a hormone called *TSH*, or *thyroid-stimulating hormone*. This causes the thyroid, a butterfly-shaped gland in the lower part of the neck, to produce an excess of the thyroid hormone thyroxine. Hyperthyroidism is eight times more common in women than in men.

The emotional symptoms of hyperthyroidism include a more intense and chronic nervousness than in hypothyroidism (discussed below), overreactions to minor crises, moodiness, frequent fear without knowing why, a sense of agitation, dread, and occasionally trembling or shaking. Some patients with serious hyperthyroidism may have symptoms resembling those of schizophrenia, in which there is little or no contact with reality.

Physical symptoms include rapid loss of weight, unusual appetite, rapid pulse, diarrhea, and muscle weakness (especially in the legs, as when climbing stairs). The classical symptoms of hyperthyroidism are staring eyes and enlargement of the neck, but these need not be present.

It is interesting to note that certain factors in upbringing and personality seem to predispose people to hyperthyroidism (this would mean that a feedback loop of the second type may precipitate the disease in some people). Individuals who later develop hyperthyroidism often have these characteristics:

- They were forced prematurely to become self-sufficient and responsible.
- They felt rejected by one or both parents and feared a loss of emotional support.
- Their early dependence needs (their needs for affection, mothering, warmth, etc.) were frustrated, and this led to feelings of insecurity and low self-esteem and to the belief that the world is a threatening place.
- They often had dominant, tight-lipped, overcontrolling mothers.

HYPOTHYROIDISM

An underactive thyroid, known as *hypothyroidism*, is caused by an inadequate production of thyroid hormone. It is most common in middle-aged women.

The emotional symptoms of hypothyroidism include mental sluggishness, nervousness, depression, irritability, impatience, and frequently dislike of everyday activities.

Physical symptoms include a sense of heaviness and lethargy, dry skin, sensitivity to cold, constipation, and thinning hair.

HYPER- AND HYPOPARATHYROIDISM

The parathyroid glands, which are four bean-size glands located on top of the thyroid gland, manufacture hormones that regulate phosphorus and calcium levels in the body. Excess hormone raises the calcium level too high, and psychotic-like behavior can result. Too little hormone lowers the calcium level to the point that a person may behave like an alcoholic. These conditions are comparatively rare.

DIABETES

Diabetes, or hypoinsulism, which affects as many as 2.5 million Americans, results from underproduction of insulin, which in turn causes an excess of sugar in the blood and urine. Diabetes takes two forms: juvenile onset (or insulin-dependent) and adult onset (or noninsulin-dependent) diabetes. The first type starts in childhood or young adulthood, and is caused by the body's failure to produce enough insulin. Juvenile onset diabetes is usually controlled by means of regular injections of insulin.

Adult onset diabetes is less serious than juvenile diabetes; it occurs more often in the elderly and especially in people who are overweight. Diabetes can appear in a person after a traumatic event: great stress, a physical accident, surgery, infection, or a severe emotional disturbance. It may also appear after a person has gone through a long period of fatigue, depression, indecision, or sense of hopelessness. Those who become diabetic may be individuals who felt strong resentment toward their parents while growing up or who were "spoiled children." Diabetic men often were dominated by their mothers while being excessively dependent on them. Adult onset diabetes is usually controlled without insulin injections, particularly during the early stages of the disease. Treatment in about one-third of noninsulin-dependent diabetics is possible by diet alone; in others, it is necessary to take oral hypoglycemic drugs that stimulate the release of insulin.

The emotional symptoms of both forms of diabetes may include apathy, depression, personality disorders, or even psychosis as a result of undersecretion of insulin.

Physical symptoms include the need to urinate frequently, day and night, unusual fatigue and weakness, tingling in hands and feet, reduced resistance to infections (especially of the urinary tract), blurred vision, impotence in men, and lack of menstrual periods in women.

HYPOGLYCEMIA

Hypoglycemia, or hyperinsulism, which affects perhaps as many as five million Americans, is caused by overproduction of insulin. Excess insulin leads to low blood sugar (literally, *hypoglycemia*). Sometimes this overproduction of insulin is caused by a tumor of the pancreas; the growth can often be removed surgically to correct the condition.

The emotional symptoms of hypoglycemia include depression and anxiety.

Physical symptoms include fast pulse, palpitations, dizziness, general weakness, faintness, stomach pain, blurred vision, and sweating. These symptoms often occur a few hours after eating and disappear after eating again.

Hypoglycemia has become almost a fad disease among "psychonutritionists." The condition is believed by most physicians, however, to be confined mainly to diabetics who have not kept to a prescribed routine and have allowed their levels of insulin to become too high. Sometimes stomach surgery, liver disease, pregnancy, and periods of high fever can cause attacks of hypoglycemia.

DISORDERS AND DISEASES AFFECTING THE BRAIN AND NERVOUS SYSTEM

EPILEPSY

The second most common physical cause of emotionally distressing symptoms, after the metabolic disorders we have just discussed, is epilepsy. Approximately 7 percent of mentally disturbed patients have some form of epilepsy.

Epilepsy affects between 1 and 2 percent of the U.S. population. Of people who have epilepsy, two-thirds appear to have no structural abnormality of the brain; in the remaining third, the disease can be traced to brain damage at birth, a severe head injury, an infection that caused brain damage, or a brain tumor.

The emotional symptoms of epilepsy can involve either anxiety or depression or both. Once a person has had a convulsive seizure, he or she may live in constant apprehension that another seizure will occur. There may be occasional, transient feelings of unreality.

Physical symptoms include peculiar stomach sensations, distorted vision, occasional bizarre behavior such as laughing for no apparent reason or sudden and unprovoked anger, loss of consciousness, and convulsions.

PARKINSONISM

Parkinson's disease often causes anxiety or depression. Physical symptoms early in the course of the disease include slowing of movement and inability to write one's name without the handwriting becoming smaller and smaller. Later symptoms include tremors, muscle stiffness or rigidity, nervousness, and tension.

MULTIPLE SCLEROSIS

Multiple sclerosis usually begins in people between the ages of twenty and forty, affecting slightly more women than men. Symptoms may disappear after one or a number of attacks, or they may get progressively worse and cause severe disability.

Emotional symptoms include anxiety, panic attacks, and depression.

Physical symptoms may involve a feeling of numbness or tingling affecting one limb or one side of the body, temporary blurring of vision, slurred speech, and difficulty or lack of control in urinating.

BRAIN TUMORS

Brain tumors may cause severe headaches, blurred or double vision, vomiting without the warning of nausea, general weakness, and, in some cases, epileptic seizures.

Emotional symptoms may involve nervousness, irritability, memory problems, and personality changes.

HEAD INJURIES

Head injuries that damage the brain generally cause headaches and dizziness.

Emotional symptoms usually involve nervousness and sometimes confusion. In more serious injuries, there may be loss of memory, depression, and decreased alertness. Severe damage to the brain can cause unconsciousness that may persist for days or weeks.

OTHER PHYSICAL DISORDERS AND CONDITIONS

PANCREATIC CANCER

Cancer of the pancreas can cause severe depression and insomnia. These emotional symptoms can occur early in the course of the disease. This kind of cancer kills nine out of ten of its victims within a year of being diagnosed. One reason for this tragedy is that pancreatic cancer frequently reaches an advanced stage before the appearance of its physical symptoms: loss of appetite and loss of weight, nausea, vomiting, and upper abdominal pain that may spread to the back. It is believed that alert psychiatrists can save many lives that otherwise would be lost as a result of pancreatic cancer by detecting the disease in its early stages.

ANEMIA

Anemia is caused by an abnormal drop in either red blood cells or hemoglobin (the main constituent of red blood cells). Iron deficiency can cause anemia, as can vitamin B_{12} or folic acid deficiency. Inherited blood disorders such as sickle-cell anemia can also lead to anemia.

The main emotional symptom of anemia is depression.

Physical symptoms include weakness, breathlessness, and heart palpitations, which may occur as the heart attempts to compensate for anemia by circulating blood faster than normal.

HEART CONDITIONS

Mitral incompetence is a heart condition in which the flaps of the mitral valve, separating the upper and lower chambers of the heart, do not close properly. The heart of a person with this disorder must therefore work harder than normal. Physical symptoms may involve shortness of breath and fatigue.

Paroxysmal tachycardia is another heart condition, in which the heartbeat suddenly speeds up to 160 beats per minute or more. An attack may last for from several minutes to several days. Physical symptoms include breathlessness, fainting, chest pain, and awareness of the rapid heartbeats.

The emotional symptoms of both mitral incompetence and paroxysmal tachycardia may involve anxiety and panic attacks.

MENOPAUSE

Menopause is not a disorder but a natural condition of aging that involves changes in hormone levels in the body. Menopause in women can cause intermittent periods of strong anxiety, chronic nervousness, depression, irritability, lack of confidence, and headaches. Physical symptoms include hot flashes, sweating, and palpitations. Male menopause is increasingly being recognized by doctors; symptoms most frequently appear when a man is in his fifties. Emotional symptoms may involve anxiety and depression; physical symptoms include hot flashes, sweating, fatigue, and insomnia.

INFECTIOUS DISEASES

Frequently, emotional symptoms are the first warnings of infectious disease. For example, fatigue and nervousness may be the only early complaints of patients who have hepatitis, infectious mononucleosis, tuberculosis, and many other diseases. Anxiety and tiredness are symptoms that deserve careful diagnostic judgment; they are not always innocuous.

REACTIONS TO MEDICATION

Both over-the-counter and prescription medications can sometimes produce emotional or mental side effects. Too, as the number of manufactured drugs increases, the potential for interactions among different medications increases greatly. Certain drug interactions produce symptoms of marked agitation, restlessness, and anxiety. Furthermore, patients who have regularly taken a particular medication may sometimes find that it begins to cause unexpected side effects. "False senility" in elderly patients, for example, is often induced by medication; when the medication is stopped, the undesirable symptoms disappear.

DRUG ADDICTION AND ALCOHOLISM

Both are runaway habits that can cause nervousness and overreactions to small crises. Ironically, individuals are usually first attracted to narcotics or alcohol in order to obtain *relief* from anxiety. But once the addictions have become firmly established, emotional symptoms of depression, irritability, sudden changes of mood, nervousness, and paranoia are common, as are memory loss and difficulty in concentrating.

Caffeine is an emotionally habit-forming drug. Real addiction—i.e., physical dependence with withdrawal symptoms—appears to be rare. Nevertheless, coffee, tea, and cola drinkers can become emotionally dependent on caffeine. The drug is a frequent cause of chronic nervousness in habitual caffeine users.

Smoking is a habit that causes a person to lose approximately $5\frac{1}{2}$ minutes of life expectancy for each cigarette smoked. Beyond this, smoking is also a common but unrecognized cause of chronic nervousness, in spite of the fact that many smokers believe smoking will help steady their nerves.

By now it should be evident that the two main signs of emotional distress—anxiety and depression—can sometimes be the symptoms of undetected physical disorders. Especially in cases of severe anxiety or depression *without* physical complaints, both therapists and clients tend to overlook the possibility of physical illness.

It is true that, at present, the majority of such cases cannot be traced to underlying physical causes; they are therefore treated by means of psychotherapy or psychiatric drug therapy. As medicine and biochemistry develop, however, mental and emotional complaints are increasingly being understood in more physical terms.

Emotional distress clearly does sometimes mask or camouflage the presence of physical disorders. If you are suffering from serious anxiety or depression, it is important to have a comprehensive physical before *beginning* psychiatric treatment. This is true especially when the onset of emotional symptoms was sudden—within a period of days or one to two weeks. It may be most useful to see a diagnostic specialist—for example, a doctor of internal medicine. But bear in mind that physicians, even those who are familiar with psychiatric problems, vary considerably in their diagnostic skills, and sometimes a second opinion can be worthwhile before you decide that the most appropriate treatment is psychotherapy.

PART II
EXPERIENCING
THERAPY

In Part II you will be able to develop an overall understanding of the main approaches to therapy available today. We will look at psychoanalysis, the first of the psychotherapies, developed by Freud at the beginning of this century; and then, in the next two chapters, discuss ten major psychotherapies. Because of their widespread use and value, individual chapters will then focus on approaches to behavioral psychotherapy, group therapy, and marriage and family counseling. The two final chapters in this section deal with the therapeutic value of exercise, biofeedback, relaxation methods, hypnosis, meditation, psychopharmacology or the use of drugs in therapy, and dietary approaches.

In the discussion of each approach to therapy you will find:

- *a concise description* of its special perspective
- information on *the kinds of problems* it is thought to be most useful in treating—and closely connected with this, but seldom taken into account—
- a description of *the kinds of individuals* who tend to profit most from that approach; and
- an account of *a successful experience in therapy,* reconstructed from the reports of clients as they look back on their treatment

HOW TO USE PART II

There are two ways you may find it profitable to use this section of the book. Perhaps you may decide to combine both of them.

First, you can use the "map" in Chapter 7 to define your goals and to suggest specific approaches to therapy that, based on your own self-diagnosis, you might find most beneficial.

On the other hand, you may not feel that mapping out your problem or goals in the way that Chapter 7 suggests is for you. Perhaps you are simply curious about the field and would like to learn more about it, or perhaps you are considering counseling or psychotherapy as an opportunity for personal growth and do not have particular difficulties or issues that you want to focus on. For you, it may be more relevant to read about a wide range of approaches and by so doing gain a clearer understanding of what the alternatives are, how they work, and what they may offer you. This "window-shopping" can then form the basis for a more informed decision later on if you want to enter counseling or psychotherapy.

THE EXPERIENCES OF CLIENTS IN THERAPY

The reports in this book that describe the personal lives and experience of real individuals in therapy have all been deliberately recast to mask all traces of their identities. Their names, life situations, ages, and other characteristics have been changed.

Descriptions of the experiences of clients in therapy have been greatly abbreviated and sometimes simplified. As we have already seen, counseling and psychotherapy last varying lengths of time. Even a very short period of therapy, over a period of weeks, will bring to light much more detail than it would be useful for us to discuss here. The personal lives of the real persons that are portrayed here are immeasurably more complex and multifaceted than short reports can bring out.

Sometimes we will use a time-lapse strategy, describing the evolution of a person's therapy over a period of many months by skipping over weeks at a time. Always the intent will be to try to convey to you how real people with real problems have come to deal with their difficulties more effectively and often, in the process, have been able to reach a richer understanding of themselves and of others.

9
PSYCHOANALYSIS

For wide-range improvements in individuals who are not severely impaired and who are articulate, reflective, patient, self-disciplined, and able to make a potentially long-term commitment to therapy.

The past hides but is present. . . .

Bernard Malamud, *A New Life*

Psychoanalysis is the root from which the large family of different theories of psychotherapy and counseling has grown. Sigmund Freud's first efforts to develop psychoanalysis began in the 1880s. He lived a long life and was active into his eighties; he died in 1939. Freud left behind one of the most important contributions to the field of mental and emotional health. It formed the historical basis for the diversity of approaches that would follow. Even when later thinkers took issue with Freud, their work in different ways relied on the foundation of his pioneering work.

Many of Freud's ideas have worked their way into our everyday vocabulary: the unconscious, the ego, repression, the Oedipus

113

complex, and so forth. His work has influenced the study of anthropology, sociology, history, philosophy, and literature.

FREUD'S THEORY

During Freud's early medical training, he went to Paris to study with a well-known neurologist, J. M. Charcot. Charcot had begun to use hypnosis to treat patients with certain physical disorders—paralysis, for example—for which there was no apparent physical cause (so-called hysterical symptoms). Working with Charcot, and later with a physician, Joseph Breuer, Freud began to suspect that these symptoms were *motivated* by earlier traumatic experiences that so distressed the patients that they were forgotten (repressed).

Freud's theory of emotional and mental illness began then to take shape around this central idea that neurotic behavior has a *purpose*: there is an underlying *motive*, the motive itself is very upsetting to the person, and so it is repressed from awareness. But it continues to gnaw away below the level of conscious awareness and eventually leads to the disturbance that brings the patient to the point at which he or she is in need of professional help. Freud believed that recovery would occur if a patient could be helped to gain insight into these painful events and feelings that had been forgotten. In a moment, we will look at two real examples.

Freud's theory has several dimensions. First, his theory offers an explanation of how the mind operates through its defense mechanisms: as we have noted, excessively painful feelings and memories are repressed. Second, his theory tries to identify the different psychologically critical stages children go through on their way to adulthood: the oral, anal, and genital stages. And third, his theory seeks to distinguish the parts of the psyche, which together underlie an individual's personality: the *ego* (the rational portion of the mind that deals with reality), the *id* (made up of basic instincts that press for gratification), and the *superego* (formed from parental influences that have been internalized).

HOW PSYCHOANALYSIS IS DONE

Together, these three so-called dynamic, developmental, and

intrapsychic dimensions of Freud's theory make up the general framework of psychoanalysis. The central technique of psychoanalysis is to help the patient become aware of motives that are unconscious. Psychoanalysis, or analysis for short, is basically an attempt to extend self-control, bringing disturbing feelings and behavior under a person's conscious management.

One of the principal techniques is free association. The patient is made to feel relaxed and comfortable—one reason a couch is sometimes used. He is encouraged to talk in an uninhibited way about his concerns and feelings. During this process, the analyst usually remains detached and restrained so as not to interfere with the patient's free expression. From time to time, the analyst shares with the patient certain of the interpretations he has developed on the basis of the patient's reports and behavior. The analyst's objective is to help the patient recover lost and painful memories that are responsible for the conflicts, weaknesses, or inabilities that cause the patient to suffer.

This process can be very hard on the patient: he or she must revisit experiences that may be very painful. Analysis requires perseverance, endurance, and courage. It is not, as we will see, for everyone or every problem.

One of the most important developments in psychoanalysis has to do with the increasing popularity of psychoanalytic psychotherapy (also called *dynamic psychotherapy*), meaning psychoanalysis that is extremely brief (12 to 20 sessions, for example). Considerably more patients are now treated with psychoanalytic psychotherapy than with traditional, intensive psychoanalysis.

TWO EXAMPLES OF PSYCHOANALYSIS

Other than the length and intensity of treatment, the main difference between Freudian psychoanalysis and brief analysis has to do with the amount of emphasis that is placed on sexual matters. Freud believed that an infant's relationship to his environment and parents is predominantly *sensual*: a baby seeks oral gratification; his attention is absorbed by what he puts into his mouth. Later, attention is focused on excretory processes; toilet-training requires the child to exercise self-regulation for the first time. Later, genital sexuality becomes the dominant interest. These sexual phases of development identify the dominant areas of attention that influence the infant, the child, and then the adult in their behavior toward others.

Brief psychoanalysis generally does not affirm Freud's sexually based (libido) theory of motivation. The second example that follows illustrates this shift of emphasis. The first example was described by Freud himself*; the second illustrates brief psychoanalysis.

A CASE FROM FREUD

Freud describes the analysis of a girl who has repressed a strong desire for sexual intercourse with her father and has, as a result, developed a bizarre pattern of behavior.

Unconsciously, the dread of actually making love with him has generalized to a dread of sexual activity of any kind. Without any conscious intent on her part, an association is formed between sexual intercourse and breaking a vase. She is not aware of the unconscious symbolic connection she has established between these acts. Similarly, she begins to associate the bolster at the head of her bed with her father and identifies her mother with the headboard.

The pressure of this repressed material impels her to go through an elaborate ritual each night before she can get to sleep. First she arranges the several vases in her room so that she feels they are well protected against being broken (thereby guarding against sexual intercourse). Then she makes sure that the bolster does not come into contact with the headboard (in this way she gains the substitute satisfaction of keeping her mother and father apart).

As her analysis proceeds, and the analyst is able—and here, timing is important—to encourage her to become conscious of her repressed feelings and generalized dread of sex, her need for the nightly ritual is gradually eliminated.

It is not difficult to think of other problems, sometimes of a handicapping kind, that, because of their obsessive or compulsive nature, interfere with normal living. Compulsive handwashing is a classical example; compulsive overeating, bulimia,

---

*Sigmund Freud, "Lecture 17," *General Introduction to Psychoanalysis* (New York: Garden City Pub. Co., 1943).

and its opposite, anorexia nervosa, as well as nymphomania, a need for sexual promiscuity, are a few others.

AN EXAMPLE OF BRIEF PSYCHOANALYSIS

Dr. Richard Chase is a psychiatrist who specializes in emotional problems of children. John and Rachel Edmonton have come to see him about their twelve-year-old son, Bobby, their only child. John is an evangelical minister in his early forties who travels a great deal, taking his family with him.

When Bobby was eight years old, he began to have strange and violent nightmares. He would go to sleep and then apparently awaken about an hour later, asking for a drink of water or expressing a need to go to the bathroom. A few minutes later, Bobby would seem to lose his balance and stumble over furniture, sometimes running into walls, crying aloud that he was "turning inside out" and was dying. Often his parents would have to restrain him to keep him from hurting himself. After a few minutes, the nightmare would end and Bobby would come out of it, a terrified, confused little boy in tears.

So far, John and Rachel, with their frequent moves, had not been able to get professional help that had made a difference. Bobby had been examined by a neurologist, and an electroencephalograph test was done to determine if some kind of epileptic disorder might be involved. The test was negative. They had also taken Bobby to a child psychologist, who said that Bobby was bright, sensitive, and precocious, that this kind of nightmare was called a *night terror* (*pavor nocturnis*), and that the problem would eventually subside.

Four years passed, and the night terrors did not. The family of three was becoming battle-scarred. Bobby hated to go to bed at night, fearing the inevitable. His parents, sometimes patient, sometimes not, used whatever ways they could, even a prescribed sedative for Bobby, so he could relax and get to sleep, to no avail.

Could Dr. Chase help?

Dr. Chase decided to meet with Bobby by himself. He found that Bobby was very willing to talk about his "bad dreams." Dr. Chase asked him to describe what happened each night.

"Oh, Doctor," Bobby began, "it's really awful. I know it's going to happen, but I can't do anything to stop it. I stay up as late as

I can, and I will do anything not to go to sleep. But when I do, I'll *kind of* wake up a little later, and I'll see Mother and Dad looking very worried. At the same time, I'll see a box, with white walls, glowing brightly, but not in the room where Mother and Dad are. It's in some space, I guess it's in my mind, a black space, with that white-colored cube just floating there. And then it begins to turn inside out. My stomach feels like it's turning inside out, and it hurts and scares me. It feels awful. I really think if the cube turned all the way inside out, I'd die. But it never does; I always wake up first."

Dr. Chase began to meet with Bobby three times a week. He gradually gained his trust. At a session during the third week of treatment, he asked Bobby if he would play a word association game with him.

DR. CHASE:	Tell me what you think of when I say, "dog."
BOBBY:	Cat.
DR. CHASE:	Black.
BOBBY:	White.
DR. CHASE:	Chair.
BOBBY:	Cushion.
DR. CHASE:	Box.
BOBBY:	House.
DR. CHASE:	Angry
BOBBY:	Mad.

Dr. Chase spent about fifteen minutes writing down some of Bobby's associations. Bobby gave back associations in the rapid-fire way Dr. Chase asked, doing this almost automatically, leaving no time to deliberate. Gradually, Dr. Chase felt he saw a pattern emerging, and he was able to confirm this from Bobby's associations in later sessions.

Toward the end of the sixth week, Dr. Chase sketched for Bobby's parents the interpretation he had developed during Bobby's short-term experience in psychoanalysis: "I believe Bobby has unconsciously been trying to tell you something in a highly symbolic form: often the mind expresses deep-seated fears in the imagery of dreams.

"I've tested Bobby in a variety of ways. Always, he appears to associate the box in his dream with home or with a house. I'm fairly certain that 'being turned inside out' symbolizes for him the process of moving out of all the houses you have moved away from. A house really *is* turned inside out when you move: all of its contents are taken out, usually in boxes.

"I believe Bobby is hurting because of your frequent moves. I think if you will stay in one place, even though I realize that you, John, would probably have to give up evangelical work, you will gradually see a real improvement in Bobby."

Dr. Chase's advice was received with a good deal of disbelief by John and Rachel, but they did, eventually, decide to try it. John became assistant minister at a local church.

Two years later, Dr. Chase received the following letter:

Dear Dr. Chase:
    Maybe you'll remember treating our son, Bobby, for what you called his "recurrent night terrors." My wife and I followed your advice: We told him we had decided to stay in Atlanta, so that he could go to the same high school for all four years.
    In about two months, Bobby's night terrors were down to about one a week. After three months had passed, the suffering our family has endured for more than five years came to an end. Bobby hasn't had another episode since then. He's doing well in school, has friends, and seems quite happy. We all are.
    It's sure a pleasure to be freed from the experience that terrorized us all.

                                    Bless you,
                                    John and Rachel Edmonton

AN ANALYST LOOKS BACK AT HIS OWN PSYCHOANALYSIS

Psychoanalysis is unique among approaches to counseling and psychotherapy in that it requires analysts, as a part of their training leading to certification, to undergo psychoanalysis themselves. Not only is this intended to be an educational experience, but it is considered essential to their competence in later professional practice: it is important that they be completely aware of what are called *countertransference* feelings toward patients. Just as patients develop toward their therapists feelings they had toward significant persons in the past—called *transference*—the analysts, no less human, do the same. Their relationships with their patients can revive some of the analysts' own conflicts. They will be unable to understand the patient clearly, free from distortions created by their own countertransference tendencies, unless they have come to understand themselves as thoroughly as it is possible to do so by means of their own psychoanalysis.

After undergoing a long and intensive period of personal analysis while in psychoanalytic training, Dr. Tilmann Moser referred to his analysis as "a successful life-saving operation for my soul." He sought relief from depression, caused, he now believes, by a troubled relationship with his parents. He describes his experience in these terms:

> Psychoanalysis is a piece of the work of conciliation with one's own origins. The important ability to be implacable, attached to the wrong place in the neurotic unforgivingness toward . . . [my] parents, has been freed for aspects of life where it can be used for efforts directed toward social change, the changing of conditions that cause avoidable suffering to countless human beings. The longtime impassable road of affection toward my parents, based on humor, has been re-opened.*

APPLICATIONS OF PSYCHOANALYSIS

In general, psychoanalysis is successful in bringing about what are called *broad-spectrum improvements*. It is less intended for abatement of specific symptoms. In other words, those with highly *specific* goals they wish to achieve through therapy tend not to be good candidates for analysis. For example, a person seeking specific and prompt relief from depression, public-speaking anxiety, or shyness may not be appropriate for psychoanalysis. Long-term, intensive psychoanalysis, because it *is* long-lasting and very detailed, can lead to very broad improvements: a sense of increased satisfaction in daily living; a stronger, more positive sense of self-esteem; a greater capacity to enjoy and be at ease with others. In the process, specific symptoms often do subside or disappear, but the focus is general, and the patient must be willing to embrace a commitment to general improvement.

On the other hand, *brief* psychoanalysis may begin by focusing on specific problems experienced by a patient, but treatment quickly widens in scope to touch on matters that affect the

---

*Tilmann Moser, *Years of Apprenticeship on the Couch: Fragments of My Psychoanalysis*, trans. by Anselm Hollo (New York: Urizen Books, 1977), p. 18.

patient's life in a general way. We saw this in Bobby's case, where recurrent night terrors revealed his general need for the greater emotional stability that comes from feeling settled, having friends, etc.

Psychoanalysis is best suited to problems that fall into two categories:

- Problems that are clearly "neurotic" in nature: they interfere with living to some degree but do not totally impair you so that your life is clearly out of control, as in cases involving psychoses (where you are no longer able to distinguish reality from fantasies and hallucinations), alcoholism, or drug addiction
- Problems that involve sexual difficulties, mood disturbances, and impairment of personal relations, assuming that you are willing to work on these problems within the wider focus that analysis usually requires

Psychoanalysis is *not* generally considered to be the treatment of choice for severe impairments, such as alcoholism, drug abuse, and psychotic disturbances, when your life is clearly out of control. Analysis is also *not* generally an appropriate form of treatment for immediate problems arising from sudden environmental changes, such as the loss of a job, or loneliness after a transfer to a new job location, or after a divorce or separation. In some instances, if problems of this kind are not resolved after a reasonable adjustment period, analysis might then be considered. Other approaches to therapy lend themselves better to specific and immediate adjustment problems, as we will see.

We have been describing the appropriateness of psychoanalysis for the treatment of certain kinds of problems, but there is an equally important, and frequently overlooked, question: whether psychoanalysis is appropriate *for the kind of person you are*. Psychoanalysis is best suited to individuals with these characteristics:

- They are verbally articulate.
- They have a sense of curiosity about themselves.
- They have a good reflective capacity and an interest in achieving insight through a careful analysis of their thoughts, feelings, behavior, and past history.

- They are comparatively unimpaired in their abilities to form relationships.
- They are able to tolerate the frustration, and endure the pain, of reexperiencing disturbing feelings and memories.
- They are willing to be patient through a potentially long period in treatment and can sustain a commitment to that process.

10
PSYCHOTHERAPY, PART I
Client-Centered Therapy, Gestalt Therapy, Transactional Analysis, Rational-Emotive Therapy, and Existential-Humanistic Therapy

The approaches to therapy we will look at in this chapter are called *humanistic therapies.* They include client-centered therapy, Gestalt therapy, transactional analysis (or TA), cognitive therapy, and existential (or existential-humanistic) psychotherapy. These approaches share the view that an effective therapist must be able to become conscious of the world as it is for the client. Doing this requires the therapist to have a heightened sensitivity to others, feel a fundamental measure of respect for them, and ideally be able to adjust to their very individual needs and concerns. All of the therapies we will examine in this chapter place priority on the client's subjective feelings and experiences.

CLIENT-CENTERED THERAPY

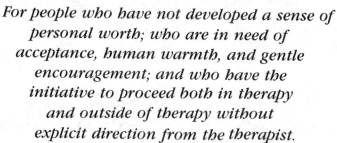

*For people who have not developed a sense of
personal worth; who are in need of
acceptance, human warmth, and gentle
encouragement; and who have the
initiative to proceed both in therapy
and outside of therapy without
explicit direction from the therapist.*

The development of client-centered, or nondirective, therapy
has largely been the work of Carl Rogers (1902-   ). His
clinical experience as a child psychologist and his later work in
training students in therapy led him to believe that people
frequently come to have personal problems as a result of the
conditional love of their parents. To receive love and approval
from their parents, children must satisfy certain *conditions of
worth* the parents lay down. If the children do not live up to the
parents' demands, they are punished by the withdrawal of the
parents' affection—a far more serious and emotionally scarring
punishment than a physical spanking. Raised in this way, people
later in life will tend to link their self-worth to internalized
parental standards. Rogers observed that the more the love
expressed by parents is conditional in this sense, the more it is
likely that a person will experience emotional difficulties later
on.

As a result, Rogers gradually developed an approach to therapy
that emphasizes "unconditional positive regard." Ideally, a
client-centered therapist is able to express a sense of complete
acceptance and respect toward the client. The therapist does not
associate positive regard with implicit conditions of worth that
the client must satisfy. In other words, client-centered therapy
attempts gradually to reverse a habit that has come to undermine
the client's sense of self-worth. It is a habit that we all, to
differing degrees, develop as parents and society teach us to
relinquish self-acceptance in favor of the conditional love or
appreciation of others. Eventually, the habit becomes so ingrained that it can jeopardize our own feelings of self-esteem.

Client-centered therapy encourages a client to grow in several
ways:

1. by feeling comfortable enough in the company of the therapist to express feelings freely and openly
2. by coming to recognize his own feelings of incongruence, of being divided against himself, often due to experiences that have encouraged a negative or insecure sense of self-worth
3. by perceiving that the therapist is an integrated, accepting person, able to convey acceptance and warmth toward the client
4. by reintegrating a sense of self, freeing himself from the distortions of self-worth brought about by love that has strings attached

AN EXAMPLE

Melissa Adams is twenty-eight years old, the district manager of a large pharmaceuticals marketing division in the Midwest. She is slender, immaculately dressed, and—as Dr. Feldman could see immediately—rigid and very uptight about herself.

Melissa came to see Dr. Feldman, a clinical psychologist, because of a growing sense of estrangement toward her husband and tension and anxiety at work. She described her upbringing in an extremely rigid, judgmental atmosphere in which her self-worth was implicitly tied to her parents' conditions of achievement. She was apparently encouraged by her parents, who realized Melissa was a bright child, to skip a grade and then to complete her undergraduate work in three years by attending summer school each summer. Her parents were very proud of her.

She admitted to having had little fun and would turn a vacation into an opportunity for achievement. She frequently could not enjoy television or the movies "because it felt frivolous." She was free from self-doubts only when hard at work, so she worked virtually all the time. Her husband wanted a family, but Melissa believed that children would be an undesirable interruption and distraction.

Melissa quickly lost her fear of the weekly meetings with Dr. Feldman. She was able to relax in his company. She felt that he cared about her as a person, whether she achieved or did not. He would not make active, directive suggestions, but rather listened to her in a genuine, positive way. During one session, Melissa asked him if he would give her some "straight advice" about her relationship with her husband. Dr. Feldman declined. He felt that telling another person what to do did not show respect for that person's individuality. He could see that Melissa was intelligent. He believed that she could trust her own decision-making abilities, and he would encourage her to believe in herself.

Over a period of a little more than a year, with weekly visits, Melissa's personality began to soften. She dressed more casually. She was more relaxed. She was beginning to enjoy herself more, although occasionally the old self-doubts would come back to assail her. But she usually was able to fend them off. Her marriage was improving, she looked forward to "a real vacation" in the near future, and she was not closed to discussing the possibility of children with her husband, although they had not yet made a decision on that issue.

APPLICATIONS OF CLIENT-CENTERED THERAPY

Client-centered therapy focuses especially on difficulties that stem from a client's negative feelings of self-worth. Client-centered therapy may be the therapy of choice especially for individuals who feel anxiety, uncertainty, and pain because of a low sense of self-esteem. A client-centered therapist can be expected to value personal genuineness, integrity, and honesty. The approach can be helpful to persons who suffer from loneliness and isolation.

Client-centered therapy is most effective for individuals with these characteristics:

- They are able to exercise initiative, both in expressing their difficulties to the therapist and in attempting to make desired changes. Most client-centered therapists will refrain from giving direction.
- They are interested primarily in personal growth rather than the removal of specific symptoms.
- They are blocked, inhibited, or rigid because they are too self-critical.
- They are not severely impaired in their abilities to relate to others.

GESTALT THERAPY

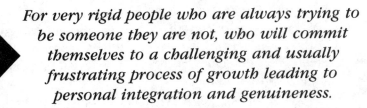

For very rigid people who are always trying to be someone they are not, who will commit themselves to a challenging and usually frustrating process of growth leading to personal integration and genuineness.

GESTALT PSYCHOLOGY

Gestalt therapy has its roots in Gestalt psychology, which was established early in this century by the German psychologists Wolfgang Köhler (1887-1967), Kurt Koffka (1886-1941), and Max Wertheimer (1880-1943). The main contribution of Gestalt psychology consisted of studies of human perception. Gestalt psychologists demonstrated that perception reveals the existence of organized wholes that cannot be reduced to the sum of their parts. They called such an organized totality a *Gestalt*. (Outside of psychology, *Gestalt* in German means "form.")

A famous example, shown below, demonstrates how an object that you see can be closely linked to its background. Here, the figure and the ground can oscillate, depending on whether you concentrate on the faces or the vase. The figure depends on its background for its identity, and vice versa.

THERAPY

Frederick (Fritz) Perls (1893-1970) brought together certain of the basic concepts of Gestalt psychology, psychoanalysis, and psychodrama, an approach to therapy developed by J. L. Moreno (1889-1974) that emphasizes role-playing, acting out of fantasies, and group interaction.

Perls transformed the Gestalt psychologists' central idea so it would serve as a basis for his approach to psychotherapy. Let's look at an example.

A man has been stranded in the desert and has become severely dehydrated. He has wandered for several days in search of water. He stumbles along, nearly blinded by the sun, seeing only vaguely defined shapes of rocks and cacti. Suddenly, out of this hazy world, something becomes clearly defined: he sees a watering hole, surrounded by low bushes. It is clearly etched in his eyes, set against the indistinct background of the hot desert. Once he has plunged his head into the water and quenched his thirst, his Gestalt is *closed*: the need that caused him to struggle for days has performed its purpose.

In this derivative sense, *Gestalt* means "a problem (figure) that arises out of a situation (background) which motivates an individual to action." If his action is successful, his Gestalt is closed: the problem is resolved, and the motivation is fulfilled. Like the Gestalt of the psychologists, the closed Gestalt of therapy signifies an organized whole. In the example, the man suffering from thirst in the desert has a Gestalt that impels him to find water. When he does, his thirst is satisfied, and the Gestalt is resolved into a whole that no longer stands in need of completion.

Perls saw life as a succession of unfinished situations, incomplete Gestalts. No sooner is one closed than another takes its place. To cope effectively with living, we must be able to deal with life's problems and challenges, yet not all of us can.

Perls used the term *growth disorders* to refer to what other therapists might call *personality disorders* or *neuroses*. He believed that emotional problems result from "getting stuck" in the natural process of growth. People get stuck in childish patterns of dependency because of a variety of childhood experiences. For example, a mother and father may withdraw the support of a stable environment while a child relies on this for a sense of security. (The example of Bobby in the chapter on psychoanalysis may come to mind.) Or, parents may force a child to accept adult responsibilities prematurely. It is as if a child were asked to walk before his sense of balance and leg strength had developed sufficiently. The child will *learn* uncertainty; his natural early fear of falling becomes pronounced and will leave a mark that can stand in his way later. Perls called such experiences *impasses*, and they form *blocks* to a person's growth.

For Perls, human personality is like a multilayered onion: From the most superficial, outside layer, moving inward, there is the usually insincere *cliché* layer ("How are you?," asked without real interest), the *role-playing* layer (the habitual masks of father, mother, businessperson, homemaker, therapist, client), the *impasse* layer (the person stripped of clichés and masks, often very frightening), the *implosive* layer (where emotions are either vented or explode inward), and the innermost layer, which makes up the *genuine* personality as it is, freed from learned pretensions. The goal of Gestalt therapy is to reach this last layer. In a word, Gestalt therapy seeks to encourage the growth of *authenticity*—a combination of a balanced sense of reality, of inner integration complemented by its outward expression, personal integrity, and of independence from the need for the approval of others.

In Gestalt therapy, self-change seems paradoxical. As long as inner conflicts continue, you try *not to be* the person you are; you cannot be genuine and are divided against yourself. Change, the Gestalt therapist claims, is possible only when you give up, at least for a time, trying not to be the person you are. There must be a firm place to stand from which to initiate change, and that place can only be the person you are right now.

WHAT GESTALT THERAPY IS LIKE

Gestalt therapy as it was developed by Perls is individual therapy done in a group setting. Gestalt therapists since Perls most commonly continue to practice therapy this way: individual members of a group are asked to volunteer to take the "hot seat"; the volunteer then becomes the focus of attention. This is not group therapy where relationships among members of the group are most imporatant (see Chapter 13). In Gestalt therapy, emphasis is on the individual, who is pushed to drop his or her masks and pretensions. Other members of the group form an audience and try to learn by example until it is time to occupy the hot seat themselves.

Perls would ask for someone in the group to sit in a chair, facing him and the audience. Then Perls would launch an attack on the client's defenses. At times, he could be almost merciless. He did not believe in mothering clients; this served only to keep their defenses intact.

Perls would notice nonverbal clues to the client's feelings. If the client was an inhibited woman, he would comment about her thighs, which were pressed firmly together. If the client was shy, he would remark about how the client held one hand in the other: Did he feel a need to have his hand held by Mother?

If the client burst into tears, Perls would make no attempt to stop the tears with reassurance but would try to make the client aware of his motivation in crying: Was it to elicit pity? Were the tears a way of hiding from self-responsibility? Were the tears another mask, standing in the way of self-acceptance, authenticity, and growth?

The objective of Gestalt therapists is to tear away clients' defensive masks and roles that usually keep them from real, sometimes painful or frightening, feelings. In this, the therapists' main technique is to *frustrate* the clients' attempts to hide behind their masks and roles and to *block* their attempts to control their therapist. Clients often do this by trying to make the therapist feel sorry for them, give them parental warmth, respond to their inadequacies, and so on. Instead, Gestalt therapy is comparatively *tough*. Perls used these instructions in beginning a workshop:

> So if you want to go crazy, commit suicide, improve, get "turned-on," or get an experience that will change your life, it's up to you. I do my thing and you do your thing. Anybody who does not want to take responsibility for this, please do not attend this session. You come here out of your own free will. I don't know how grown up you are, but the essence of a grown-up person is to be able to take responsibility for himself—his thoughts, feelings, and so on. Any objections? . . . O.K.*

---

*Frederick Perls, *Gestalt Therapy Verbatim* (Lafayette, CA: Real People Press, 1969), p. 79.

By refusing to give unnecessary emotional support even when clients cry for it, Gestalt therapists convey through their behavior that clients do have what it takes to stand on their own two feet. Ideally, Gestalt therapists are genuine, mature people; they refrain from interfering in the lives of others and expect them to be self-supporting. They try to impress on their clients that they do not exist to live up to the expectations of others, nor do others exist to live up to theirs.

APPLICATIONS OF GESTALT THERAPY

Gestalt therapy is most effective in treating persons with these characteristics:

- They tend to be very rigid—restrained, overcontrolled, perfectionistic—or depressed, or phobic. That is, they have certain well-defined fears; for example, fear of public speaking, of insects, of sexual intercourse.
- They have become stultified in their relations with others and have pent-up feelings in need of release.
- They obtain little joy or satisfaction from living; their lives lack emotional intensity.
- They are not excessively frightened by group activity.

Specific conditions Gestalt therapy often treats include these:

- psychosomatic disorders, such as stomach pain, colitis, back and neck spasms, and migraines
- behavior problems in children
- difficulties in coping with persons in authority
- shyness and passivity
- emotional difficulties arising from poverty and from the deprivations suffered by minority groups
- rigid, conflict-torn family situations
- crisis intervention: treating individuals in despair who have lost the will to live or are suicidal

Gestalt therapy is *not* generally the treatment of choice for people whose lives are out of control or who show signs of psychosis. Gestalt therapy relies on your capacity to make your own practical life decisions, to tolerate the stress and frustration of being in the hot seat, and to benefit from being challenged by the therapist to confront your own pretenses, distortions, and confusions. People who have lost these capacities for the time being due to problems such as alcoholism, drugs, and loss of touch with reality tend not to benefit from Gestalt techniques.

TRANSACTIONAL ANALYSIS

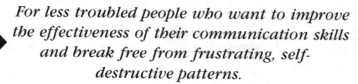

For less troubled people who want to improve the effectiveness of their communication skills and break free from frustrating, self-destructive patterns.

Transactional analysis has perhaps done more than any of the other main approaches to therapy to increase the sensitivity of the public to the psychological dimensions of human relationships. It has achieved widespread popularity in a short time largely because of its simple, commonsense vocabulary that is easy to apply to personal, family, and group situations.

Eric Berne (1910-1970) completed his medical training in 1935, then finished his psychiatric residency at Yale in 1941. He soon separated himself from psychoanalysis and began to formulate his theory of transactional analysis (TA).

By the mid-sixties, TA was gaining in popularity: Berne wrote his book, *Games People Play*, primarily for professionals, but it became a best-seller filling a need for an easy-to-understand and easy-to-apply approach to therapy.

TA is based on the premise that human personality has three parts: Berne called them the *Parent, Adult,* and *Child.* Although similar in meaning to Freud's *superego, ego,* and *id,* Berne's terms were intended to name dimensions of personality that could be observed directly; his three "ego states" are not theoretical constructs.

The Child ego state is the source of fun, humor, creativity, wishful thinking, and irresponsibility. It is impulsive and resists control.

The Parent ego state is the repository of values, attitudes, and expectations inherited from one's parents. *Shoulds, oughts,* hands-on-hips, and finger-wagging gestures are common expressions of the Parent.

The Adult ego state is the source of reason, logic, and unemotional evaluation. It forms the basis for decision making and predicting outcomes.

Only one ego state can be in control of our emotions or behavior at a time.

Berne observed that many emotional difficulties in individual clients result from problems involving their ego states. Some personality problems come about because a person cannot separate his or her ego states and switches from one to another erratically and uncontrollably. For example, a young mother begins—in a calm rational way—to describe the behavior of her nine-year-old son. She talks about his impertinent and disrespectful behavior, and, as she does, she becomes enraged, her face turns beet-red, and she yells at her therapist that someday she is going to give her boy a beating he'll never forget! Transactional analysis would try to show her that she tends to slip from her reasonable Adult state to the state of an angry Parent who demands complete respect and subservience. Berne called this structural problem of the personality *confusion*.

Exclusion is another structural problem. An individual rigidly adheres to one ego state, locking out the other two. A Don Juan gives free expression to his Child, while his Adult and Parent states are suppressed. A workaholic, on the other hand, permits

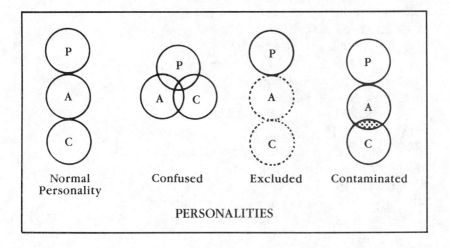

Normal Personality Confused Excluded Contaminated

PERSONALITIES

his Parent to block the expression of his Adult and Child ego states.

Contamination is a third personality problem. One ego state subverts another. A woman cannot commit herself fully to her chosen profession because her Child has undermined her sense of determination by persuading her that a wealthy knight in white armor will soon appear to relieve her of the need to exert herself.

WHAT TRANSACTIONAL ANALYSIS IS LIKE

Transactional analysis normally begins with "structural analysis" in which clients are taught how to distinguish ego states that may be confused, excluded, or contaminated. This phase of therapy is sometimes done on an individual basis and sometimes in a group workshop or classroom environment. Therapy then proceeds to transactional analysis proper, in which frustrating or painful forms of communication and unsatisfying life directions are discussed. Most commonly this is done in a group setting, since a group encourages a variety of different styles of communication.

TA teaches clients to determine which ego state is active at a given moment—in themselves and in others with whom they are trying to communicate. *Transactions* or communication patterns between people are the focus of TA. Some typical transactions are diagrammed on the facing page.

In (a) on the facing page, person 1 communicates in an Adult mode and receives an Adult response from person 2: "Where are you going?" "To the cleaner's."

In (b), a Parental boss receives a petulant response from the Child ego state of an employee: "What took you so long?" "My little boy is sick, and there's just too much work for one secretary."

In (c), an Adult-to-Adult message receives a Child-to-Parent reply; this is an example of *crossed transaction*. It is one of the most common sources of frustration and conflict in family and professional life. For example, a therapist says, "You seem to be late for your appointment today." (Adult-to-Adult, or A-A.) The

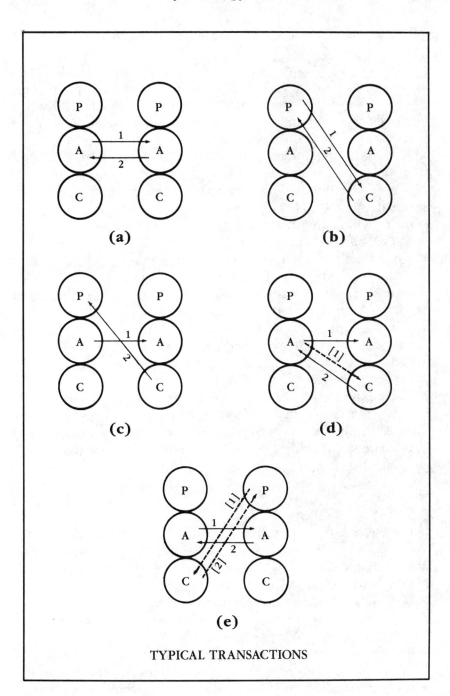

TYPICAL TRANSACTIONS

client replies, "You're just like my father, always picking on me." (C-P.)

Diagram (d) illustrates communication that involves an *ulterior* message. For example, a psychologically clever salesman is showing hair driers to a woman. She tells him how much she is prepared to spend and then asks, "How much is that one?" The salesman (arrow 1 in the diagram) replies: "You wouldn't be able to afford that model." His response is based on his customer's stated budget limitations and appears to be Adult-to-Adult. However, the hidden message (dotted arrow [1]) is directed to his customer's Child state, which, as he predicts, causes her to reply rebelliously (arrow 2), "That's the one I want."

In (e), another example of this class of communications that are not what they appear to be, there are two ulterior transactions. A secretary returns a few minutes late from lunch. Her boss asks, apparently Adult-to-Adult (arrow 1), "What time is it?" They both know what the hidden message is. The secretary answers sharply (arrow 2): "It's 1:15." The ulterior message from the boss is "Are you late again?" (P-C: arrow [1].) The secretary's covert or hidden reply is "Get off my back: you're always criticizing." (C-P: arrow [2].)

The central objective of TA, then, is to make clients aware of these and other patterns or games that their habitual ways of communicating reveal. By doing this, clients find that communication becomes less problematic and more effective as they learn to control their responses.

AN EXAMPLE

Joyce was forty-one when she decided to take her seventeen-year-old only son, Joe, to see Dr. Goldstein, a transactional analyst. For about five years, ever since his father died, Joe and his mother had quarreled a great deal.

Dr. Goldstein met with Joyce, then with her son, and then with them both. After he listened to their complaints about one another, he agreed to try to help.

For six weeks, Joe and his mother met once a week with Dr. Goldstein as "TA students." They were to put family problems on a back burner; their energy was devoted to learning to apply the concepts of transactional analysis. Dr. Goldstein had them analyze many examples of communication.

During a second six-week period, Joyce and her son were coached to learn to talk to one another more effectively. Here are some samples of their automatic patterns of response *before* they began to use TA:

> SON: The soup's too salty. (A-A or C-P)
> MOTHER: I don't know why I work so hard! All you do is complain! I'm just not appreciated! (C-P)

> SON: Mom, here's the sports jacket I bought for graduation. (A-A)
> MOTHER: You can't go in *that!* We're taking that jacket back. I can't trust you to buy clothes for yourself. Let's go! (P-C)

> MOTHER: We're going to dinner tonight at Esther and Gary's. Get out of those jeans; we have to leave in fifteen minutes. (P-C)
> SON: But Mom, I told you last Wednesday that Fred and I are going camping this weekend. We're leaving in Fred's car in just an hour. (A-A or C-P)
> MOTHER: I don't remember anything like that. Esther and Gary are *expecting* us. You're always wrecking our plans! (C-P)

> MOTHER: Mmm, isn't this the most delicious soufflé you've ever tasted? (C-P)
> SON: That's it, compliment yourself! (C-P)
> MOTHER: Well, if I don't, no one else will! You don't know how lucky you are, having a mother who really knows how to cook. (C-P)
> SON: I sure hope I don't learn how to be modest from you! (C-P)

The problems weren't hard for Dr. Goldstein to spot: Joyce had low self-esteem, was easily hurt, and, when she was, put her son down (the salty soup). She wanted to be indispensable to him and was unwilling to let him grow up (the sports jacket). She had little respect for Joe's plans, especially if they interfered with her desires (Joe's camping trip). She felt unappreciated and had grown to be resentful of her role as mother (the soufflé).

Joe, on the other hand, was feeling the natural rebelliousness of a seventeen-year-old. He needed some free rein, even if he made some mistakes. His mother was always "getting in his hair" or "getting under his skin."

The sample transactions above led each of them to anger and hurt. Seldom did Dr. Goldstein see Joe and his mother communicate Adult-to-Adult. Instead, their transactions crossed and re-crossed, and resentments piled up.

Joyce saw Dr. Goldstein without Joe present for several weeks. She learned from Dr. Goldstein that her expectations toward her son were inappropriate; she needed to strengthen her sense of self-worth outside of her family role. She was excessively dependent on her son for recognition and appreciation. Especially since her husband died, she was easily hurt when her desires for appreciation were not satisfied by Joe, so she put him down. What she needed to do was to strengthen her Adult and weaken the domination of her self-pitying Child and overcritical Parent ego states.

Dr. Goldstein then met with Joe for several sessions. Joe began to see his mother in a different light. Dr. Goldstein made him aware of his mother's sadness in being left alone and of her needs to feel worthwhile.

During the joint sessions that followed, Dr. Goldstein typically would ask them to recall recent conversations or exchanges that had been unpleasant. He would ask them to analyze these in TA terms and then would push mother and son to imagine more appropriate and less uptight ways of responding.

After several months of joint therapy, their former pattern of transactions began to look very different:

SON: Mom, there's too much mustard on the ham. (A-A or C-P)

MOTHER: Well, then it's OK with me if you want to scrape some off. (A-A or P-C)

SON: How do you like my new tie? (A-A)

MOTHER: I'd need a lot of courage to wear it myself, but I'm not you! (A-A or C-C)

SON: Mom, your roast is delicious. It's great to have a mother who's a good cook! (A-A)

MOTHER: Thanks, Joe. I guess now I've learned that you really hate soufflé! (A-A)

APPLICATIONS OF TRANSACTIONAL ANALYSIS

TA has been used in individual and group therapy, in nonclinical settings to help business executives improve communication skills, and also in prisons. It has been used to treat a wide range of problems, including these:

- personality trait problems: e.g., shy, lonely, depressed, overbearing, or hostile individuals
- troubled relationships in couples and families
- fears of withdrawal of affection and of abandonment
- drug abuse
- phobias
- difficulties in relating to authority figures, such as a boss, a teacher, a parent
- adaptation problems in individuals with counterculture attitudes and values

Few controlled evaluative studies have been done to determine how effective TA really is. At this time, and in this author's judgment, TA is most useful as an *educational therapy* to assist less severely troubled individuals with communication problems by helping them sharpen their perceptions of their own ego states and the ego states of others. TA is most effective for clients who are able to exercise responsibility for themselves. TA appears to be especially useful in helping individuals who are caught in frustrating relationships to break free from self-destructive patterns or games.

COGNITIVE THERAPY:
RATIONAL-EMOTIVE THERAPY

 For people who tend to think and judge in very rigid ways, who are frequently intense and uptight, and who tend to magnify and exaggerate evils.

Man is not disturbed by events, but by the view he takes of them.

Epictetus, *Enchiridion*

"It is absolutely essential to you to be loved by members of your family and to be appreciated by your friends and employer."

"You must be consistently competent and nearly perfect in all your endeavors."

"Some people are really bad, their actions should be restricted, and they should be punished when they do wrong."

"It is terrible when things are not the way you would like them to be."

"Events outside your control are largely responsible for how you feel."

"You should be anxious in relation to what is uncertain, unknown, or potentially dangerous."

"It is much easier to avoid problems than to face life's difficulties and responsibilities."

"It is necessary to have something greater or stronger than yourself to rely on."

"The present is largely determined by past events."

"Happiness comes when one has complete leisure."

"If you don't work hard to please others, they will abandon you."

"If people don't approve of you, you ought to question your self-worth."

By telling ourselves things like these, we create our own unhappiness, frustration, and anger; that is the point of view of cognitive therapy. During the 1950s, Albert Ellis (1913-   ) developed a theory of personality that claims that people are largely responsible for their emotional reactions. They tell themselves that things *ought* to be different, that people *should* do certain things, and that what they desire they *must* have. Life, for people whose thoughts are filled with *shoulds*, *oughts*, and *musts*, is full of disappointment, annoyance, and hurt.

Ellis observed that, as time goes by, we tend to reinforce an emotional pattern that amplifies our sensitivities more and more. The emotional reactions we create in ourselves become more exaggerated, distorted, and self-destructive.

But, like any habits, these mental (or cognitive) habits can be broken. Cognitive therapy attempts to do this.

Ellis called his own approach *rational-emotive therapy*. By this, he acknowledged that people have both rational and emotional dimensions. Their emotions and thoughts (cognitions) are so thoroughly intertwined that they cannot be clearly separated. Yet mental evaluations and ideas are given so much power that cognitive habits are responsible for emotional responses. It is thinking that makes it so.

Rational-emotive therapy is the most widespread approach to cognitive therapy, so we will examine Ellis's approach in some detail.

The main technique of rational-emotive therapy, and of cognitive therapy in general, is to focus clients' attention on their belief systems, their views about what "should" and "ought" to be, their cognitive "filters" through which they interpret, in a semiautomatic way, the world around them. If the "activating event" is a failure or a rejection, for example, a client's *rational* belief system will lead to feelings of regret, sorrow, disappointment, or annoyance; if an individual's beliefs are *irrational*, on the other hand, he or she may instead feel depression, worthlessness, futility, and severe anxiety. For rational-emotive therapy, emotional good health depends on the rationality of the way a person receives and interprets events.

WHAT RATIONAL-EMOTIVE THERAPY IS LIKE

Therapy usually begins with individual sessions. Once clients have learned how to identify mental habits that create disturbing emotions, therapy is normally continued in groups, where new attitudes and forms of behavior can be practiced in a kind of microcosm of the larger world. Rational-emotive therapy that is done in a group context is not, however, "group therapy," since the therapist's focus is on individual styles of thinking, not on relationships among members of the group.

During therapy, clients are very quickly challenged to give evidence for their irrational beliefs. The rational-emotive therapist will openly and ruthlessly oppose the foolish absolutes that clients express and make it clear how they are upsetting themselves emotionally by insisting on such nonsense. It is not considered essential that the therapist be a kind, warm, support-

ive person. In fact, rational-emotive therapy encourages therapists to show their impatience with irrational beliefs that cannot
be defended empirically or logically. Once clients are shown
that many of their beliefs cause them misery and disappointment, they are asked to *dispute*—silently, in their own minds—
their irrational beliefs whenever they find the old habits taking
over. It takes time to extinguish old habits; it doesn't happen
overnight. Clients need patience and tenacity to oppose their old
reflexes and replace them with rational, realistic beliefs.

An hour a week in rational-emotive therapy is really, then, like
a tutorial session with a teacher. The client-students talk about
their feelings; the therapist criticizes underlying irrational beliefs and makes it clear to the clients what a rational response
would be. Then the clients are asked to practice applying
rational beliefs on their own, outside of therapy. Gradually, a
more rational way of looking at things takes the place of the old
habits.

AN EXAMPLE

Joan Hendley is single, twenty-nine years old, and assistant
manager of a bank. She has come to Dr. Kovac because of chronic
depression, a sense of low self-worth, and feelings of insecurity
and anxiety. Lately, she has begun to drink heavily and regularly
feels the need to use sleeping tablets.

The following is a sample of their dialogue during their first
session of rational-emotive therapy:

DR. K.: Well, what would you like to start on?
JOAN: It's hard to put it into words. I guess it's that I've been
depressed a lot, about *everything*. I feel like there's no
purpose to my life. I don't know where to go or how
to decide.
DR. K.: So, right now you don't know where you're headed.
What's so terrible about that? It would be *nice* if you
knew, but you don't. Is that *awful*?
JOAN: Yes, it is! Everybody should have a purpose!
DR. K.: Why *should* they? Most people go through life without
much of a sense of purpose.
JOAN: Well, that's what I believe in.
DR. K.: Look, Joan, you appear to me to be an intelligent person.
You and I can agree that it would be more satisfying
for you to have a sense of direction, but you take this

one more step, and it's a *very* big step! You think it's *terrible* that you don't feel there's a purpose to your life right now. You think you *should* have a purpose, and I suspect you're punishing yourself because you don't live up to that *should.*

JOAN: But most people believe in things like that.

DR. K.: And a lot of them end up feeling miserable! I know: I've seen dozens of people sitting where you are, and their thinking is chock-full of *oughts, shoulds,* and *musts.* And that's what makes them feel upset. They feel much better when they can come to say to themselves, "It would be nicer, or more pleasant, or better if things were different."

JOAN: You mean, if I can get rid of *shoulds* and *musts* in my *thinking,* I'd *feel* better?

DR. K.: That's exactly what I'm saying. If you were to follow what I've told you, you'd seldom be upset again, and probably never enough to get yourself really depressed.

JOAN: Uh-huh. I'm not sure I really see how that can be. I feel pretty stupid.

DR. K.: So here you go again! You think of yourself as a pretty bright person, and so you say to yourself, "I ought to be able to catch on to anything pretty fast." And now here you are, and you're not all that sure you've followed everything already, and so you tell yourself, "Oh my, I must be stupid."

JOAN: [Nods appreciatively, laughs.]

DR. K.: You don't *have to* upset yourself. You can *choose* what you tell yourself, and then you'll have control over what you *feel.*
Tell me about your job. You're in the role of a leader, aren't you?

JOAN: Yes.

DR. K.: But you don't think you're doing a great job?

JOAN: No, I don't.

DR. K.: But *they* think you're doing OK, isn't that correct?

JOAN: Yes, but my job seems to be taking more and more out of me. [Begins to cry.]

DR. K.: Well, it seems like you're doing your job OK; it's just that you, from *your* point of view, aren't perfect! So *therefore* it's all just empty pretense: you're just faking it! But, if you'll give up your nutty perfectionism, you'd be in the clear, because you're obviously satisfying people at work; you're satisfying *their* expectations. But since you feel bad about yourself, you say to yourself, "Well, they just haven't found me out! When

they do, I'm in for it." And so you live in a state of
fear.

JOAN: That's it.

DR. K.: It's all because of your unreasonable *expectations*. Can
you see that?

JOAN: [At least temporarily convinced.] Yes, I think I can!

DR. K.: This is what I'd like to work on with you. It's going to
take some self-discipline on your part, but together we
can help you get rid of some mental habits that bring
you unhappiness. They don't serve a useful purpose,
and they drag you down.

Why don't you tell me more specifically what upsets
you at work?

APPLICATIONS OF RATIONAL-EMOTIVE THERAPY

Although rational-emotive therapy has been used to treat
many different kinds of problems, Ellis admits that his approach
is most effective for the treatment of clients with a single major
symptom or clients who are only moderately disturbed. In
addition, Ellis does advocate rational-emotive therapy for individuals whose patterns of irrational thought are severe, but for
such individuals—when they can be helped—therapy is a long-
term process.

From evaluative studies completed so far, it appears that
rational-emotive therapy is especially effective in reducing anxieties resulting from such things as public speaking, relating to
others on an individual basis, and facing old age. Other specific
applications of rational-emotive therapy include these:

- problems of maladjustment, where you have increasing
  difficulty coping with either an already familiar
  environment or a situation new to you
- marital problems and sexual difficulties
- psychosomatic problems
- anxiety
- depression
- problems of criminals and deliquents

Individuals who are most effectively treated with forms of
cognitive therapy tend to have one or more of these personal
characteristics:

- They tend to think in very rigid ways.
- They are inclined to think in all-black, or all-white terms. They are absolutists who think in terms of *what is right* and *what is wrong*. Life, for them, is an uncompromising affair.
- They are often perfectionists about themselves, so they tend to have unrealistic expectations of others as well. They are idealistic.
- Their behavior is frequently uptight, intense, judgmental, and intolerant *or* shy, self-effacing, and inclined to self-condemnation.
- They tend to think that if there is one bad apple, the whole bushel must be rotten. They tend to magnify and exaggerate evils.
- They confuse what they would like to have with what they believe they absolutely *need*. They are demanding and exacting.

EXISTENTIAL-HUMANISTIC PSYCHOTHERAPY

 For individuals who suffer from feelings of acute loneliness and emptiness, who have lost faith in themselves or others, and who tend to be analytical and introverted.

There is no single, well-defined theory accepted by most existential therapists. Instead, existential psychotherapy is a point of view, a general philosophy that attempts to describe what it means to be human and to live meaningfully in the world.

There is, nevertheless, a consensus among existential therapists concerning the objectives of the approach. Existential therapy seeks to help clients achieve these goals:

- to accept and make constructive use of their own personal *freedom*
- to become *authentic* individuals, shedding the conventions and conformities that obscure the real persons they are
- to establish human relationships based on *honesty* and *personal integrity*
- to be *fully present* in the immediacy of the moment

• to learn to *accept* the natural limits of life

Existential therapy cannot be described in terms of a group of techniques commonly used by therapists. In fact, existential therapists are inclined to resist the formulation and application of specific techniques of therapy, believing that psychotherapy is essentially a human endeavor and that the drive to formulate techniques is basically a dehumanizing, objectifying interest.

To understand existential therapy, then, we ought not to expect to encounter a set of specific techniques. What really characterizes existential therapy are its self-consciously endorsed attitudes about life. They include these realizations:

• Anxiety frequently motivates individuals to change their lives. Anxiety often is present to tell you that you need to change; it is not necessarily a bad feeling from which no good will come.
• Eventually each of us will die, and clutching life anxiously will stand in the way of finding real meaning in living.
• Past events need not control what you feel and do now; you are free to change old, unsatisfying patterns.
• Guilt is often a sign that you have missed opportunities for personal growth: you have not been true to yourself and have "sinned against yourself" in some important way.
• If you are to become a mature and genuine person, you must discard the *lies* you have cultivated. Among these is living the lie of trying *not to be* the person you really are; another is the lie of trying to be a person you are *not*, and there are many others.
• To be content within the limitations of life, it is vital that you have a sense of your own value. You become inauthentic if you base your sense of self-esteem on what others think of you.

It is obvious that *individual responsibility* is central to existential therapy. You are responsible for the person you choose to become. You may choose to be genuine, or you may choose to lie to yourself and others. It is when you abdicate responsibility for becoming authentic that you will often come to feel anxiety and a sense of guilt. Anxiety and guilt are often present, in other words, when there is a fundamental lack of congruence, of being whole, of being in accord with yourself.

The main contributors to existential psychotherapy have been the Swiss analysts Ludwig Binswanger (1881-1966) and Medard Boss (1903-   ), along with Rollo May (1909-   ), who was the founder of existential psychotherapy in America. Today, existential psychotherapy is practiced under a variety of names: *humanistic psychology, experiential psychotherapy*, and also in the context of the related approaches, logotherapy and reality therapy (see Chapter 11).

WHAT EXISTENTIAL THERAPY IS LIKE

Existential psychotherapy is usually individual therapy, with sessions commonly scheduled a few times a week, as in psychoanalysis. Existential therapy often shows its psychoanalytic origins: as in analysis, existential psychotherapy focuses largely on anxiety and the suppressed issues that anxiety veils. Existential therapists will push clients to confront anxiety directly; they will try to understand the clients' anxiety in relation to the lies that clients tell themselves in order to protect themselves from more anxiety.

As we have already seen, existential therapists very commonly regard anxiety and depression as *promising* symptoms because they can shake clients out of unfulfilling patterns of living. Anxiety and depression, instead of being viewed as undesirable symptoms to be eliminated, can motivate people to change and grow. Consequently, existential therapists tend to disapprove of the use of drugs in therapy. If clients take pills to reduce anxiety, for example, they will reduce the awareness of motivating pain that, if faced squarely, may bring about a more meaningful, satisfying life.

Here is an example of the way an existential therapist forces a client to face issues head-on. What the therapist is thinking is in brackets.

CLIENT: I don't know why I stay with my job. It just makes me depressed. All I do is tell you the same things over and over. I'm not getting anywhere.

THERAPIST: [She is complaining because I'm not curing her. She has to do this herself.] To be frank, I'm impatient,

CLIENT: too. We talk, but you're not able to act. [She has to see that I can't take responsibility for her procrastinating].

CLIENT: What do you think I ought to do? I can't keep living like this.

THERAPIST: [I can't make her decisions for her.] I can't tell you which way to go. I do know that you've been avoiding a decision. I believe you're going to take charge of your life but, until then, we may both feel impatient. . . .
What *do* you want to do? [She has to be pushed to make up her mind. She's ready now to decide but is understandably scared.]

CLIENT: I want to stop worrying, stop feeling so anxious and upset.

THERAPIST: [She'd like me to mother her.] Look, Diane, you've been coming to see me for three months now. You know what I think about feeling upset: if you're upset, there's something bothering you that you need to pay attention to. We both know you dislike your job and that you stay on mainly because you're afraid of a change. We can talk a long time about your unhappiness at work and about your fear of change, but eventually it will be time to stop talking and to try some alternatives. Do you think you're ready? I think you are.

CLIENT: (Sighs.) I guess you're right. I seem to be dragging my feet. If I want a satisfying job, I'm just going to have to try something else. Can we talk about some of my alternatives, then, and I'll try to stop complaining!

THERAPIST: [Now she's starting to face up to the challenge.]

APPLICATIONS OF EXISTENTIAL PSYCHOTHERAPY

These are some of the difficulties existential psychotherapy is designed to treat:

- feelings of *real estrangement or alienation* from others—from your immediate family and friends or from neighbors or colleagues at work
- a sense of *acute loneliness*, of being cut off from humanity and from normal everyday activities and interactions
- an awareness that your life has become an *empty pattern*

of habit, that your activities or work no longer feel
meaningful or valuable
* an inability to *accept* the realities that limit life; for
example, anxiety experienced by older persons as they
become more aware of the need to face the reality that life
will end or anger and frustration experienced by
individuals who must cope with real limitations—persons
with physical impairments and chronic pain, individuals
whose opportunities are limited by poverty, by their ties of
responsibility to others, or by social disadvantage

Individuals who benefit most from existential psychotherapy
tend to have these characteristics:

* They are reflective and analytical.
* They tend to be introverted.
* They have *lost faith*—in their sense of social commitment,
in their identity and role within their families, in their
belief that their work is of value, or in their religion.

11

PSYCHOTHERAPY, PART II
Logotherapy, Reality Therapy, Adlerian Therapy, Emotional Flooding Therapies, Direct Decision Therapy

In this second chapter devoted to major approaches to psychotherapy, we will look at logotherapy, reality therapy, Adlerian therapy, the family of emotional flooding therapies, and direct decision therapy. Like the five psychotherapies described in Chapter 10, these focus special attention on a client's personal style of relating to the world and others. They all seek to help a person to free himself or herself from troubling feelings and negative attitudes and to replace these with a stronger and more confident self-concept. Each therapy is a different path to that goal.

LOGOTHERAPY

▶ *For reflective individuals who are sensitive to values and who are in search of a richer sense of meaning in life.* ◀

He who has a *why* to live for can bear with almost any *how*.
Friedrich Nietzsche

Viktor Frankl (1905-   ) is worthy of much respect and admiration. Out of three terrible years of suffering in a concentration camp, during which his mother, father, brother, and wife were taken from him, Dr. Frankl developed logotherapy (from the Greek *logos*, roughly equivalent to "meaning"). Logotherapy is an approach to therapy that addresses our inherent need for meaning and value in living. The belief that sustained Dr. Frankl during this period of intense suffering was the conviction that people, in spite of great adversity, anguish, and the loss of all they hold dear, can remain free within themselves and are able to maintain, and even to strengthen, their sense of self-respect and integrity. To communicate how it is possible to do this became Dr. Frankl's lifework.

Logotherapy is a therapy of meaning for those who are unable to find a reason for living. It is a form of therapy related to existential analysis (see Chapter 10), but it is specific in its concern for helping clients find what it is that really matters to them, that makes hardships and pain worthwhile.

If Freudian psychoanalysis looks to the past for insight, logotherapy focuses instead on the future, on a person's *life task*. In this, there is no abstract and general answer to the question "What is the meaning of life?"

> For the meaning of life differs from man to man, from day to day and from hour to hour. What matters, therefore, is not the meaning of life in general but rather the specific meaning of a person's life at a given moment. To put the question in general terms would be comparable to the question posed to a chess master, "Tell me, Master, what is the best move in the world?" There simply is no such thing as the best or even a good move apart from a particular situation in a game and the particular personality of one's opponent. The same holds for human existence. . . . Everyone has his own specific vocation or mission in life; everyone must carry out a concrete assignment that demands fulfillment. . . . Ultimately, a man should not ask what the meaning of life is, but rather must recognize that it is *he* who is asked. In a word, each man is questioned by life; and he can only answer to life by *answering for* his own life; to life he can only respond by being responsible.*

---

*Viktor E. Frankl, *Man's Search for Meaning: An Introduction to Logotherapy* (New York: Washington Square Press, 1963), pp. 170-171.

Dr. Frankl liked to compare logotherapy to the role of the eye specialist: the logotherapist's role is to help the patient see more clearly the range of lived values and meaning available to him.

WHAT LOGOTHERAPY IS LIKE

An elderly physician came to Viktor Frankl to ask for help with severe depression. His wife, whom he loved above all else, had died two years before. His sense of loss would not heal. Could Dr. Frankl help him?

Dr. Frankl responded with a question: "What would have happened, Doctor, if you had died first, and your wife had had to survive you?"

"Oh," he said, "for her this would have been terrible; how she would have suffered!"

"You see, Doctor, such a suffering has been spared her, and it is you who have spared her this suffering; but now, you have to pay for it by surviving and mourning her."

The physician said nothing, but rose to his feet, shook Dr. Frankl's hand, and calmly left his office. "Suffering ceases to be suffering in some way at the moment it finds a meaning, such as the meaning of sacrifice."[*] It is the basic concern of logotherapy to help patients see the meaning in their lives.

Logotherapy is known for two techniques endorsed by Viktor Frankl. He called them *dereflection* and *paradoxical intention*.

Many emotional problems have their roots in what psychotherapists call *anticipatory anxiety*: a woman who is afraid of blushing when she enters a room filled with people will tend to blush. A man who fears impotence and who tries to achieve an erection will often fail. A woman who willfully tries to achieve orgasm also will frequently fail. These are examples of excessive, or hyper-, reflection. Excessive, anxious attention is paid to what we fear or wish, bringing about the very thing we are trying to avoid.

Frankl developed specific ways of refocusing or rechanneling this excessive attention. *Dereflection* could take the form, for example, of persuading the blushing woman to concentrate on particular things when she enters a crowded room: to look for acquaintances, to admire what someone may be wearing, or to

---

[*]Frankl, *Man's Search for Meaning*, pp. 178-179.

look for objects in the room to appreciate, for example. In the case of impotence or frigidity, often a shift of attention from yourself to your partner's pleasure will eliminate anticipatory anxiety.

Frankl describes an attempt to help a bookkeeper who was in real despair and close to suicide. For several years he had suffered from writer's cramp: very real muscular cramps that reduced his legible script to an illegible scrawl. He was in danger of losing his job.

He was treated with *paradoxical intention.* He was asked to write in an intentionally illegible scrawl. But he found that when he deliberately tried to scrawl, he could not. Within two days, his writer's cramp had vanished. Similar approaches have been very effective—and long-lasting—in certain cases of severe stuttering, uncontrolled shaking, washing compulsions, insomnia, sexual difficulties, and other problems.

Logotherapists tend to be warm, accepting individuals. They will often use humor. Yet they are trained to confront individuals: to push their clients to face their inner feelings of futility and despair, and then, out of their often overlooked and underestimated inner resources and moral strength, to *will* that their lives become meaningful. Logotherapists try to encourage clients to see more clearly what it is that gives them a sense of value in living and to use what they see to direct themselves toward more satisfying and personally fulfilling lives.

APPLICATIONS OF LOGOTHERAPY

As we have already observed, logotherapy has been used to treat a wide range of individual problems involving a loss of faith in the value of living, behavior that no longer is under voluntary control, or behavior that frustrates your desires.

Logotherapy is especially well suited to helping individuals with *noögenic neuroses,* Frankl's term for personal problems that have their basis in conflicts between opposing values. Noögenic (from the Greek *nous,* meaning "spirit" or "mind") neuroses have their origin in personal moral or spiritual, but not necessarily religious, conflicts. They lead to a feeling of existential frustration: a person's will to find meaning is blocked. When sufficient pressure is built up, anxiety and depression can follow. You can imagine how pressure might build up in the inner lives of a business executive who wishes she had a family instead of a career identity, a university professor who yearns to be an artist, or a financially successful businessman who despises his own pretenses and opportunism.

> I asked the poor creatures who listened to me attentively in the darkness of the hut to face up to the seriousness of our position. They must not lose hope but should keep their courage in the certainty that the hopelessness of our struggle did not detract from its dignity and meaning. I said that someone looks down on each of us in difficult hours—a friend, a wife, somebody alive or dead, or a God—and he would not expect us to disappoint him. He would hope to find us suffering proudly—not miserably.*

REALITY THERAPY

 For persons able to make a commitment to a plan for life improvement, whether they have emotional or behavioral problems or simply want to develop a success-identity.

. . . [U]nhappiness is the result and not the cause of irresponsibility.

William Glasser, *Reality Therapy*

Reality therapy was developed in the 1950s by psychiatrist William Glasser (1925-   ). His approach to therapy evolved as a result of his work with delinquent teenage girls, with clients in private practice, and with severely troubled patients in a VA hospital.

Reality therapy, as the name implies, attempts to help by strengthening a person's practical understanding of reality and by encouraging concrete planning that will bring about an improved sense of personal adjustment to reality. It emphasizes a very practical, feet-on-the-ground focus on the present: a person's past experience cannot be rewritten. Reality therapists do not believe in the essential value of psychoanalytic interpretation, dream analysis, nondirective counseling, or intellectual

---

*Frankl, *Man's Search for Meaning*, p. 132.

insight. A reality therapist focuses on the present, specifically on attempts patients may now be making to become more success-ful *from their own points of view*. If a patient is not able to make definite plans of this kind and cannot sustain a commitment to them, the focus of reality therapy will be to encourage the patient to begin to do this. It is an approach that believes that a strong sense of personal identity can come only from *doing*: if an individual is able to develop a degree of self-responsibility that is solid and enterprising, a feeling of personal success and effec-tiveness will follow.

Reality therapists are opposed to making diagnoses. A diagnos-tic label frequently adds a burden to individuals who are already burdened by emotional, family, or adjustment problems. Glasser notes, for example, that being labeled a schizophrenic "can be worse than the disease as far as incapacitating one in the course of life's activities."[*]

Reality therapists can resist diagnosing and labeling their clients because their approach claims that personal psychologi-cal difficulties, except those due to physical illness (see Chapter 8), result from a lack of personal discipline and responsibility. People are often caught in the habit of blaming their failures on their families, their lack of opportunity, their race, poverty, and other outside forces. It is a habit with a dead end: it ignores the potential success that can come from initiative motivated by responsibility and moral courage. As Ernest Hemingway said when asked if he ever anticipated failure, "If you anticipate failure, you'll have it."

THE EXPERIENCE OF REALITY THERAPY

It isn't hard to gain a feeling for what reality therapy is like. These are the basic principles of the approach:

The relationship between therapist and client must be per-sonal. The therapist tries to make clear that he is a genuine person who has, in some areas of his life, been able to plan effectively and to develop a sense of personal success.

The focus of individual sessions is on what the client *does*, not on what he or she may *feel*. Behavior can be changed much more

---

[*]William Glasser and Leonard M. Zunin, "Reality Therapy," in Raymond J. Corsini, ed., *Current Psychotherapies* (Itasca, IL: F. E. Peacock Publishers, 1979), p. 329.

directly than feelings, and feelings soon fall into place once behavior is more satisfying. What is important is for the client to develop intelligent plans and then to work to carry them through. If certain goals are not realized, the therapist's concern is to encourage the client to take the next practical step, rather than to spend time and energy analyzing what went wrong.

The reality therapist accepts that the first steps are often halting ones. It is important not to be disconcerted by occasional stumbling and a few falls. What is essential is a commitment to self-discipline and progress, refusing to punish yourself when a plan may not succeed, but going beyond it with a positive attitude that eventually can become a habit.

Glasser gives this illustration of the persistent refocusing on practical issues that characterizes reality therapy: a teenage girl expresses to her therapist that she would like to look for a job. The therapist does not respond, "Good, let me know how it works out," but instead begins the following exchange.*

> THERAPIST: What day next week?
> GIRL: I don't know. I thought Monday or Tuesday.
> THERAPIST: Which day? Monday or Tuesday?
> GIRL: Well, I guess Tuesday.
> THERAPIST: You guess, or will it be Tuesday?
> GIRL: Tuesday.
> THERAPIST: What time Tuesday?
> GIRL: Well, sometime in the morning.
> THERAPIST: What time in the morning?
> GIRL: Oh, well, 9:30.
> THERAPIST: Fine, that is a good time to begin looking for a job. What do you plan to wear?

In another example of reality therapy, a patient says, "I feel depressed and miserable." Instead of responding, "How long have you felt this way?" or "What have you been feeling depressed about?," a reality therapist might ask, "What have you been doing that continues to make you depressed?" or "Why aren't you even *more* depressed?" With both of these responses, the therapist makes it clear that he believes the client can influence his or her feelings.

Often therapists, no matter what their approach, will say to

---

*Glasser and Zunin, "Reality Therapy," *Current Psychotherapies*, p. 324.

clients who are going through a difficult time that they may phone after hours if there is an emergency. A reality therapist may, in addition, also say, "I hope you'll call me if you have had a special success."

APPLICATIONS OF REALITY THERAPY

Reality therapy has been used in connection with these types of problems:

- individual problems involving anxiety, marital conflicts, maladjustment, and some psychoses where a person is comparatively out of touch with reality and may have hallucinations or delusions
- teenage delinquency
- difficulties faced by women who have recently been widowed
- designing school programs that stress the development of individual identity based on a sense of personal success

Reality therapists believe that their approach is of value to people who want to develop a more successful pattern of living, of managing their own affairs, and of coping effectively with challenges at work and with problems of everyday living. Reality therapy has also been used in industry with organizational problems and with difficulties experienced by individual employees.

Reality therapy is not useful in treating problems in which there is severe withdrawal (as in autism) or cases involving serious mental retardation. To be effective, reality therapy presupposes that clients are able to communicate and are both willing and able to cultivate habits of self-discipline and personal responsibility.

ADLERIAN PSYCHOTHERAPY

For individuals interested in personal growth, especially in social directions, and for persons with low self-esteem who feel blocked and discouraged about life.

The greatest principle of living is to love one's neighbor as oneself.

Rabbi Akiva, writing 2,000 years ago

Alfred Adler (1870-1937) was a contemporary of Freud. Early in his career, Adler was invited by Freud to participate in his special circle of professionals interested in the development of psychoanalysis. Adler's already formulated views were not in accord with Freud's, their differences became more pronounced, and Adler eventually separated himself from psychoanalysis. Freud was embittered and became a lifelong enemy of Adler.

In contrast to Freud's technical and abstract theory, Adler's is humanistic, open, and concrete. Where Freudian analysis believes that emotional disturbances have a sexual basis, Adlerian therapy claims that neurosis comes about through distorted perceptions and from habits and attitudes that are *learned*. In Adler's system of *individual psychology*, there is no concern for unconscious processes or for internal divisions of the self into id, superego, and ego. Adlerians stress that a person forms a unity and must be treated as a whole.

Adler's approach to psychotherapy is based on the view that feelings of inferiority are normal. They exist in children, and they continue to be present in adults who may feel weak psychologically, socially, or because of physical limitations. To compensate for feelings of inferiority, adults strive for superiority by dealing effectively with the world, or they become deeply discouraged (however, they are not considered to be "sick") and lose contact with positive, constructive activities.

Adler also postulated that emotional difficulties come about when you are convinced that you simply cannot solve the problems of life in a way that is compatible with a need to be superior in some way. Certain attempts to compensate for feelings of inferiority can lead to emotional problems later. They include seeking a feeling of superiority by requiring attention from others, striving for power over others, taking revenge, and giving up—declaring that you cannot cope because of personal deficiencies and weakness. Children from families where there is distrust, domination, abuse, or neglect tend to choose these paths.

Another facet of Adler's approach is that individuals who

cannot compensate for feelings of inferiority are inclined to make a number of "basic mistakes" in perceiving the world. They will overgeneralize ("Nobody cares about me."), depreciate their worth ("I'm just a housewife."), set unrealistic goals ("I should please everyone."), distort ("You have to lie to get ahead."), and hold faulty values ("Win, even if you have to climb over others.").

Finally, Adler felt that, over the course of their lives, many people strengthen these basic mistakes while in pursuit of the ultimately unsatisfying desires for attention, power, revenge, or escape. Their styles of living may lead to depression, chronic anxiety, crime, alcoholism, drug abuse, and other problems.

WHAT ADLERIAN THERAPY IS LIKE

Adlerian therapists try to help people change unfulfilling patterns of living in several ways.

First, and perhaps most important, is the belief that therapy should do more than help clients with immediate problems. It should help them develop an adequate philosophy of life, encourage them to cultivate an approach to living that is self-sustaining, positive, and inherently *social* in focus. The paradox of inferiority and low self-esteem is that the suffering they cause disappears once people can forget themselves and begin living to some extent for others. Adler would remind his clients to "consider from time to time how you can give another person pleasure."* Adlerian therapy stresses the importance of social goals. For Adler, we are foremost social creatures; our individual identities can be developed and our problems resolved only in a social context.

Since Adler believed that most emotional difficulties we experience result from feelings of inferiority that have led to discouragement, the second goal of Adlerian therapists is to offer *encouragement.* They are as much concerned with mirroring clients' strengths as they are with analyzing their problems. Adlerian therapists will devote a good deal of attention to identifying and encouraging the personal assets of each client.

Adler suggested several techniques that have also come to be used by other schools of psychotherapy:

---

*Alfred Adler, *Problems of Neurosis* (New York: Harper and Row, 1964), p. 101.

Acting "As If"

Frequently, clients express a wish to begin acting in new ways—to be more assertive, to make an effort to break out of confining patterns of living, to conquer certain fears. However, they usually feel that the new behaviors are phony, so they are reluctant to try. Adler suggested that clients try a new behavior for the next week only as they would try on new clothing: they need only act *as if*. Adler found that, as clients began to act differently, they would begin to feel differently. When their feelings were positive, they tended to make new ways of behaving part of themselves. (Behavior modification, described in the next chapter, builds on this idea.)

Paradoxical Intention

We encountered this technique, also called *negative practice*, in the preceding section on logotherapy. It can be a very effective technique when certain habits can no longer be controlled. If you suffered from insomnia, you would be asked to focus your attention on staying awake: to put an end to the habit, you would be asked to amplify it. Oddly enough, in many cases, this judo-like dropping of resistance and redirection of attention can bring involuntary behavior back under control.

The Push-Button Technique

Many of us have unpleasant thoughts and emotions that refuse to leave us. We find ourselves on familiar tracks that we know lead to sadness, regret, anger, panic, or frustration. But we can't seem to subdue what Zen calls "these chattering monkeys of the mind." Adler taught clients that they *could* create whatever feelings in themselves they wished, simply by deciding what to think. It is possible, with some practice, to imagine a happy or peaceful memory or scene and to direct your attention to it when negative thoughts try to dominate. We all have this push button available. Like all exercises in self-discipline, it strengthens us the more we use it. (Cognitive therapy, discussed in Chapter 10, is especially concerned with this influence of thoughts on emotions.)

SETTINGS FOR THERAPY

Adlerians use a variety of settings for therapy. Individual

therapy is common, but sometimes two therapists may work together with one client, an approach that gives clients an experience of cooperation between professionals who may perceive them differently. Adlerian workshops are popular with parents concerned with problems in rearing children. Other workshops exist for married couples. Adlerians have often been innovative: Rudolf Dreikurs, a well-known student of Adler, was, for example, one of the first therapists to use group therapy in private practice.

APPLICATIONS OF ADLERIAN PSYCHOTHERAPY

Because Adler did not view human problems as forms of sickness, Adlerians see emotional and behavioral difficulties as blocks that people encounter in their attempts to realize themselves. Many of the problems Adlerian therapists treat are therefore considered to be *normal* problems of living faced by *normal* people. Many clients enter therapy to learn about themselves and to grow.

Adlerians have worked with a wide range of clients with a wide range of human problems:

- clients interested in personal development
- individuals who have become deeply discouraged about their lives
- couples and families
- delinquents and criminals

EMOTIONAL FLOODING THERAPIES

Today there are three main varieties of emotional flooding therapies: bioenergetics, primal therapy, and implosive therapy. They share the central belief that, by taxing you, pushing you to experience frustration, anger, or anxiety, the therapist may help you achieve a lasting sense of emotional relief and well-being.

These three therapies do, however, vary a good deal in the techniques they use to encourage clients to experience strong emotions. Bioenergetics makes use of an unusual approach to physical exercise. Primal therapy encourages clients to relive early painful memories. Implosive therapy asks clients to use imagery to increase, in a controlled manner, feelings that cause emotional distress. These approaches share the assumption that emotional difficulties can be helped by a direct release of feelings that have come to be blocked.

BIOENERGETICS

 For rigid, inhibited people who have pent-up feelings in need of release.

Alexander Lowen (1910-   ) was trained as a physician and then as a psychoanalyst under the direction of Austrian psycho-analyst Wilhelm Reich (1897-1957). Reich believed that emotional problems resulted from sexual repression. He was a social revolutionary in his attempts to bring about sexual freedom. He became a controversial figure and was not able to put his ideas on a serious and professionally respectable footing.

Lowen was interested in the therapeutic implications of Reich's work. He developed an approach to therapy that emphasizes not sexual liberation and pleasure as Reich did, but a sense of freedom that he felt could result only from an approach to the body that allows you to drop tense muscular armor and to feel integrated and fully alive. Lowen found that emotionally troubled people were physically knotted and rigid and tended to breathe in a shallow and constricted way.

Lowen devised a variety of physical exercises, such as holding your body in an arched position until exhaustion sets in, making contact with the floor only with hands, head, and feet. These exercises can cause enough stress to arouse intense emotions: crying out, collapsing, feeling rage or tenderness. As these pent-up feelings are released, many clients often discover an increase in positive emotional strength.

Bioenergetic therapists offer individual therapy as well as workshops. They tend to act as teachers, pointing out very bluntly how a client's physical rigidities reflect rigid qualities of personality: "Your chest muscles are this tense because you have been defending yourself so long, like a boxer," or "Your jaw muscles ache because you've been biting back angry impulses."

Because of its physical approach to human emotions, bioenergetics has been regarded as the West's therapeutic version of yoga. (For a discussion of yoga, see Chapter 15.)

Applications of Bioenergetics

Bioenergetics appears to be most useful for people with any of these characteristics:

- Their feelings are markedly inhibited, or they feel deadened emotionally.
- They feel impaired sexually or do not experience orgasm for nonphysical reasons.
- They are rigid, uptight, and inclined to be obsessive perfectionists.
- They have pent-up feelings of anger, hostility, or grief that are in need of an outlet.

Bioenergetics is not the treatment of choice when deeper insight and self-knowledge are important. Bioenergetic therapists are not in general especially concerned with a client's personal history, family and work environment, or specific adaptation problems.

PRIMAL THERAPY

 For individuals who continue to suffer from childhood pain.

Arthur Janov (1924-   ) was psychoanalytically trained as a clinical psychologist and psychiatric social worker. He had been practicing for seventeen years when a shy and withdrawn client in a group therapy session let out a piercing, primitive scream. The inhibited client experienced a sense of release and insight. This event fascinated Janov and eventually transformed his professional perspective.

He developed an approach to therapy that encourages patients to reexperience repressed painful memories from childhood. Janov calls these *primal* pains: they come about when a child's emotional needs repeatedly are not met. The inner suffering that results is suppressed; the pain cannot be dissipated. It takes energy to continue to block out painful feelings. The constant expenditure of energy then shows up in conscious tension. Janov came to believe that emotional problems in adults stem from their unwillingness to experience feelings that a child would find crushing but—though painful—can now be faced. When primal pain is faced, Janov claims, individuals gain a degree of freedom and maturity they could not otherwise achieve.

Janov's primal therapy is best known for the "primal scream" we mentioned above that some patients let out when they confront the pain they have suppressed for so long. Primal therapy encourages a repeated cathartic release of pent-up feelings. During the first three critical weeks of therapy (which normally cost in excess of $2,000), the primal therapist is on call twenty-four hours a day for a single patient. The patient is isolated for the first week in a hotel room, without TV, cigarettes, alcohol, sex, or companionship, and has daily therapy sessions with the therapist that last from two to three-and-a-half hours. Patients then spend six to twelve months in a primal therapy group.

Janov has been criticized for his apparent desire for public charisma and for capitalizing on advertising hype. He tends not to reveal in writing details of his procedures in therapy and will share his professional secrets only with initiates at his primal therapy institute. Comparatively few therapists have had this special training. However, many therapists offer what they claim is the equivalent of primal therapy, which they call *intensive feeling therapy*. They have the same format for therapy: isolation in a hotel room, three weeks' exclusive attention to each client, and the resulting high fees.

Applications of Primal Therapy

Primal therapy has been used to treat these problems:

- chronic depression and anxiety
- compulsions
- phobias
- drug addiction
- problems of homosexuals
- marital problems

Like bioenergetics, primal therapy is best suited for individuals who have repressed or pent-up feelings they have not found ways to release.

It is important to bear in mind that primal therapy is initially one of the most expensive therapies, since it devotes exclusive attention to each client at the beginning of therapy. It may not be the therapy of choice for more verbal, intellectual clients who want to develop an understanding of themselves beyond an experience of catharsis.

IMPLOSIVE THERAPY

For people with phobias.

This emotional flooding therapy was developed by Thomas Stampfl (1923-   ). Stampfl was trained as a clinical psychologist at Loyola of Chicago and was influenced by both psychoanalysis and the psychology of learning. Early in his career, he became convinced that clients with phobias tend to reinforce their fears by automatically avoiding what they fear. He developed an approach to help people face the situations, feelings, or memories they most fear.

Stampfl's approach is most easily understood in the light of recent experimental work on animal avoidance behavior. A dog, for example, is confined in a cage that is divided in two. A low wall separates the two halves of the cage, over which the dog can jump. On one side there is a bell that rings just before the dog receives an electric shock. The dog promptly learns that he can avoid the shock by jumping to the other side of the cage. Soon he will learn to do this automatically, whenever the bell rings. What is significant from a psychologist's point of view is that the dog will continue for a long time to jump to the opposite side of the cage, even once no further shocks are given. The dog's fear is maintained in force only by his own memory.

Animal psychologists have found a quick way to end the dog's fear: ring the bell, but *prevent* the dog from jumping to the other side of the cage. Once the anxiety-stricken animal realizes that he is no longer going to be shocked, the old habit based on fear simply disappears.

Implosive therapists make use of an equivalent technique with human beings. Patients are asked to imagine, as vividly as possible, that they are facing the very thing they chronically have tried to avoid. For example, an individual may have suffered from a terrifying fear of elevators for years. The therapist tries to use exaggerated imagery to produce maximum anxiety. He might ask the patient to imagine being stuck in an elevator fifty floors up, having the elevator shake and abruptly fall a foot, then have the lights go out, and so on. By *maintaining* this contrived elevator nightmare long enough, implosive therapists claim that, frequently, the level of anxiety of patients quickly and dramatically falls, and they lose their exaggerated fears.

Implosive therapists are therefore not primarily concerned with being genuine, sympathetic, or mothering. They focus their energy and attention on pushing clients to confront the worst fears and catastrophes they can imagine. All the while, clients are aware both that the intense anxiety they experience is an *intended* goal of therapy and that the therapist is convinced they are much stronger than they have thought.

Implosive therapy is usually done on an individual basis and is comparatively brief, usually lasting less than a dozen sessions. It should be mentioned that, when not successful, implosive therapy may occasionally *sensitize* clients to feel even more anxiety than they did at the outset. It therefore tends to be a higher-risk treatment, but it can be remarkably effective. Visualizing anxiety-producing events also has successfully been used by individuals on their own. (For more information, see "Appendix B: Suggestions for Further Reading.")

Applications of Implosive Therapy

Implosive therapy is especially appropriate for the treatment of phobic individuals who characteristically tend to avoid certain kinds of behavior, situations, or objects because of the severe anxiety and agitation these produce in them. Implosive therapy, when effective, can be dramatically effective in a comparatively short time. However, less arduous approaches to therapy can often be as effective and may involve less risk of increasing a client's existing anxiety. Alternative short-term therapies especially well suited to the treatment of phobias include behavior modification (Chapter 12), Gestalt therapy (Chapter 10), reality therapy (earlier in this chapter), primal therapy (earlier in this chapter), and biofeedback, relaxation training, and hypnosis (Chapter 15).

DIRECT DECISION THERAPY

 For individuals capable of exercising determination and self-discipline who earnestly desire to change.

[I]f there's one thing my experience as a psychotherapist has taught me, it is that no one has to be a victim. However important external factors like health, physical appearance, and upbringing may be, they don't have to determine the happiness quotient in anyone's life story. The way we experience our lives is, quite simply, up to us.

Harold Greenwald, *The Happy Person*

The majority of academic and research psychologists regard themselves basically as Freudians. Yet most psychiatrists, psychotherapists, social workers, and counselors have moved beyond Freud's formal categories and made use of their own common sense and interpretive abilities. Harold Greenwald's work probably represents the approach of more therapists and counselors today than any other theorist's. His conception of therapy is casual, simple, and often good-humored.

Greenwald (1910-   ) was originally trained as a psychoanalyst. As Greenwald gained professional experience, however, his perspective began to change. He gradually came to believe that many patients had, at some critical moment, made a *decision* to "go crazy." There was a point when they could exercise control, and at that moment, they chose to be depressed or anxious, to withdraw completely into catatonia, to become schizophrenic, alcoholic, or whatever their decision might be.

I discovered in working with people who have had psychotic breaks . . . that most of them described a particular moment when there was a choice of whether to stay in control or let go. . . . You will find, again and again, if you speak to patients who have broken down, and if you search for it, that there is always

a point at which they had a choice, and it is at that point that
they still have the possibility of controlling themselves. If they
have confidence in their ability to control themselves they can
exercise it.*

This *choice point* that people experience became the focus of
Dr. Greenwald's direct decision therapy.

AN EXAMPLE

Here is one of the most dramatic examples of his approach: Dr.
Greenwald had been invited to give a demonstration of direct
decision therapy at a mental hospital in Norway. He asked for a
volunteer from the inmates, someone who could speak English.
A twenty-year-old patient named Marie came forward. She had
the appearance of a back ward schizophrenic. She was haggard,
wild-eyed, and unkempt. Here is Dr. Greenwald's description of
their opening conversation:**

> I gestured toward a chair. "Won't you sit down, please?"
> "When I'm ready. I'll sit when I'm ready."
> "Would you tell me your name?"
> She waved an arm toward the staff member seated behind me.
> "You heard him. Marie, my name is MARIE!"
> "I'm sorry, Marie, I didn't catch it at first. Now I wonder if
> there is anything I can do for you. Would you like me to help
> you?"
> "You can't help me, none of you can help me. Why don't you
> *leave me alone*? WHY ARE YOU ALWAYS AT ME? . . ."
> She rushed on, shouting at the top of her voice and using a
> mixture of expletives and obscenities that showed an admirable
> command of English as well as Norwegian.
> Nothing I could do could make the situation worse, so I
> decided to try something drastic. I outshouted her.
> "CUT IT OUT, MARIE! YOU KNOW YOU DON'T HAVE TO
> TALK LIKE THAT."
> She stopped suddenly and focused on me for the first time.
> The muscles in her face relaxed ever so slightly, and her eyes

*Harold Greenwald, "Treatment of the Psychopath," in Raymond J. Corsini, ed.,
Readings in Current Personality Theory (Itasca, IL: F. E. Peacock Publishers,
1978), p. 355.
**Harold Greenwald and Elizabeth Rich, *The Happy Person* (New York: Stein
and Day, 1984), pp. 180-181.

showed awareness and intelligence.

"How'd you know?"

I stared at her for a minute, giving her my best foxy-grandpa look. "It takes one to know one," I said finally—at which point Marie's face broke into a grin.

"You mean *you're* crazy? You too?"

"Perhaps. And perhaps the only difference between you and me is that I know how to act sane."

Marie seemed to like the sound of that. She tightened the sash of her bathrobe and sat down.

As Marie calmed down, she agreed that she would like Dr. Greenwald to help her. She wanted badly to leave the institution.

DR. G.: If you really want to get out, Marie, you'll have to make a very simple decision.

MARIE: What's that?

DR. G: Decide to act sane.

Dr. Greenwald asked her to think of the benefits, the payoffs, that came to her as a result of her crazy behavior. There were a number of major payoffs: she didn't have to look after herself, didn't have to look for a job, didn't have to listen to her mother.

The upshot was that Marie decided to give up being crazy and to return to everyday living. It would have been easy for Dr. Greenwald to conclude that she had been faking all the years she was in the mental institution. But she had not been play-acting. Yet her illness began through a *choice* she had made, and it ended the same way.

Leaving the hospital world was not easy for her. In fact, it was often very difficult. But she stayed with her decision and often had to reaffirm it. She married and had a child. She wrote to Dr. Greenwald:

I found myself beginning to drift off, drift out of my life, the way I used to. And—I didn't! I decided to be the kind of person, the kind of wife and mother, that I want to be. Not perfect, just what's possible. And if I drift off, I won't be able to hear my daughter, I'll be just like my mother was with me.

Marie went back to school and earned a degree in psychology. After her experience, she was, she felt (as did Dr. Greenwald), in a special position to be helpful to other people in suffering.

WHAT DIRECT DECISION THERAPY IS LIKE

On your own or with professional help, the truth about you—
whoever you are—is that you carry within yourself the resources to heal your most grievous pains, overcome your most
paralyzing fears, devise ingenious solutions to your most
burdensome problems.

                    Harold Greenwald, *The Happy Person*

During the first session with a client, Dr. Greenwald often says
something like, "Do you want me to concentrate on your
problems, or would you like us to work together in making you
happy?" Immediately, he suggests to clients that in fact they are
able to change and become happier.

Dr. Greenwald describes seven phases that direct decision
therapy involves:

1. Decide what you want in order to be happy (or happier).
2. Find the decision behind the problem: what has your
   implicit decision been in your life that has established an
   unhappy, or less happy, pattern? Greenwald calls these *life
   decisions*: they form the center around which you organize
   your life. They are responsible for your attitudes, perceptions, what you value most, and your behavior.
       If your life decision is to suffer, you will interpret
   everything that happens to you as more suffering-to-be-
   endured. If you are praised, you may question whether the
   praise has an ulterior motive. "Sufferers . . . have the ability
   to snatch disaster from every victory.*
3. When was the original decision made? Did your life decision come from your upbringing? Did you inherit it from
   your parents?
4. Identify the payoffs for the decision. Even extreme unhappiness—chronic clinical depression—can have real payoffs:
   release you from responsibilities, gain you attention from
   others, allow you to return to the comfort of childhood
   dependency, etc. Anxiety can give you good reasons for

---

*Greenwald and Rich, *The Happy Person*, p. 29.

disqualifying yourself from stressful situations and reinforce your belief that you cannot cope.

5. What are your alternatives to the behavior that is causing a
problem? It is often hard to see that you are *not* really
trapped in a state of unhappiness. There are always alternatives.

6. Choose your alternative and put it into practice. Trust
yourself. "[H]appy people have a sense that whatever
happens, things will eventually work out. In short, they
trust themselves to react in their own best interest."*

7. Support yourself in carrying out your decision. Habits die
slowly. You must be patient. Your decision has to be made
over and over again, just as an overweight person who loves
food must decide again and again to say "No" to this dessert
today, the baked potato tomorrow. Gradually, the strength
of your decision builds as *you* build strength into it.

APPLICATIONS OF DIRECT DECISION THERAPY

As we have seen, direct decision therapy is based on the
assumption that you are *able* to begin to exercise self-discipline
and that you are *willing* to give up the real payoffs that being
emotionally troubled frequently does achieve.

These interrelated things—ability and willingness to change—
simply are not present in many people who enter therapy. They
come to therapy for a variety of other, often unconscious,
reasons: for temporary comforting, for escape from an upsetting
situation or environment, or for a chance to release painful
feelings and to express painful thoughts. Clients come in order
to procrastinate; they come to prove to themselves that they
simply *can't* change and that the therapist just isn't good enough.
They come out of anger, frustration, despair. But comparatively
few enter therapy because they really are persuaded they *can*
change and are committed to bringing change about.

These people are unquestionably the most promising candidates for *any* approach to psychotherapy. Clients who come to
therapy for other reasons make up the daily challenge and the
daily frustration, concern, worry, and hope of the therapist. The
therapist believes that, in time, and with proper treatment,

---

*Greenwald and Rich, *The Happy Person*, p. 29.

people who are imprisoned within walls of their own habits can rally the determination and faith to tear them down and to gain a measure of personal freedom.

In this author's judgment, direct decision therapy, perhaps more than any other approach, relies on a client's determination and perseverance. If these personality qualities are there, or if they can successfully be encouraged by a good therapist, the approach can be effective with a very wide range of problems.

> [W]hat . . . many . . . patients proved to me is that, given the choice to be happy, many unhappy people are able to decide that happiness is what they want. Then . . . they develop the ability to experience their problems in a different way. *

---

*Greenwald and Rich, *The Happy Person*, p. 53.

12
BEHAVIORAL
PSYCHOTHERAPY

*For people who want prompt relief
from specific symptoms and who have
the incentive and discipline to practice
new patterns of behavior.*

[M]uch of our suffering is just so obscure . . . frigidity, social
anxiety, isolation, boredom, dissatisfaction with life—in all
such states we may see no correlation between the inner
feeling and the way we live, yet no such feeling can be
independent of behavior; and if only we find connections we
may begin to see how a change in the way we live will make for
a change in the way we feel.

Alan Wheelis, *The Desert*

Many of us today feel forced to adapt to ways of living that will
lead to unhappiness, loneliness, fear, and illness. Is unlocking all
five bolts on one's apartment door in the morning, checking that
the can of Mace is in your purse, joining the sidewalk crowd to
the subway, hoping you are not mugged (or worse), and then
spending the daylight hours in a windowless office, in an
atmosphere of tension, pressure, competitiveness, and cigarette

smoke, with time out for caffeine (or, again, worse) and then a lunch soaked in alcohol a desirable and healthy way to live?

Behavioral psychotherapy seems to have been developed to respond especially to twentieth-century needs.

> Clients usually respond . . . with a great sense of relief on finding they are not seen as sick or weak; they appreciate the positive orientation toward changing the problematic situation rather than dwelling on it.[*]

Behavioral psychotherapy is best known for focusing on symptoms as its main target, rather than viewing symptoms as signs of underlying problems. Like most generalities, this one has its exceptions; some behavioral psychotherapists are very much concerned with understanding the underlying causes of an individual's difficulties. Nevertheless, behavioral therapies do tend to aim for concrete, specific, and prompt relief of symptoms. They frequently are effective, and they are based on techniques that have been tested extensively.

THE THREE SCHOOLS

Today there are three main schools of behavioral psychotherapy:

COUNTER-CONDITIONING

Also called *reciprocal inhibition*, this approach was developed by Joseph Wolpe (1915-   ), a Jewish psychiatrist trained in South Africa. Anxiety is offset by means of desensitization, assertiveness training, and sex therapy. As the basis for desensitization, deep relaxation is used to inhibit anxiety. Assertiveness training is used to counteract anxiety due to excessive shyness or aggressiveness by helping individuals form balanced habits of assertiveness that are neither submissive nor hostile. Sex therapy makes use of techniques of relaxation and desensitization to permit clients to feel sexual arousal and, in this way, to overcome sexual anxiety.

---

[*]Dianne L. Chambless and Alan J. Goldstein, "Behavioral Psychotherapy," in Raymond J. Corsini, ed., *Current Psychotherapies* (Itasca, Il.: F. E. Peacock Publishers, 1979), p. 234.

BEHAVIOR MODIFICATION

This approach was derived from the work of American behaviorist B. F. Skinner (1904-   ) and others, who attempted to show that most emotional problems result from situations in which a person has been punished. He or she comes to fear these situations and develops emotional symptoms in an effort to escape from them. In behavior modification, attempts are made to change behavior through the use of rewards or punishments.

COGNITIVE APPROACHES TO BEHAVIOR CHANGE

These approaches make use of techniques developed outside of behavioral psychotherapy, especially those of Albert Ellis's rational-emotive therapy (see Chapter 10). These cognitive approaches are based on the belief that a person can gain control over undesirable behavior and psychosomatic problems by learning new habits of thinking.

These three schools of behavioral psychotherapy claim that the problems leading people to enter therapy are *learned* and can be unlearned through systematic training. In particular, anxiety—the primary source of emotional discomfort—can become a learned habit. When this happens, anxiety is linked to stimuli that in themselves are usually harmless. A person may come to feel extremely anxious, for example, when in the presence of people in authority, when in bed with a sex partner, when near dogs or insects, when criticized by others, when in a confined space, or in any number of other situations. Anxiety in these situations is learned, and it gradually becomes an involuntary habit. But the habit frequently can be broken and eliminated.

WHAT BEHAVIORAL PSYCHOTHERAPY IS LIKE

COUNTER-CONDITIONING

When you are exposed to a situation that you believe is threatening, your blood pressure and pulse rate go up, your muscle tension increases, the blood supply to your large muscle groups increases, circulation to your stomach and genitals is reduced, your pupils may dilate, your mouth may get dry. A startling noise or a physical shock can produce these symptoms. They are the physical manifestations of anxiety, and they are the focus of counter-conditioning techniques.

Anxiety *generalizes* very easily. If you were repeatedly punished for playing with dirt as a child, dirt can evoke strong anxiety in you as an adult. If you were bitten by a dog, the sight of a dog years later may make you feel anxious. Anxiety can come to be associated with almost any experience. What is particularly destructive about this is that you soon find yourself caught in a vicious circle: a certain situation makes you anxious, you try to avoid the situation and the anxiety it produces in you, and as you do this, you build up *secondary* anxiety—you get anxious that you'll get anxious. So anxiety compounds, feeding on itself, fueling itself.

Counter-conditioning therapists have found that, to varying degrees, we are all capable of inhibiting anxiety. A behavior therapist tries to teach you how to do this, eventually so that you can use relaxation techniques on your own.

The following are the main phases of desensitization therapy— assertiveness training and sex therapy are similar, gradual, and reassuring processes:

1. You are taught how to achieve a state of relatively complete physical relaxation. Many therapists will tape relaxation instructions so that you can practice daily at home for twenty to thirty minutes. Some therapists will instruct you to *tense* your arms, hold the tension for ten seconds or so, then relax and feel the resulting sense of relaxation, the sense of relief from tension and strain. Or, some therapists use *suggestion*, asking you to imagine that your arms are becoming heavier and heavier, encouraging you to relax deeply. Each of your major muscle groups is relaxed in turn until you feel fully relaxed. This first phase of therapy usually takes from two to six sessions.

2. Next a hierarchy is constructed by the therapist for each individual client, ranking situations or stimuli from most to least anxiety-producing. A person who fears to leave the sense of security of home already is aware of such a hierarchy: low anxiety may be felt on the front steps, greater anxiety when going out to the mailbox, more

anxiety in walking around the block, and extreme anxiety when facing a trip or a move to another residence.

3. The last phase is the actual process of desensitization. You are asked to relax deeply with eyes closed, usually in a recliner in the therapist's office. You are asked to imagine a scene taken from the low-anxiety end of your hierarchy. The therapist tries to describe the scene as realistically and vividly as possible. If you begin to feel anxious, you can raise an index finger, and then the therapist will shift away from the imagined scene and will turn back to relaxation instructions. When you are again relaxed, the process continues until, in time, you are able to imagine a scene high on the hierarchy, but still sustain deep relaxation.

Once this process of desensitization can be accomplished in the office, you begin anew, but now with actual situations—first with those low on your hierarchy and then working your way toward situations that used to cause you high anxiety. Frequently, behavior therapists will accompany their clients outside the office, helping them to remain relaxed—e.g., while riding elevators, in crowds, even sometimes on airline flights if fear of flying is the problem.

BEHAVIOR MODIFICATION

The central idea behind behavior modification is that undesirable habits of behavior will gradually be eliminated if, consistently, they are not rewarded or even are punished. Conversely, desirable habits are encouraged when they consistently are reinforced or rewarded.

Therapists who use behavior modification techniques may recommend both punishments and rewards to clients. If you are a chronic smoker or overeater, for example, you may be given a small device with which to shock yourself moderately each time you reach for a cigarette or a second helping. Or, you may be asked to deposit $100 with the therapist, and a certain amount will be donated to your most disliked political group each time you go astray.

Rewards, on the other hand, include material rewards that clients may promise themselves once a habit is successfully under control for a certain length of time. Most therapists

encourage you eventually to substitute inner satisfactions: pride
in your slim appearance or improved health, strengthened self-
confidence, growth of sexual satisfaction, and, most importantly,
a developing sense of self-respect as you learn to gain control
over anxiety, frustration, or dissatisfaction.

Behavior therapists also use *distraction* techniques. They
encourage you to do things that are incompatible with the
problem you wish to resolve. Bicycling or lovemaking may prove
to be good antidotes for some individuals who overeat. Hiking or
jogging, or physical reassurance, massage, or relaxing baths may
lessen anxiety. Laughter releases tensions and offers its own
special kind of encouragement and healthier perspective.

Behavior modification requires strong initiative and discipline
on the part of the client. More than these, it requires that you be
willing to let go of old habits that have been unsatisfying or
destructive and work to form new, more rewarding habits. At
first, forcing yourself to behave in new ways may feel like
pretense or dishonesty. This is a common experience and should
not be allowed to block your desire to change. Unfamiliar and
even uncomfortable ways of behaving do become familiar and
more comfortable the more they are practiced. If these new ways
of behaving come to offer satisfactions or compensations that old
habits did not, they will gradually be absorbed into your own
sense of personal identity. What at first may feel to you like an
act slowly is made a part of your personality until a habit is
established that feels entirely natural. This takes time, patience,
practice, and more practice.

COGNITIVE APPROACHES TO BEHAVIOR CHANGE

Behavioral psychotherapists use a variety of techniques designed to help clients control their own behavior and individual
physical responses more effectively.

Biofeedback

Biofeedback can help many people gain control over habitual,
automatic processes. Biofeedback equipment can be used to
teach you how to reduce tension, develop skills to bring about
relaxation, or cope more successfully with chronic pain. (For a
detailed discussion of biofeedback, see Chapter 15.)

Thought Stopping

Thought stopping can help you break chains of negative and self-undermining thoughts. Thought stopping is a technique that begins by having you think out loud during therapy sessions. If you repeatedly express negative, troubling thoughts, the therapist shouts, "Stop!" In this way, you are made acutely aware of self-destructive thinking habits. You gradually learn to stop yourself from trapping yourself in upsetting thoughts by silently commanding your mind to "stop!" It is a simple but often effective technique, related to two techniques we have already discussed: the push-button technique of Adlerian psychotherapy (see Chapter 11) and the technique of disputing your own irrational beliefs in rational-emotive therapy (see Chapter 10).

Problem Solving and Decision Making

These techniques have been developed to help clients solve personal problems and make life decisions more effectively. Behavioral therapists who offer assistance of this kind emphasize the importance in problem solving and decision making of several factors.

One is refraining from implementing solutions or decisions until you have clearly defined and understood your problem or situation. Another is becoming aware of emotional blocks to solving problems and making decisions. For example, procrastinating serves to protect people from facing risks. Individuals are frequently also deterred from solving practical problems because they are emotionally distracted by other difficulties that demand attention first. And people are inclined to jump at one possible solution that then acts as a blinder to seeing other potentially more promising alternatives.

Behavioral therapists also believe you must realize that, often, difficulties you experience when trying to solve problems or make decisions are due to conflicts between incompatible goals or values. Sometimes one objective cannot be achieved without compromising another. They also believe you must develop abilities to imagine a wider range of alternatives. And finally, they believe you must become better able both to foresee likely personal consequences of implementing a particular solution or decision and to evaluate these in relation to what is personally most important.

AN EXAMPLE OF BEHAVIORAL PSYCHOTHERAPY

Anne Holt was thirty-two when she came to see Dr. Cantwell. She was noticeably anxious, wringing her hands, tense, and easily startled, as when a car's exhaust backfired in the street below. She complained of feeling unloved by her husband and was always in dread of his criticisms. She also felt her mother-in-law was very critical of her. Anne wanted to get away from the house but had quit two jobs in succession, in each instance when her boss's criticism of her work upset her.

Dr. Cantwell explained the rationale behind desensitization to her and taught Anne how to practice systematic muscle relaxation, beginning by tensing her hands, then relaxing them, tensing them, then relaxing them again, and doing this with her arms, shoulders, calf muscles, thighs, abdomen, jaw, neck muscles, cheek, and mouth muscles. He recorded his instructions on a tape for her to use at home.

After five weeks of daily practice, Anne was usually able to relax deeply in less than a minute. Dr. Cantwell, in the meantime, had gained a clearer idea of what troubled Anne, and he had made up the following hierarchy:

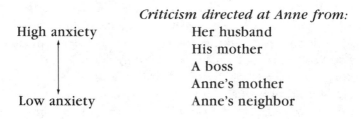

	Criticism directed at Anne from:
High anxiety	Her husband
↑	His mother
	A boss
↓	Anne's mother
Low anxiety	Anne's neighbor

Dr. Cantwell decided to use a combination of desensitization and assertiveness training with Anne. During half of each weekly session with Dr. Cantwell, Anne was asked to relax in a recliner with her eyes closed, and Dr. Cantwell would then describe situations low on her hierarchy. Anne was to try to maintain her sense of relaxation *in spite of* Dr. Cantwell's description of an imagined situation involving Anne's neighbor. She was to imagine that her neighbor, who was very fastidious about her own yard, knocked at Anne's door to complain about Anne's habit of setting the trash out the night before pickup. Gradually, in a similarly concrete way, Dr. Cantwell had Anne imagine her mother criticizing Anne for using the same sponge for wiping up in the kitchen as for washing the dishes; a boss asking Anne to retype a business letter using another format that he preferred; Anne's mother-in-law "dropping the hint" that her son liked to have his T-shirts ironed; Anne's husband complaining because Anne always overcooked the soft-boiled eggs.

During the second half of each session with Anne, Dr. Cantwell played roles with Anne in which he taught her how to assert herself more in situations involving criticism. In one session, for example, he took the part of Anne's mother and chose a typical remark she might make: "Annie, dear, don't you think it would be smarter to use a different sponge for wiping the kitchen counter? You should use a separate one for the dishes." Dr. Cantwell then asked Anne to think of a way she could reply to her mother's "nice" criticism, without feeling bad about herself, without "getting hooked."

ANNE: Well, one way you've taught me would be to use humor: I could say to her, "Mom, anytime you'd like to come over to do the dishes, it would be fine with me." And then laugh.

DR. C.: That's a good approach. But you don't want to be offensive; you don't want to laugh *mockingly. How* you do this is important. You want to set a good-natured feeling. Humor can be very useful to offset the sting of criticism. Can you think of a different way to reply to your mother, in addition to humor?

ANNE: Well, let's see. . . . Yes, well, I could go with her suggestion and not interpret what she says to me as criticism at all. I could say, "Mom, thanks for the idea. Maybe I'll do that."

DR. C.: Sounds very good. That's another way. The more alternatives you can prepare yourself with ahead of time, the less likely she will hook you, leaving you with nothing to say and simply feeling bad. Would you try to think of one more alternative? What other tact could you take?

ANNE: (After a moment of silence.) I can't think of another.

DR. C.: How about telling your mother how you actually feel when she criticizes you? How *do* you feel?

ANNE: Well, I wish she'd say some positive things instead, at least sometimes. That would be nice.

DR. C.: Great. How could you tell her that?

ANNE: Well, I could say, "Mom, you know, you give me a lot of suggestions. Some are OK, now and then, but, to be

honest, I'd really like to hear some praise sometimes.
Do you think you could find some things to
compliment me on? I don't want any false praise, but I
need to hear some encouraging things from people I
love."

DR. C.:   Anne, you're doing very well: . . . Humor, reinterpreting
so you don't feel criticized, and talking about criticism
from a more detached point of view. You're definitely
learning how to cope with criticism much better.

APPLICATIONS OF BEHAVIORAL PSYCHOTHERAPY

Desensitization is normally used in the context of individual
therapy. Behavior modification and cognitive approaches to
behavior change are frequently used in groups. People with
problems in common—smoking, obesity, phobias, etc.—are
sometimes grouped together. Often, however, a mixture in
groups is desirable. For example, it is frequently helpful for shy
people to be part of a group in which they may watch others who
can model more assertive ways of acting. (For more about group
therapy, see Chapter 13.)

Behavioral approaches to therapy must be tailored to the
individuality of each client; whatever goals are established have
to be in accord with the client's own desires. Behavioral psychotherapy presupposes that clients will practice instructions and
new behaviors between sessions and that they can maintain an
adequate level of motivation, both while in treatment and after
treatment ends, so that new habits of behaving or thinking can
become effective and reliable parts of their own personalities.

In general, behavioral approaches to therapy have been *less*
effective in treating panic attacks, chronic depression, substance
abuse (smoking, for example, is one of the habits most resistant
to formal therapy), and psychosis.

COUNTER-CONDITIONING

This approach, which includes desensitization, assertiveness
training, and sex therapy, has been used effectively in treating
these problems:

• phobias
• psychosomatic complaints

- sex, marriage, and family problems
- passivity and shyness
- personality trait problems: lonely, anxious, hostile, or overbearing individuals

BEHAVIOR MODIFICATION

This approach has been used successfully in connection with these problems:

- sexually deviant behavior
- children's problems, school discipline, academic performance, and juvenile delinquency
- problems of the mentally retarded and of psychotically regressed individuals
- some instances of obesity, alcoholism, and smoking
- schizophrenia
- stuttering

COGNITIVE APPROACHES TO BEHAVIOR CHANGE

These approaches have, for example, been used to treat such problems as:

- anxiety and depression
- adjustment problems
- marital and sexual difficulties
- psychosomatic problems

The popular conception of behavioral therapists is that they tend to be coldly scientific and mechanical. Yet a number of studies show that they are inclined to be warm individuals who show positive regard for their clients. In general they tend to be empathetic and self-congruent. These qualities are very much needed if we as clients are to feel encouraged to face one of the most difficult challenges life can pose for us: to change ourselves.

13
GROUP THERAPY

 *Especially well suited to people who are
outer-directed but lonely, who want to
develop their interpersonal skills,
and who would like to learn about
themselves from the perceptions of others.*

Group therapy is ancient. For as long as men have gathered together to share their experiences, thoughts, and feelings and to give one another comfort, group therapy has existed. As an approach to modern psychotherapy, however, it was in its infancy fifty years ago. No single great mind stands behind group therapy; it has been and continues to be innovative, flexible, and free from ties to any particular orthodox school of thought.

Clients who are attracted to group therapy and who often benefit from group experience tend to have these characteristics:

- They are passive in their interactions with others. They are more comfortable being told what to do than facing the need to decide for themselves.
- They are often lonely or socially isolated. Individual

184

therapy, with its one-to-one relationship between therapist and client, does not encourage some clients enough for them to feel like members of humanity. They tend to feel sorry for themselves while in individual therapy or to judge themselves harshly for their need for help. Being with other clients in a group situation answers their needs better.

• They are outer-directed people: what others think of them is crucial to how they think about themselves. Inner-directed individuals are likely to feel more interested in and comfortable with individual therapy.

For people who are relatively passive, lonely, yet outer-directed, group therapy has some distinct advantages:

• It gives them a place within a group of people—they are no longer alone.
• It gives them opportunities to express themselves freely, confront other people, and say things that they otherwise might not be able to express, thanks to the close and confidential environment of the group.
• They can hear how a variety of other people perceive them. They are not limited to the observations, ideas, and recommendations of a single therapist.
• They often feel more at ease in a group. They feel less fear or intimidation in the presence of the authority figure the therapist represents.
• They may benefit from the experiences of other group members who have similar problems or who have very different kinds of difficulties. Knowing that they are not troubled minorities of one can be a comfort; knowing that other people have problems in areas where they don't can be reassuring.

In general, group therapy can give you insight provided by the thoughts and perceptions of others; it can help you develop social ties if you feel isolated; and it can offer group support if you need emotional bolstering in order to cope with difficult situations, undertake decisions that may frighten you, and face more calmly and confidently the many challenges life can present. But it can also help you deal with more specific problems, such as facing an especially stressful situation—the death of someone very close to you, divorce or separation, serious illness, unemployment, drug addiction, or alcoholism. Or perhaps you have problems relating to others, such as having a history of being fired from job after job despite your efforts to hold them. For that matter, group therapy can even offer information about job opportunities, how to develop occupational skills, how to apply for a job, and how to keep a position you hold.

Some psychologists have commented that the popularity and the need for the kind of experience that group therapy offers are due to the decline of community life and to the virtual disappearance of extended families living physically and emotionally close to one another.

Group therapy is offered in private practice, in hospitals, and in halfway houses; in psychiatric and counseling centers, in clinics and hospital wards for patients with diabetes, AIDS, epilepsy, arthritis, heart conditions, paralysis, blindness; in prisons and juvenile detention centers; and in schools, for students with behavior problems and truancy. Group therapy is often used for marriage, family, and child-guidance counseling and to help families in which a member is physically or emotionally disabled. Group therapy is used by churches for family guidance and for spiritual counseling. It is used in virtually any area where people share problems: victims of crime and physical abuse, former patients, the aged, children of the aged, those who are discriminated against—the list goes on.

So, group therapy cuts across virtually the whole range of human problems. Because it is used in so many areas, it is impossible to define it as a single approach—many distinct approaches actually may be involved.

Many of the approaches to psychotherapy we have already looked at are used in groups. There are psychoanalytically oriented groups, Adlerian groups, Gestalt groups, groups that use behavior modification, and others. Perhaps the most useful way to understand group therapy is to liken it to education. Many sorts of things can be taught, and many can be learned. Group therapy may be understood most clearly in relation to what kinds of learning and teaching really go on in it.

Since group approaches to problem solving include many applications beyond our scope here—in industry, religion, schools, etc.—we will look more closely at these forms of group therapy used in psychotherapy: brief group psychotherapy, T-groups, human potential groups, self-help groups, and the use of specialized approaches to psychotherapy in a group setting. (Marriage and family therapy, special forms of group therapy, are of interest to a large number of people, so they are discussed separately, in Chapter 14.)

BRIEF GROUP PSYCHOTHERAPY

Also known as *short-term encounter groups*, brief group psychotherapy is intended for people who face life crises, who are motivated to change, and who are comparatively free of individual emotional disorders. Normally, there are about ten sessions. People who find short-term group therapy useful generally have well-defined problems to solve. Their experience in group therapy encourages them to become involved in new activities, join clubs, perhaps do volunteer work after being recently widowed, divorced, or separated; to take specific steps to find employment; or to practice new ways of behaving—to become more assertive, to implement a weight-loss plan, to return to school after raising a family, or to change careers.

T-GROUPS

Training groups were an outgrowth of the National Training Laboratories, an organization formed in 1947 by social psychologists who were interested in improving education. T-groups were made up of "normally adjusted people" who were interested in improving their communication skills so they could become more competent in difficult interpersonal situations.

T-groups gradually widened their focus and became the basis for the practical orientation of many therapy groups today. Clients who feel isolated or alienated, find it hard to relate to others, lack a sense of meaning and direction, and do not have strong self-discipline often are attracted to T-groups.

HUMAN POTENTIAL GROUPS

These groups have probably done the most to give group therapy its popular image. "Growth centers" are usually rural retreats where psychological growth of participants is encouraged. Visits last from a weekend to several weeks. The first center was called Lifewynn, organized in the 1920s at a summer camp in New York's Adirondack Mountains. The best-known growth center is the Esalen Institute in Big Sur, California, formed in 1962 by Michael Murphy. Its program combines Gestalt therapy with Eastern meditation (see Chapter 15). Other similar growth centers have sprung up across the country. In addition to these, the est (Erhard Seminars Training) organization has attracted a good deal of public attention and controversy. The est approach is eclectic, combining Eastern thought, Gestalt therapy, transactional analysis, psychoanalysis, Jungian philosophy, positive thinking, meditation, and other approaches. Some est leaders have been described as charismatic, proselytizing personalities who claim to be able to lead participants to salvation.

SELF-HELP GROUPS

There are self-help groups to aid you with many different kinds of problems. They provide group moral support for members with shared problems. They are not intended to bring about deep-seated personality change. Alcoholics Anonymous (AA), founded in 1934, probably is the most well-known self-help organization. Recovery, Inc., also known as the Association of Nervous and Former Mental Patients, was formed in 1936 by psychiatrist Abraham A. Low. Meetings focus on members' conscious control of symptoms; Recovery, Inc., frequently encourages members to become involved in volunteer social work.

There are many other self-help organizations—for the handicapped, widows, battered wives, diabetics, victims of AIDS, hemophiliacs, homosexuals, drug addicts, and others. (For further information see "Appendix A: Agencies and Organizations That Can Help.")

PSYCHOTHERAPY IN A GROUP SETTING

Most of the approaches to psychotherapy that we have discussed provide treatment in the form of group therapy in addition to individual therapy. Group therapy is frequently offered, for example, by psychoanalysts, client-centered therapists, Gestalt therapists, transactional analysts, rational-emotive therapists and general cognitive therapists, existential-humanistic therapists, reality therapists, Adlerian psychotherapists, emotional flooding therapists, and behavior modification therapists. In the remainder of this chapter, we will discuss how group therapy is handled by the main psychotherapies.

WHAT GROUP THERAPY IS LIKE

Although your experience with group therapy will vary depending on which school of therapy you have chosen, you will find some common elements regardless of the approach.

Initially, there is likely to be a period of group confusion, awkward periods of silence, some polite superficial conversation, and often a frustrating lack of overall organization and continuity. Different group members will speak up, and what they say may have absolutely nothing to do with what the previous speaker has said; people are waiting for the chance to talk about themselves and tend to concentrate so much on what they are preparing to say that they don't pay attention to what others have been saying.

Gradually, a more organized style of interacting comes into being through the directive efforts of the therapist or as a result of general group frustration over the lack of coherence. At the same time, group members will begin to feel more at ease with one another and will in time begin to lift their public masks and reveal more of their private selves—their often hard-to-admit feelings of loneliness, pain, anxiety, depression, etc.—and to express their personal needs.

Frequently, the first steps in the direction of expressing private feelings will involve attacks on the therapist for not structuring the group's interactions more or attacks on one member for monopolizing group sessions. Experienced group therapists realize that these common negative attacks are understandable tests of the trustworthiness and the safety of the group as a place to express personal feelings. If an atmosphere of acceptance is established, and these initial complaints are allowed to occur without catastrophe, some group members will usually then begin to open up, to reveal some deeper feelings. One member may begin to talk about her unhappy marriage, a man about his gambling obsession, another about his loneliness since his wife died.

At about this time it is common for group members to begin to tell one another how they feel about each other, how they see one another. Some of these comments will be positive, some negative. Here are some examples:

"You have a really nice smile."

"You remind me of my father, all these *shoulds, oughts,* and rules!"

"You never say much, so I feel you're just sitting there judging us."

"You make me nervous, biting your nails all the time."

"Every time you say something, you put yourself or somebody else down."

As this process continues, one or two group members will begin to take an interest in the personal problems of some of the others and express a desire to help. They will ask questions for more information, express sympathy or empathy, and begin to offer suggestions. It is at this point that the process of group interaction begins to acquire a focus on healing and problem solving. Frequently, these expressions of desire to help one member will encourage him or her for the first time to begin to accept the kind of person he or she has been, to realize that "I *have* been too hard on myself because I'm so damned perfectionistic," "I *am* a controller; I want other people to do things *my* way," or "I live in a suit of armor; I'm just afraid of other people."

As members of the group come to know one another as real personalities, they tend to become impatient whenever anyone tries to put on his public mask again. The group demands and expects members to be honest about themselves. Feelings can run hot whenever Fred tries to make Alice accept his suggestions because he *knows* what she really needs. Group members can show quick impatience with Judy whenever she tries to persuade herself, even though her husband has severely beaten her several times, that her marriage is *really* OK.

Group members quickly gain a good deal of information about how others see them and feel about them. As a result of an implicit commitment to honesty, some members' ways of behaving gradually change: a rough tone of voice becomes less abrasive and calmer; offensive gestures and judging looks disappear; self-centeredness gives way to a certain amount of sympathy and interest in other people.

Some of the values of group therapy are sensitively expressed in this passage from a letter written by a client to his group:

> "I have come to the conclusion that my experiences with you have profoundly affected me. I am truly grateful. This is different from personal therapy. None of you *had* to care about me. None of you had to seek me out and let me know of things you thought would help me. Yet you did, and as a result it has far more meaning than anything I have so far experienced. When I feel the need to hold back and not live spontaneously, for whatever reasons, I remember that twelve persons . . . said to let go and . . . be myself and of all the unbelievable things they even loved me. . . . This has given me the *courage* to come out of myself many times since then. . . ."*

THE RISKS

Unfortunately, like many healing processes, group therapy is not for everyone. There are recognized *risks* of entering group therapy.

When members leave the intimacy of their group and return to the "real world," they may feel disappointed and discouraged. Their experience has given them the opportunity to dispense with social masks, to become more authentic, to see the lies and pretenses of others more clearly. But the vast majority of people outside the group have not learned these things and *do* live behind masks they are not even conscious of. When you gain from a learning experience a perspective you can share with comparatively few people, you're likely to feel discontented and alienated.

You should also be aware that some of the changes that occur in group therapy simply may not last very long after the group stops meeting because the emotional and moral support offered by the group are no longer there. Or, group therapy may make you aware for the first time of personal problems you had ignored or evaded, leaving you hanging when the group terminates. So group therapy may bring about a need to solve problems that, before the group experience, you didn't even

---

*Quoted in Carl R. Rogers, *Carl Rogers on Encounter Groups* (New York: Harper and Row, 1970), p. 33.

know you had. These problems may then motivate you to enter individual therapy.

Finally, if you enter group therapy but your spouse does not, your experience could bring marital tensions into the open, leaving your spouse at a disadvantage. Your spouse, who is unfamiliar with what transpired during your group sessions, may react defensively and without empathy to your desire to talk about your feelings.

GROUP TECHNIQUES

The techniques discussed below are commonly used in group therapy.

Content Analysis

A member of the group describes a problem he or she is having, and the therapist and other members make problem-solving suggestions. Their focus may be on why the person does *not* want to solve the problem or on how the person brought the problem on and maintains it.

Group Process

After a series of interactions, comments, suggestions, and personal observations by group members, the therapist will ask the group to stand back and look at the pattern of their communication. The group may become aware of the way one member is consistently overlooked and is not given a fair share of attention because of shyness or because another more forceful member dominates the group's attention.

Models

One member can work on personal problems in group therapy by noting how another member goes about handling a similar problem and then trying to learn from that example.

Analysis of Nonverbals

The group therapist and members of the group can often help make an individual better aware of how his or her behavior has contributed to personal problems. For example, Jim tends to be shy, makes poor eye contact with people, has bad posture, and speaks indistinctly because he has a habit of covering his mouth with his fingers. The impression he makes on people is weak. By helping him pay attention to these nonverbal habits, group members can encourage Jim to change so he will be more successful, for example, at job interviews and generally feel more confident.

APPLICATIONS OF GROUP THERAPY

As we have seen, group therapy is most helpful to people with these characteristics:

- They are lonely, socially isolated, or passive.
- Their sense of worth depends greatly on what others think of them.
- They would like to improve their interpersonal skills.
- They may be drawn to group therapy for the practical reason that it tends to be less expensive than individual therapy.

Group therapy has the distinct advantage of providing clients with multiple points of view; they receive feedback from the therapist as well as from other members of the group.

Group therapy is potentially useful for a very wide range of problems. This is evident from the fact that most approaches to psychotherapy offer therapy in a group setting. Group therapy is generally *not* the treatment of choice for these individuals:

- persons lacking communication skills
- those who lack the motivation to attend group sessions regularly or who refuse to keep information about other group members confidential outside of the group
- people who are severely disturbed
- individuals who are intellectually impaired
- those suffering from chronic depression
- psychopathic or sociopathic adolescents (who do not have a sense of social conscience)

Group therapy, as we have noted, also appeals *less* to inner-directed individuals and is therefore less likely to be helpful to them.

14
MARRIAGE AND FAMILY THERAPY

 For couples and families with problems of communication, strain, and conflict, and for individuals whose difficulties are best resolved with the participation of other family members.

The family is the basic source of health or sickness.
Vincent D. Foley, *Current Psychotherapies*

During the last forty years there has been a gradual shift away from an emphasis on individual therapy to a belief that many emotional difficulties people experience have their roots—and, often, also their solutions—in their marriages or families. As this shift in emphasis grew, many therapists saw that marriage and family relationships make up units, or systems, each with a personality of its own. Members of a family gain their identities from their roles in the family system. This systems view made it possible for therapists to understand families and marriages more clearly as interdependent, interlocking, functioning wholes.

Marriage and family therapy treats emotional disorders in terms of the interdependent relationships among members. The marriage or family system is thought of as a unit with properties that reach beyond the sum of the personal qualities of the individuals who make it up. Usually, one person in a family or marriage is more troubled; his or her symptoms are more pronounced. The husband tends to feel his wife has "the problem," or vice versa. Mother and father feel that little Richard is "the problem." However, therapists believe that the problems experienced and expressed by the "sick" person are really signs that something is wrong with the whole system. A "heart problem" is frequently part of a larger problem, such as poor diet or excessive stress, and the same is true for couples or families. One person's distress tells the therapist that, often, something is troubling both husband and wife or all the members of a family.

This interdependence between partners of a marriage or members of a family system frequently leads to a complex situation in which emotional difficulties are contagious, one person's improvement is connected with another's getting worse, or treating one person separately draws the members of a relationship apart.

One of the very difficult problems troubled couples or families face is that emotional disturbance can often "spread." Repeatedly, therapists observe that there is a kind of subtle transmission from one generation to the next of inner conflicts and difficulties in coping with life. And beyond this, there are intimate connections between the emotional makeup and emotional balance of married partners or family members. For example, it is all too common for the partner of a chronically depressed person also to fall into a serious depression. Marriage and family therapists are therefore inclined to see the emotional disturbance of one member in terms of a troubled, ineffective pattern of interaction.

Because of their close ties, sometimes one person's behavior, attitudes, or feelings get better while another family member develops new symptoms or problems. We will look at a real example of this in a moment.

Marriage and family therapists have noticed that, when one person in a marriage or family is treated separately, the family members frequently are drawn apart instead of brought closer together. Therefore, therapists generally feel it is essential to see husband and wife together or to involve both parents and children in therapy.

The purpose of marriage or family therapy is not only to resolve existing problems but also to help clients cultivate a new way of communicating and interacting together. Marriage therapy and family therapy of course seek to relieve emotional distress by helping to reduce or end conflicts and to lessen anxiety, frustration, anger, or resentments. But beyond these, marriage and family therapists try to show clients how to complement one another's personal needs. They also attempt to strengthen bonds between them so that they are able to face crises and emotional upsets with greater strength, balance, and courage. And they try to redirect clients' values in a way that will support the personal growth of each person.

How long marriage or family therapy will take depends primarily on the goals of the couple or family:

- to reduce tensions: perhaps six sessions
- to reduce symptoms such as emotional distress or behavioral problems: ten to fifteen sessions
- to improve communication habits: twenty-five to thirty sessions over six to eight months
- to restructure relationships so that members of the family system will have more independence and will cultivate an awareness that they do have separate identities: forty sessions or more

WHAT MARRIAGE AND FAMILY THERAPIES ARE LIKE

Marriage therapy and family therapy are distinct from group therapy in two important ways. First, unlike in group therapy, the clients in marriage or family therapy have a shared history and, if therapy is successful, will be able to enjoy a shared future. Second, in marriage and family therapy, the therapist is more active and directive than in group therapy. Any changes made by members of a group come about because of interactions among the group members; a group therapist acts as a moderator or facilitator, while the role of a marriage or family therapist resembles that of a teacher.

Marriage and family therapy focuses on *present* interactions between husband and wife or among family members. It is not that the past is judged to be unimportant, but it is not generally useful to pay a great deal of attention to what has already happened. What causes problems *now* are the current patterns and habits of interaction in the family or marriage. A wife may have been drinking for fifteen years because her mother undermined her sense of self-confidence, but the fact is that she no longer lives with her mother. However, she *did* choose to live with a man who continued her mother's pattern of undermining abuse. A marriage therapist will focus on present difficulties and, by doing this, may be able to help her resolve her drinking problem by improving a troubled relationship with her husband.

Jay Haley, a leading contemporary marriage and family therapist, has expressed the belief that concentrating on feelings and thinking will not lead to change, that empathy on the part of the therapist does not correct problems, and that insight often just provides an excuse for intellectual rationalization and game-playing.*

Because the patterns of behavior of a troubled couple or family tend to be very rigid, therapists have found that strongly directive techniques are most effective. Their focus is on developing interventions—or therapeutic strategies—that will have a real impact on the complex patterns of interaction that have come to paralyze a couple or a family.

What seems to help in marriage and family therapy is ingenuity on the part of the therapist that will give him or her power or control over a situation that is out of control. One way to do this is to force clients into a paradoxical situation. For example, the therapist may prescribe that a couple or members of a family *continue* their present unsatisfying behavior. As a result, they may (and very likely will) rebel so that desired change comes about.**

All family therapy *is* marriage therapy to a certain extent. And so, suppose we first look more closely at what marriage therapy is like.

---

*Jay Haley, "Marriage Therapy," in Gerald D. Erickson and Terrance P. Hogan, eds., *Family Therapy: An Introduction to Theory and Technique* (Monterey, CA: Brooks/Cole, 1972), pp. 180-210.

**As we have seen, logotherapy and Adlerian therapy both make use of this technique, as do family therapists, as we will see later on.

MARRIAGE THERAPY

Marriage therapy is generally advisable* when the husband or wife has sought help in individual counseling but this has not been helpful. Sometimes the marital relationship itself inhibits, or even undermines, the improvement of the most troubled person. For example, individual therapy did nothing to help one woman who was suffering from severe chronic anxiety. When her husband was asked to participate in treatment, it was found that he abused his wife continuously but subtly. Whenever she spoke, he would criticize her views and indirectly slight her worth; when he lost something, he would often accuse her of misplacing it. The problem she had come for help with turned out to be marital rather than individual.

If you are unable or unwilling to communicate openly and adequately with a therapist, marriage therapy may encourage your spouse to become more involved in the process of therapy. Often, having the other marital partner present will stimulate an otherwise silent client to express himself or herself, especially to correct what the other partner has to say!

If you suddenly become severely troubled at the time of a marital conflict, marriage therapy may be useful. A spouse who falls into a deep depression immediately after a quarrel may be troubled in a way that marriage therapy can treat.

Finally, marriage therapy is of course essential if a husband and wife are in conflict and serious distress and cannot resolve their differences. Frequently, one spouse (usually the wife) will want marriage therapy; the other will come, but reluctantly. However, both usually *will* come, because if one is in distress the other is affected.

Conflicts in marriage frequently come about because of disagreements having to do with the couple's rules for living together, especially regarding how each is to treat the other. Who sets the rules is often another area of conflict, as are incompatible rules. For example, a wife insists that her husband stop being a "mama's boy" and demeans him for being dominated by a woman; yet it is *she* who seeks to dominate her husband by insisting that *he* be more domineering.

In marriage therapy (and also in family therapy), therapists

---

*See Jay Haley, "Marriage Therapy," pp. 180-210.

encounter a great deal of resistance to change on the part of their clients. (Alas, so do all other therapists!) A main reason for resistance is that, in a marital relationship or family system, change in one member's feelings and behavior will tend to affect another's, often in unsuspected ways. Change disturbs the established balance of their system, a balance that does serve some purposes.

Jane Dowland, for example, went to see Dr. Carlton because of her husband's depression. Phil had lost his job and now spent most of his time at home, feeling sorry for himself and collecting unemployment benefits. Jane was easily upset and felt terribly insecure. Dr. Carlton recommended that Phil accompany Jane to the next session. After seeing Phil, Dr. Carlton referred him to a psychiatrist, who was able to treat Phil's depression effectively in four months' time with medication. Jane, however, continued to feel severely (and perhaps even more) anxious, although Phil's symptoms were now under control and he was back at work.

Dr. Carlton recommended marriage therapy to Jane and Phil. They saw Dr. Carlton once a week for three months. It became clear to Dr. Carlton, and eventually clear to Jane, that without realizing it she had used Phil's depression as an excuse for her own anxiety so that she could evade responsibility for herself. She came to realize that she had been unable to resolve her own conflicting needs—whether to have children in spite of Phil's disinterest in children or whether to commit herself to developing a career.

Treating Phil's depression led Jane to become aware of her own problems. The balance in their relationship was changed by therapy: Jane found out that Phil's depression was really a problem that served a purpose for her—without it, she needed help for herself.

Because of the complex, interwoven nature of a marital relationship, it is often difficult to separate the problems each partner may experience. One partner's symptoms may mask the other's problem. Or, one person's problem may be perpetuated by the other's behavior, interfering with the resolution of the problem. Further, each partner may encourage distress in the other as a result of differing expectations concerning rules of living together and who sets them.

FAMILY THERAPY

In family therapy, the "identified patient" is seen as but a symptom, and the system itself (the family) is viewed as the client.

Vincent D. Foley, *Current Psychotherapies*

Very often, one family member is labeled the one with the problem, the one who is "sick." When the family decides to enter therapy, it is usual for family members to feel troubled, scared, and confused. They realize that something is wrong, but they are uncertain about what is amiss and don't know what to do. The usual response to this perplexity is to push the "identified patient" forward—usually a child who is "the problem"— and try to make him or her the focus of treatment.

As the members of the family are interviewed, individually and together, the therapist is able to assemble a coherent picture of the family, its typical ways of interacting, the habitual, automatic patterns of response of one family member to another, the family's values and beliefs. What one member tries to hide another often will express.

The family therapist has a difficult double role, as both observer and participant. He or she needs to be able to notice what the styles of interaction of individual family members are and *at the same time* interact with members of the family. The therapist tries to bring about meaningful emotional interchange, create an atmosphere of trust and rapport, and reduce the feeling that family members are threatened.

In time, the therapist is able to show the members of a family how they tend to interrelate inappropriately, how their own ineffective defenses cause them to hurt one another. To do this, the therapist has to be able to cut through the vicious circles of resentment, anger, blame, frustration, and intimidation that frequently hold families in a death grip.

THE THERAPIST'S FUNCTIONS

In both marriage and family therapy therapists must:

• establish a sense of rapport and trusting communication between clients and themselves

- use this rapport to bring out the conflicts, frustrations, and inadequate means of communication that burden their clients
- see through denials, rationalizations, and excuses
- push family members to put out in the open feelings and pains they have kept from one another
- bring to a halt the family's tendency to focus on one person as a scapegoat, "the problem"
- act in understanding, calm, and emotionally supportive ways and help supply the emotional stability that the couple or family temporarily lacks
- try to exemplify or personify for clients what it is to be adult, mature, caring, and able to relate openly and without feeling threatened

MARRIAGE AND FAMILY THERAPY TECHNIQUES

Marriage and family therapists may use a variety of techniques to encourage their clients to change in constructive ways. For example, it is becoming more common to *videotape sessions* so that couples and families may become more aware of their automatic, self-destructive patterns of interaction—which makes it easier to change them.

Family therapists also sometimes make *home visits*: often, being in their own familiar surroundings will encourage family members to let down their defenses and more clearly define the problems that need to be resolved. Another innovation that is becoming more widespread is *multifamily therapy*. Two or three families participate together in an especially modified form of group therapy so that each family can see its own problems in clearer perspective and learn by seeing more or less troubled interactions among members of another family.

Techniques drawn from *behavior modification* are frequently used in family therapy, especially when family difficulties seem to be localized around the behavior of rebellious or delinquent children.

Paradoxical intention, discussed in Chapter 11, can also be very helpful in marriage and family therapy. Instead of trying to restore a state of balance between husband and wife or among family members—something that usually stimulates the couple or family to fight to hold on to its old habits—a therapist encourages a state of imbalance so that the unbalanced system falls of its own weight. The cure, paradoxically, may lie in intensifying the problem. For example, a wife has migraines that prevent her from doing her family chores. A child throws up when he is forced to go to school. Both claim that they "just can't help it." The therapist's response might be, "I realize you can't help it. What I want you to do, Alice, when you feel household chores are just too much, is to go to bed and permit yourself to have a migraine. Don't fight it. Go ahead and have a bad headache. It gives you some relief, so I want you to do this through your own choice. And you, Johnny, I want you to go into the bathroom before you leave for school and throw up. It is unpleasant, but it hasn't hurt you. If you need to, stick your finger down your throat. I want you to take control and *make* yourself throw up each morning before going to school. And you, Alice, you won't interfere or try to mother him; let him alone. But do remind him to go and throw up." In a very short time, the results of these paradoxical strategies can be surprisingly effective.

APPLICATIONS OF MARRIAGE AND FAMILY THERAPY

As in all approaches to therapy, the effectiveness of marriage and family therapy depends on the strength of the clients' desire to overcome the difficulties that have motivated them to ask for help. Goodwill and commitment to change may or may not be there. Sometimes a therapist can help clients become aware of their deep-seated but habitually ignored feelings of warmth toward one another. At other times, marriage therapy may lead to separation and divorce, if a couple comes to realize that their goals really are not compatible and what each needs or wants from the relationship the other is not able or willing to give. Marriage therapy and family therapy are not magic wands that can be waved over trouble to make things better. Therapists can make specific recommendations, they can help a couple or family become explicitly aware of destructive patterns, they can point to and illustrate constructive ways of interacting, and they can sometimes use therapeutic strategies to break old habits and make room for care and sensitivity to the needs of wife, husband, and children. These interventions from a therapist can be very helpful, perhaps even crucial, but they are, at most, *catalysts* for change: real and lasting changes can only come from clients themselves. Marriage or family therapy is ideally an educational experience. What wife, husband, and children do with what they have learned is, in the end, up to them.

Family therapy has been especially effective in dealing with these problems:

- problems due to conflicts among family members
- emotional disturbances in children
- some cases of schizophrenia where members of the family are frequently not well-individuated—each person's identity is so bound up with the outlooks and behavior of other family members that no one has a clear sense of his or her own personal identity and separateness
- problems that are interlocking, where the difficulties of one member of the family cannot be resolved without the cooperation of the others
- problems experienced by a family when a child becomes old enough to leave home

Family therapy has been much *less* effective in treating paranoia in one member of the family, and behavioral problems stemming from sexual disorders.

Marriage therapy has been effective in helping couples with any of these characteristics or problems:

- They communicate and interact in ways that lead to conflict, frustration, anger, and unhappiness.
- They are insufficiently sensitive to one another's needs.
- They have unstated and conflicting expectations concerning their relationships.
- They will work together to help one partner overcome individual difficulties.

15

CHANNELING AWARENESS:
Exercise, Biofeedback, Relaxation Training, Hypnosis, and Meditation

All of these approaches to therapy serve to *channel* awareness in particular ways, to provide a point of focus for the mind. They are all processes that eliminate distractions and enable you to direct your awareness in ways that are basically different from normal, everyday waking consciousness. Special kinds of absorption or concentration characterize the therapeutic uses of exercise, biofeedback, relaxation training, hypnosis, and meditation.

THE PSYCHOTHERAPY OF EXERCISE

 For some individuals who already are or who are willing to become physically fit, sustained vigorous exercise can significantly decrease symptoms of tension, anxiety, and depression.

It is my contention that, just as prayer, meditation, dream analysis and some drug experiences open doors into these areas not usually accessible to us, under the appropriate circumstances slow long-distance running opens similar doors. The subjective experience of the runner appears the same, and he becomes revitalized or reenergized in a psychological or spiritual or creative sense. . . . It is clear to me that this is a distinct form of psychotherapy.

Thaddeus Kostrubala, *The Joy of Running*

Many studies have been made and a small mountain of literature has accumulated about the physical effects of exercise. However, little attention has been paid to its psychological aspects, particularly in connection with the kinds of symptoms and problems that bring people to psychotherapy.

Psychiatrist Thaddeus Kostrubala (1930-   ) has been one of the pioneering contributors to the study of exercise as a form of psychotherapy. Dr. Kostrubala is a dedicated runner who has completed many marathons and who uses running as a therapeutic approach in his practice.

Much of the modest amount of research on the psychotherapeutic value of exercise has focused on running, probably for these reasons. First, slow long-distance running seems to be an anatomically natural activity for us, with our two comparatively long legs. Second, running appears to be an especially effective way to derive specific therapeutic benefits from an aerobic activity. And, of course, running has recently become very popular.

Most exercise physiologists claim that the physical, and very likely also the psychological, effects of other aerobic forms of exercise, such as bicycling, swimming, and cross-country skiing, are essentially equivalent to running. So, until we know otherwise, we will assume that what is true of running is true of other types of exercise that make similar demands on the body, and we will focus here on running.

Dr. Kostrubala has attempted to describe a particular approach to running that seems to have definite psychotherapeutic value. More is involved than donning a pair of running shoes and starting out, as we will see.

Dr. Kostrubala has found that running is emotionally or mentally therapeutic under certain conditions. First, you need to make sure that you are in *medically good condition* to begin a therapeutic running program. It would be prudent to have a thorough physical and, if you are over forty, also a stress test. You need to do warm-up exercises, which any good book on running describes in detail, and then you need to build up your endurance—gradually and patiently—until you can run a *minimum* of three times a week for an hour each time, without stopping, and with a pulse rate of at least 75 percent of your maximum heart rate. (Your maximum heart rate is 220 beats per minute minus your age. If you are 40 years old, your maximum heart rate is 180. Seventy-five percent of 180 yields a pulse rate of 135 beats per minute. If you are 40, you would want to run for an hour so as to maintain a pulse rate of 135 beats per minute during your run. By way of encouragement, you may want to know that 75 percent of a person's maximum heart rate represents, for almost everyone, a slow, easy jog.) Second, you must have a *noncompetitive attitude* toward running. Whether you're comparing yourself to others or just trying to beat your own running record, a competitive drive rivets your attention on a goal separate from yourself. This misplaced emphasis will undermine the therapeutic value of the activity.

You also should either run alone or with someone who won't distract you by talking. Direct your attention within—to the rhythm of your pace, the regularity of your breathing, maintaining relaxation in your shoulders, back, and feet. To prevent distraction it is also important to run in an area or around a track that is familiar to you. For slow long-distance running to have a therapeutic effect, you cannot be a sightseer. The novelty of unfamiliar surroundings will distract you from being inner-directed, which is therapeutically important.

Finally, be aware of the physical risks. If you begin to feel dizzy, stop running. In hot weather, dizziness is a first warning sign of heat exhaustion, which can lead to heatstroke. If you feel a snap in one of your running muscles, stop. An internal snapping or popping noise can mean that a muscle or tendon has torn, or a small bone has broken. Make sure you are all right before resuming. If you have a cramplike pain in your side, which is very common, try slowing down, exhaling forcefully, giving a yell, or singing. You can often keep going, and the pain will subside. If it does not, or it gets worse, you'll need to stop to rest.

WHAT RUNNING AS THERAPY FEELS LIKE

The psychological effects of regular, slow long-distance running can be impressive if you follow the directions above.

During the first twenty minutes, you may feel slow and stiff and not very inspired about the run. You may find yourself in a sour mood. (There is even a term for this phase: *dysphoria.*)

Persuade yourself that it is not important and keep going.

Between twenty and thirty minutes, if you are dysphoric, that feeling may peak; some people even begin to cry. This is not necessarily depression; it may actually feel good. (Another reason to run alone: other people won't understand and may want to "rescue" you from your therapeutic endeavor.)

At some point, after about thirty minutes of running, you will probably find that your mind refuses to do any more problem solving. You stop worrying, problems you may have been dwelling on simply begin to feel distasteful, and your mind clears. (After a good run, when you do return to the problem, you may well find that it is less difficult to think through.)

Between thirty and forty minutes, many people begin to feel more "open"—their breathing begins to come more freely, and their whole system seems to work more smoothly and with less effort. This can be a wonderful feeling.

After you have been running for forty minutes, the first alterations in your consciousness may begin. Your senses begin to feel more alert, more alive. Things seem more vivid—the colors of leaves, the song of a bird, the freshness of the air. Runners who have experienced this say that this natural, vivid, fresh sense of perception is unique; to some extent it may resemble the experience that comes from meditation, biofeedback, or drugs. This experience seems not to occur before forty minutes of running. It may be an experience of mild euphoria, or you may feel it as a marked increase in aesthetic sensitivity or as a sense of growing inner serenity.

APPLICATIONS OF EXERCISE AS PSYCHOTHERAPY

I'm sure that these experiences are closely related to meditation. The clearing of consciousness, the ability to find a central focus within, the delight of a clear mind, the sense of refreshment of the soul are reported both by those who practice meditation and by long-distance runners. The difference between the two techniques is in the physical effects of the running. It is as if those who meditate have found one half of the picture. The runners who just compete and do not reach for the psychological aspects have found the other half. The runners who are able to slow down and search for the psychic aspects will have both—the soul and the body.

Thaddeus Kostrubala, *The Joy of Running*

Even though aerobic exercise such as slow long-distance running can produce a feeling of moderate depression during the first thirty minutes, people who have moderate, lingering depressions in daily life often find that, as described above, depression disappears after about forty minutes. Anger and hostility also seem to be much reduced after about thirty minutes of running.

The repetitive rhythm and sustained exertion of slow long-distance running appear to tire the conscious mind. Many anxieties, tensions, worries, feelings of guilt, anger, and depression lift. The easily distracted, constantly nervous and shifting focus of everyday consciousness gives way to a sense of integration, of being one with yourself and the activity of running.

> O chestnut tree, great rooted blossomer,
> Are you the leaf, the blossom or the bole?
> O body swayed to music, O brightening glance,
> How can we know the dancer from the dance?
>
> W. B. Yeats, *Among School Children*

The therapeutic use of running appears to offer the following benefits:

- increases mental energy, acuity, and concentration
- strengthens self-confidence and a sense of personal worth
- increases a capacity for work so that you feel less tired at the end of the day
- diminishes smoking, drinking, and other unhealthy habits
- helps those with eating disorders—who either are overweight or dangerously underweight—change their eating habits
- lessens or lifts depression
- improves relationships that were destructive or motivates people to separate
- reduces or eliminates confused and irrational thought processes in some schizophrenic patients

Treating Depression

In particular, running as described here appears to be especially effective in treating depression: " . . . it's hard to run and feel sorry for yourself at the same time."* Running tends to increase your sense of independence and self-confidence, which have been weakened if you have been depressed. Psychotherapy and drug therapy, in contrast, may encourage *dependency* on the therapist or psychiatrist.

Dr. Kostrubala has noticed that long-distance running often greatly reduces or even eliminates the typical early morning awakening and insomnia of the chronically depressed person. This particularly painful symptom involves jarring awake to a new day to be faced—a day of anxiety, fears, and hopelessness to be combated. If you have experienced this, you are probably familiar with waking up too early, at what the Swedes call "the hour of the wolf," lying in bed, exhausting yourself with crushing worries, despair, and tears, and beginning the day in a state of emotional exhaustion. Kostrubala has found that as depressed people cultivate the habit of long-distance running, these early morning ordeals often gradually subside and disappear.

A British medical group led by Dr. Malcolm Carruthers discovered that individuals who exercise vigorously produce increased levels of the hormone epinephrine, which counteracts depression. Apparently, strong exercise for even ten minutes doubles the normal level of epinephrine; the effects of the heightened level of the hormone can be fairly long-lasting.

Another study, by psychiatrist John Greist at the University of Wisconsin, revealed that one group of seriously depressed patients benefited more from a ten-week session of therapeutic running than another group benefited from traditional therapy.

To summarize research findings on exercise as a treatment for depression:

- To be effective, vigorous exercise must be done regularly no less than three times a week, and preferably at least five times a week, for periods lasting between thirty minutes and an hour. (Dr. Kostrubala uses an hour as a goal.)
- Although running and running combined with walking are the most commonly used therapeutic forms of exercise, any regular aerobic exercise is likely to produce the same

---

*James Fixx, *The Complete Book of Running* (New York: Random House, 1977), p. 16.

antidepressant effects when done for proportional periods of exertion.

• Studies over the past ten years show that lessening depression by means of exercise is most successful for persons with mild to moderate depression, but vigorous exercise tends *not* to benefit patients with *severe* depression.*

Lessening Anxiety

Therapeutic running also tends appreciably to lessen anxiety. A research study conducted by Dr. Herbert A. deVries of the University of Southern California School of Medicine and Gene M. Adams of USC's Gerontology Center found that fifteen minutes of moderate exercise diminished anxiety more in people aged fifty-two to seventy than did 400-milligram doses of meprobamate, a widely prescribed tranquilizer.

For Schizophrenics

Therapeutic running also seems to benefit schizophrenic patients. Schizophrenia is a complex, difficult-to-treat illness that affects approximately 1 percent of the world's population. It is no respecter of particular cultures. There are many forms of the illness, but all are characterized by disabling blockages to normal human interrelation, strange behavior, loss of contact with reality, and withdrawal, paranoia, or hallucinations. Again, Dr. Kostrubala has attempted to help patients with this condition through a combined program of medication, psychotherapy, and therapeutic running. Although he is careful to emphasize that controlled studies have yet to be made, his judgment about the patients he has treated is that

> . . . using this form of running therapy . . . [I] have seen them change dramatically. They begin to lose their symptoms; medication can be reduced and often discontinued; and they have picked up the course of their lives until several are no longer recognizable as schizophrenics at all—even by professional observers.**

---

*John H. Griest and James W. Jefferson, *Depression and Its Treatment* (Washington, DC: American Psychiatric Press, 1984), p. 63.

**Thaddeus Kostrubala, *The Joy of Running* (Philadelphia: J. B. Lippincott, 1976), p. 129.

... I have come to the conclusion that running, done in a particular way, is a natural form of psychotherapy.*

The Risks

Since therapeutic running appears to be of psychiatric value, it is not surprising that it, like any attempt to heal, may have potential risks. Aside from the obvious potential for sports-related injuries, there is a specific risk: physical addiction. Dr. William Glasser, whose approach to psychotherapy we discussed in the section dealing with reality therapy (Chapter 11), agrees with Kostrubala that therapeutic running *is* addictive. Glasser calls it a *positive* addiction, since—unlike the use of alcohol, barbiturates, and opiates—running is constructive and thera-peutic.** However, like alcoholism and drug addiction, thera-peutic running *does* produce very real withdrawal symptoms if a dedicated runner cannot continue to run, whether temporarily because of an injury or illness or permanently. Withdrawal symptoms can be surprisingly severe: primarily, strong anxiety and insomnia, but sometimes also restlessness, sweating, weight gain or loss, and/or depression.

BIOFEEDBACK

 In psychotherapy, especially useful for clients with problems involving anxiety, depression, phobias, and insomnia, who will benefit from learning how to lessen their own tension.

Most of us can draw a relatively clear line between the physiological processes we can control and those we cannot. Unless an illness or accident or handicap interferes, we have voluntary control over many muscles, but there are many that, fortunately, work without our conscious intercession: the heart beats day and night, our lungs fill and empty, our digestive processes are automatic. Except for people who have voluntary control over the muscles that move their ears, we are all more or

---

*Kostrubala, *The Joy of Running*, p. 119
**William Glasser, *Positive Addiction* (New York: Harper and Row, 1976), Chapter 5. (Chapter 6 is devoted to another positive addiction, meditation.)

less equally endowed, and equally limited, in what physical processes we are able to influence.

Until the development of biofeedback, there was only one way to extend self-control beyond the normal range: through the disciplined and time-consuming practice of yoga. Experienced practitioners of yoga claim that studying yoga over a period of years has given them a sense of personal integration and mental centering similar to what we will see in connection with the practice of meditation. Physical and emotional flexibility also seem to result from long-term yoga practice.

Some yogis have extended their range of control over inner, normally involuntary processes in dramatic ways. Some can cause their heart rate to increase to five times its resting rate. Some are able to cause a ten-degree temperature difference between the thumb and little finger of the same hand: one side is flushed and hot, the other side cool and pale. Many other forms of self-control have been documented,* but acquiring these special skills through the practice of yoga takes years of discipline, concentration, and tenacity. But the years of dedication seem also to be indispensable if one is to develop the qualities of inner tranquility and strength sought by yogis.

Biofeedback has greatly shortened the yogis' road to conscious control of some physical processes, and, in turn, it has become the main contribution technology has made so far to psychotherapy. Many of the physical processes that biofeedback training can help you learn rather quickly to control influence your emotional well-being. Biofeedback equipment can enable you to learn, for example, how to *will* a state of muscular relaxation, how to gain a measure of control over your physical response to stress or pain, even how to raise or lower your blood pressure or heart or respiration rate.

To use biofeedback equipment, electrodes are taped to the areas of your body that are to be monitored. They may measure such things as skin temperature, skin moisture, muscle tension, pulse and breathing rates, or brain wave patterns. The feedback from which you learn to control normally involuntary processes occurs when the measurements made by the instruments are externalized for you: you are able to *see* a pattern on a television

---

*See, e.g., Mircea Eliade, *Yoga: Immortality and Freedom* (Princeton, NJ: Princeton University Press, 1958).

monitor or oscilloscope or *hear* a changing tone that gives you immediate information about your physical responses. In other words, biofeedback is an electronic way of representing inner processes externally that are usually automatic, involuntary, and unconscious.

PHYSICAL APPLICATIONS

Frequently, and relatively quickly, many people are able to learn how to control many of their internal responses very well. Biofeedback can sometimes be an alternative to using medication to reduce tension or pain. Its range of applications has grown tremendously. Here are some examples of its uses:

A woman was badly injured in an automobile accident. On one side of her face her facial nerve was severed, leaving her unable to move any part of the left side of her face and unable to close or blink her left eye. Surgeons decided to splice the severed facial nerve to a nerve in her neck-shoulder muscle. Once this was done, the woman could shrug or twitch her shoulder, and in this way cause the paralyzed side of her face to move, and blink her left eye. However, the movements of the left side of her face were uncoordinated, spastic, and not synchronous with the movements of the uninjured right side of her face.

Biofeedback training seemed to offer a possible solution. Electrodes were taped to the injured side of her face. The electrical activity of muscles in the damaged area was displayed on a screen, along with the pattern that *would* be produced by undamaged facial nerves and muscles. The woman's task was to watch the two patterns and somehow learn by inner experiment how to control the left side of her face so its movements would match the normal pattern and would then coordinate with movements of the other side.

Her training lasted for several months. Because of her persistence and hard work, she was successful in learning to match the "normal" pattern; she was now able to move the two sides of her face in symmetrical harmony.

Other successful physical applications of biofeedback therapy include these:

- controlling high blood pressure
- learning to raise blood pressure in cases of spinal injuries

that block the automatic raising of blood pressure when a person stands up (excessively low pressure causes them to faint)
- coping more effectively with asthma attacks
- eliminating migraine headaches
- helping children with cerebral palsy control muscle spasms
- helping stroke victims with proprioception problems (in which they lose the sense of where their arms and legs are in space)
- teaching patients with circulation problems (e.g., blood clots in the legs) to dilate their blood vessels, regaining movement and reducing pain
- assisting stutterers by helping them become aware of unnecessary and interfering muscle contractions they have come to make habitually when they speak and teaching them how to relax these muscles
- reducing tension and pain in arthritis patients

To date, of all the areas to which it has been applied, biofeedback has been *most* successful for patients who are physically paralyzed or have movement disorders.

PSYCHOTHERAPEUTIC APPLICATIONS

Biofeedback has been used successfully in psychotherapy in these ways:

- teaching general relaxation methods, which can be useful to many people who have problems that involve anxiety, depression, or phobias
- assisting people with insomnia, also through relaxation techniques
- teaching people how to recognize effective meditation by making them aware of periods during sessions of meditation when their brain wave patterns slow (see the last section in this chapter, on meditation)

Increasingly, biofeedback is being used to treat emotional disorders in conjunction with both psychotherapy and medication. It is one of the ways available to us to enlarge the range of our conscious control over ourselves and our lives.

RELAXATION TRAINING

 Primarily a coping strategy to help people continue to function in an environment of stress.

The pervasive phenomenon of stress is the hidden epidemic of the United States and other highly industrialized countries. It is associated with high blood pressure, hardening of the arteries, strokes, ulcers, colitis, and a host of other physical conditions. And severe stress endured too long leads to emotional breakdown.

All physical materials can be loaded or stressed to a certain point beyond which they distort, snap, fracture, or break. Stress loads human beings physically as well as emotionally. *Any* change—whether for good or for ill—is a stressor. As human beings, we are not simple engineering materials that form simple cracks or breaks, and when stressful events are strong enough, we begin to crack or break in ways that are considerably more complex. Physical disease, emotional disorders, and mental illnesses are the cracks or breaks that occur in human "material."

Statistics show that common forms of severe stress *do* cause us to break. For example, compared with others the same age, ten times more people die during the year following the death of their husbands or wives. In the year after a divorce, ex-spouses have an illness rate twelve times higher than married people the same ages. In addition, chronic anger, anxiety, and depression appear to weaken the body's immune system, increasing the likelihood of serious disease.

Individuals do, of course, have different emotional breaking points, but we know that prolonged high levels of anxiety erode a person's psychological integration. What results is "nervous breakdown"—a term that is vague and means little more than a blown fuse due to emotional overload. The aftermath of such an overload may leave a person with depression, anxiety, and the inability to function "as usual" for a considerable period of time.

Relaxation training, along with the other therapies discussed in this chapter, is an antidote or prevention for human breakage brought about by excessive stress. The central belief on which relaxation training is based is that you cannot be tense and anxious if you are physically very relaxed.

There are two main approaches to relaxation training. (We have already briefly discussed them in Chapter 12 in connection with desensitization.) In both approaches you begin by reclining or lying down in a quiet room. Relaxation can then be achieved through tension and release or through suggestion. In the former, you tense a given muscle group, holding the tension for five to ten seconds, then release the tension and experience the relief from tension, or relaxation. In the latter, you consciously suggest to yourself that a group of muscles feels warm, heavy, very heavy, and relaxed, sinking into the recliner or bed or floor. Both approaches aim to achieve two things: to bring about deep, progressive muscular relaxation and to increase your sensitivity to the presence of tension in your body when it exists.

Relaxation training is a learned skill. If you practice it regularly—that is, daily, for at least several weeks—you can gain increased control over your major muscle groups—those of the arms, legs, shoulders, back, abdomen, neck, and face. You gradually learn to recognize even low levels of tension in these muscles so that the tension can be eliminated consciously.

Eventually, as you learn how to control physical relaxation, you are able to achieve deep relaxation in increasingly shorter periods of time. After regular practice over a period of months, many people, when they face a suddenly upsetting situation, can quickly offset their emotional and physical reactions to stress by inducing a calm and relaxed state in themselves. They are able to neutralize the stressor's potential for doing damage. If you can learn to do this, you have learned a skill in controlling your own life that is of great value. It is a survival skill that can help you protect yourself against being worn down by stressful events that otherwise eventually lead to learned habits of anxiety and tension. Once formed, these habits can be very difficult to get rid of.

For emotionally disturbed persons, relaxation training techniques are useful primarily as an adjunct to psychotherapy or drug therapy and can be helpful in reducing tension and anxiety. They are ways of treating *symptoms*; they can help you continue to cope with stressful situations. It is another question whether it is in your best interest to *continue* in a situation that causes you enough stress that relaxation training becomes a needed crutch. Sometimes it is wiser to change an unsatisfactory situation or to attempt to change your attitudes, values, or behavior than it is to learn skills so that you can keep doing the same stressful and perhaps unsatisfying thing day after day. Relaxation training is a *coping strategy*. By itself, it cannot resolve the fundamental question: whether it is better to learn how to numb yourself to an unhappy situation, to leave it, or to face the possibility that your stress is caused by inner conflicts and unrealistic attitudes rather than external factors.

If you cannot or do not want to leave a stressful environment, techniques of relaxation training may benefit you. If you feel the main problems are within you, then psychotherapy may be the best alternative. And sometimes, throwing in the towel, deciding in favor of a change of career, marriage, place to live, or way of life may be most therapeutic and personally fulfilling.

It can often be hard to know which alternative is best. Counseling may help. Talking with good friends may help. Letting time pass may help. Usually, ignoring discomfort will *not* help; stress has a way of compounding and wearing you down. Waiting too long, usually out of fear of facing a need for some form of change, is itself a source of internal stress—of worry and anxiety that will not go away until you do something to put a stop to doing nothing.

HYPNOSIS

 An approach to therapy that can have far-reaching beneficial effects for people with many different kinds of problems, especially useful for persons who are strongly motivated to change and can feel a deep sense of confidence in the humanity and competence of their therapist.

Hypnosis is very old. Ancient Egyptian records indicate that priests maintained temples of sleep devoted to healing the ill and troubled. The priests are thought to have used hypnotic induction of sleep and to have offered assurance that patients would get well.

Many centuries later, Franz Anton Mesmer (1734-1815) developed a method for inducing a hypnotic trance state (he associated it with sleepwalking) and claimed that therapy often was more effective when patients were in a trance. Hypnosis was later used by Jean-Martin Charcot (1825-1893) at the Paris Hospital of Salpêtrière; Charcot was one of Freud's teachers. During World War II, hypnosis was used to treat soldiers with amnesia, paralysis, and pain. Since then, it has been used frequently by clinical psychologists and psychotherapists.

Much is still not understood about the mental and physiological mechanisms involved in hypnosis. They are difficult to define because they seem to assume many different forms in different people, depending on their personalities and their moods at the time.

Hypnosis probably occurs in daydreaming to some extent; it probably is also involved when a mother lulls her child to sleep or when a customer succumbs to suggestions from a salesperson. We all seem to be—vaguely and to some degree—familiar with the phenomenon, yet we remain, paradoxically, ignorant of its existence.

WHAT HYPNOSIS IS LIKE

For most people, the experience of hypnosis is something of a letdown. They anticipate that they will experience something extraordinary in a trance state, and yet what actually happens is very similar to their probably familiar experience of drifting into a state of relaxed distraction from time to time when daydreaming. Often what happens is that our attention is focused on an object, and we gradually relax and begin to drift into a state of partial awareness. The phone may then ring, but for a moment it can be unclear whether we are just imagining this.

The hypnotic state induced by a trained hypnotherapist is very similar. When in a hypnotic trance, you never become unconscious; your mind continues to be active. As you go gradually into a deeper trance, your breathing and heart rates tend to slow, and you feel increasingly more deeply relaxed. Usually, the experience is one of being lulled into a state of calm repose. Sometimes—for example, in former surgery patients who have had unpleasant experiences with anesthesia—hypnosis may cause people to become anxious or frightened and to refuse to continue.

You relax physically while in a hypnotic trance. You will slump in your chair; your breathing becomes slow and deep; you move very little. In other cultures, however, trance states take very different forms. Behavior may become ecstatic, even violent; individuals may begin to dance frenetically and to spin about, as in the case of Algerian dervishes. But in Western society, hypnotic trance usually takes the form of deep, passive relaxation.

After their first experience with hypnosis, most people tend to disbelieve that they have really been in a trance state. They realize they have been pleasantly relaxed, but they feel that "hypnosis" has not occurred. Clients who are suspicious, hostile, or feel threatened by the experience, or who do not trust the therapist, tend to resist hypnosis. Frequently, on the other hand, clients who are extremely anxious and feel greatly in need of help turn out to be especially good candidates for hypnosis.

If their first experience with hypnosis is comfortable, safe, and pleasant, clients will usually allow themselves to drift into a deeper trance state in subsequent sessions.

Many techniques exist to induce hypnosis. Commonly, they make use of the well-known method in which you are asked to fix your attention on an object—a coin, a stone, a pendant—while the hypnotherapist speaks softly in a monotone, suggesting that you are relaxing ever more deeply, that your eyes are getting heavy, and so on.

Milton H. Erickson (1901-1980) has been one of the leading American contributors to recent developments in clinical hypnosis. His ideas have been among the most creative, imaginative, and subtle in the field. He is well known for his *indirect* induction techniques, which, because of the complex and unusual perspective they reflect, we cannot deal with at any length here. They are techniques that frequently induce a trance state *without* the client's being in the slightest way aware that this is happening. Dr. Erickson is often able to induce hypnosis only by means of a *handshake.* An example may give some general idea of his approach. Dr. Erickson describes this technique:

When I begin shaking hands, I do so normally. The "hypnotic touch" then begins when I let loose. The letting loose becomes transformed from a firm grip into a gentle touch by the thumb, a lingering drawing away of the little finger, the faint brushing of the subject's hand with the middle finger—just enough vague sensation to attract the attention. As the subject gives attention to the touch with your thumb, you shift to a touch with your little finger. As your subject's attention follows that, you shift to a touch with your middle finger and then again to the thumb. . . .

The subject's withdrawal from the handshake is arrested by his attention arousal, which establishes . . . an expectancy.

Then almost, but not quite simultaneously (to ensure separate neural recognition), you touch the undersurface of the hand (wrist) so gently that it barely suggests an upward push. This is followed by a similar utterly slight downward touch, and then I sever contact so gently that the subject does not know exactly when—and the subject's hand is left going neither up nor down, but cataleptic. Sometimes I give a lateral and medial touch so that the hand is even more rigidly cataleptic. . . .

There are several colleagues who won't shake hands with me, unless I assure them first, because they developed a profound glove anaesthesia when I used this procedure on them. I shook hands with them, looked them in the eyes, . . . rapidly immobilized my facial expression, and then focused my eyes on a spot far behind them. I then slowly and imperceptibly removed my hand from theirs and slowly moved to one side out of their direct line of vision.*

Here is a characteristic reaction of one of Erickson's colleagues to his procedure:

I had heard about you and I wanted to meet you and you looked so interested and you shook hands so warmly. All of a sudden my arm was gone and your face changed and got so far away. Then the left side of your head began to disappear, and I could see only the right side of your face until that slowly vanished also. . . . Your face slowly came back, and you came close and smiled. . . . Then I noticed my hand and asked you about it because I couldn't feel my whole arm. You said to keep it that way just a little while for the experience.**

APPLICATIONS OF HYPNOSIS

It is much easier to bring about a hypnotic trance than to know how to make effective therapeutic use of the trance state once it is produced. Depending on the depth of trance that you will accept, these are the kinds of goals that can be achieved:

In a light trance, your eyes are closed, you are physically

---

*Milton H. Erickson, Ernest L. Rossi, and Sheila I. Rossi, *Hypnotic Realities: The Induction of Clinical Hypnosis and Forms of Indirect Suggestion* (New York: Irvington Publishers, 1976), pp. 108-109.

relaxed, and it is possible to convey to you, for example, that you are unable to move an arm. At this stage, the therapist can often be effective in offering you support and encouraging you to begin to make changes in your behavior.

In a medium trance, relaxation is still deeper. A partial anesthesia of a hand or arm can be achieved, and you will comply in a slow, semiautomatic way with instructions from the therapist. In this state, many clients can learn rather quickly how to bring about *self*-hypnosis, which they can then practice on their own. At this stage, it is sometimes possible to suggest gradual personality changes.

In a deep trance, more extensive anesthesias are possible. A therapist can encourage you to experience emotional changes, to hallucinate, and to regress to a younger age—i.e., to reexperience memories of past events and to feel and behave as you did at that time. In a deep trance state, it is possible to use hypnotic desensitization techniques to help you overcome anxieties and fears.

Hypnotherapy lends itself well to use on your own. Once you have learned how to induce light trance states on your own, you can begin to suggest certain attitudes, feelings, or behavioral changes you would like to bring about in yourself. Being successful at this—as with any skill—requires regular practice and regular and gradual strengthening of the habits that are being formed. Some psychotherapists will make a cassette recording for the individual client to use at home on a daily basis.

Hypnosis has been used to treat many problems, including these:

ulcers
frigidity
impotence
headaches and migraines
insomnia
arthritic pain
colitis
tachycardia
obesity
depression
phobias
antisocial behavior

disturbed children
amnesia
stuttering
nervous tics
sexual inhibitions
dental anxiety and pain
heart palpitations
abdominal cramps
tension and anxiety
overeating
reduction or elimination of smoking

Both men and women are equally hypnotizable. Children are generally better subjects than adults. As already noted, clients who are more anxious tend to accept hypnotic suggestion more readily. Clients who are motivated to change respond best to hypnotic suggestion. Individuals who are imaginative, who had fictitious companions in childhood, who read a good deal, and who can become readily absorbed in nature are inclined to make good subjects. Good rapport between client and therapist and a sense of trust in the therapist's goodwill and ability contribute greatly to successful hypnotherapy.

Russian-born Lewis R. Wolberg (1905-   ) is a leading New York hypnotherapist who was originally trained as a psychoanalyst. He is recognized for the comprehensiveness and eclecticism of his approach. After forty years of practice, he came to see its main limitation:

Because hypnosis is so dramatic a phenomenon, it is easy to overestimate its potential. A great many things may be accomplished with a subject in a trance, even the removal of psychologically determined symptoms. . . . But almost immediately after hypnosis has ended, or shortly thereafter, the symptoms will return *if the subject has a psychological need for them.* [italics added] . . .

Quite often patients on disability compensation are sent to me by insurance companies for hypnotic examination and treatment. Almost invariably, these casualties cling to their symptoms with the desperation of a drowning man hanging on to a raft. . . .

There are other secondary gains a person may get out of holding onto his symptoms. The need to punish himself for his guilt feelings, the desire to abandon an adult adjustment and return to the protective blanket of infancy in order to be taken care of. . . . Symptoms do not magically vanish; they must be worn down. It is essential to replace them with productive habits.*

MEDITATION

 For individuals who are able to make a long-range commitment to the practice of a discipline that, over a period of many months and years, can strengthen them and help them to become more fully integrated and centered.

Don't go outside yourself, return into yourself. The dwelling place of truth is the inner man.

Saint Augustine, *The True Religion*

Meditation is a systematic discipline that attempts to help people move toward the goal of self-realization. It is not the creation of one individual or group. Techniques of meditation have evolved over many centuries and in different parts of the world. And yet these techniques bear striking similarities to each other, whether they originated in the temples and monasteries of India, Japan, Europe, or the Middle East.

Meditation is not a relaxed act of "contemplating one's navel"; it more closely resembles athletic training. It is a form of progressive mental exercise that has as its goal a strengthening of a person's self-confidence, inner strength, and the mind's ability to focus and concentrate. Meditation takes considerable endurance. It is essentially a discipline. It requires fortitude, perseverance, and a strong will. Like athletic ability, skills in meditation cannot be developed without regular practice. Because its effects are felt only gradually, meditation needs a long-term commitment to sustain it, and this ultimately must be based on faith in its eventual value.

The disciplined and regular practice of meditation over a period of many months appears to lead to a sense of personal integration, a sense of being more firmly *centered* in yourself,

---

*Wolberg, *Hypnosis*, pp. 237-239.

more confident and aware of your connection with all that is. Experienced practitioners of meditation claim to feel a greater degree of personal security; they feel more at ease with themselves. They claim to feel serenity, zest in living, and inner peace and joy in work, which they seem to be able to do more efficiently, with greater energy and interest.

WHAT THE PRACTICE OF MEDITATION IS LIKE

Techniques of meditation share the goal of disciplining the mind to do one thing at a time. Until you have made a serious attempt to meditate, you will very likely be unaware of how perpetually distracted your attention is. We seldom make the effort to stand apart from our thoughts, to take note of how numerous and varied they are and how chaotically they tumble into and out of our consciousness. It is exceedingly hard work to quiet these "chattering monkeys of the mind." Quieting the overactive and undisciplined mind is a challenging task. It takes energy and a great deal of practice.

There are many approaches to meditation. Here, we will look at three.*

Breath Counting

Breath counting is one way to train your mind to control and focus attention. The object is to be doing one thing, and one thing only, becoming fully involved in that single purpose. Start by finding a comfortable position, sitting or lying down. Place a clock or watch where you can see it without having to turn your head. Usually with eyes closed, you then begin to count your breaths, silently: "one" as you slowly exhale the first breath, "two" as you exhale the second, etc. After you get to "four," start with "one" again. The purpose is to be doing *only* this, only breathing and counting. You will quickly find that your mind rebels; it will stray and wander whenever your concentration and attention falter. It is a recalcitrant entity. You will be doing well in the beginning if you can succeed for only a few seconds

---

*See the excellent introduction to the practice of meditation by Lawrence LeShan, *How to Meditate: A Guide to Self-Discovery* (Boston: Little, Brown & Co., 1974). Dr. LeShan is a psychotherapist in New York City who teaches many of his clients meditation as part of their therapy.

at a time in being conscious *only* of your counting. Distractions will subvert your will in a split second. You will find yourself thinking of a host of things: what to do tomorrow morning, whether you are doing well or badly at meditation, whether it is silly to be doing this, what's for dinner, taxes, work, or that itch on your forehead. Again and again you will have to return your mind to the task at hand. Very quickly, you'll begin to realize that meditation *is* hard work. It is frustrating and demanding.

Practice doing this for fifteen minutes a day. After a few weeks, increase to twenty minutes. After another four weeks, spend twenty-five to thirty minutes a day. Once you can do this, continue to practice daily for another month. It will take that long before you will begin to sense whether this approach to meditation is going to be useful to you.

The Meditation of Contemplation

This is an alternative approach to meditation. Again, the purpose is to discipline your mind by means of focused attention. In this approach, you try to focus attention on a physical object. Pick a natural object—a shell, a small stone, a pressed leaf. Now, with the object a foot or two from you, simply *look* at it. The purpose is to look at the object actively, to keep your attention fixed on it, but to be wakeful and alert. Do not stare at one place on the object or strain your eyes. Explore the object, *look* at it, attend to it. As usual, you'll find plenty to distract you—stiffness, the need to move, sleepiness, slipping into thinking about problems you need to solve. Each time your mind drifts out of track, gently bring your attention back to the object. Try this for ten minutes a day for two weeks, then fifteen minutes a day for a month, then twenty minutes for the next month. By then, you will know if this approach will help you. Be prepared for some effective sessions and some discouraging ones. Remember that no one said meditation would be easy.

The Meditation of the Bubble

This is an ancient form of meditation that, again, seeks to discipline the mind by developing your ability to focus on one thing at a time. In this meditation, you concentrate on your own stream of consciousness. Imagine yourself sitting quietly on the bottom of a clear lake. Each of your thoughts and feelings forms a bubble that slowly rises to the surface of the lake. As each comes to your mind, watch it closely and think only of it for the five seconds or so that it takes to rise to the surface. Be aware of the slow rhythm of the bubbles. Try to spend approximately equal amounts of time attending to each bubble. If the same thought, the same bubble, rises several times, this is OK. If you continue, the repetition will pass. If nothing comes to mind for a time, this, too, is OK. Form an empty bubble. Try this meditation for ten minutes a day for two weeks, then increase to twenty minutes a day for one or two months. By then, you will know if this approach to meditation is beneficial to you.

THE BENEFITS OF MEDITATION

How *will* you recognize whether an approach to meditation has value for you? Any changes that occur in you will be gradual; you must be patient. If, after most sessions of meditation, you feel generally more integrated, calmer, more at ease, this is a good sign. Over a period of time, if you are working hard at an approach to meditation that seems to fit your temperament, these periods of feeling peaceful, alert, and comfortable in the world will gradually become more evident to you.

Physiologically, meditation appears to lead to a deeply relaxed state of alert concentration. Your respiration and heart rates slow, the level of lactate in the blood (associated with tension and anxiety) drops lower, and there is an increase in slow alpha brain waves, associated with profound relaxation.

What is important, no matter what approach to meditation you try, is to stay with that approach long enough to determine its potential value for you. Doing a meditation once or a few times is like jogging once or twice: you can't expect to derive any benefit from exercising a couple of times. Meditation is the practice and expression of discipline; deciding to practice regularly and then carrying out your decision are just as important as the approach you take to meditation.

16
DRUG AND NUTRITION THERAPIES

DRUG THERAPY:
BALANCING EMOTIONS WITH CHEMISTRY

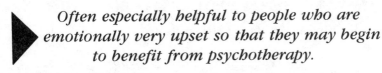 *Often especially helpful to people who are emotionally very upset so that they may begin to benefit from psychotherapy.*

During the past thirty years, biochemistry and pharmacology have made many important contributions to the treatment of mental and emotional disorders. There is no question that *psychotropic*—literally "mind-turning" or mind-influencing—drugs can help many people during periods of emotional or mental suffering.

Psychotropic drugs can be used by themselves or in conjunction with psychotherapy. Frequently, drugs are used to help reduce the severity of symptoms in patients so that they may benefit from psychotherapy. Effective psychotherapy requires you to be comparatively calm, rational, and able to make well-thought-out decisions. These things are not possible if you are terribly agitated, are despondent and crying much of the time, or may have disturbing hallucinations and are no longer in touch with reality.

The aim of drug therapy is, eventually, to eliminate the need for medication. In this respect, psychopharmacology is similar to psychotherapy: both would like to help the patient so that he no longer needs either one. It is not always possible to do this, however. Some disorders are, at present anyway, chronic conditions. People with parkinsonism or epilepsy may have to take medication indefinitely. But the general trend is to use psychotropic drugs as temporary measures to bring symptoms quickly under control so that psychotherapy can be started.

The only professionals who are legally authorized to prescribe psychotropic drugs are physicians and, in particular, psychiatrists. However, psychotherapists are now being trained to be sensitive to conditions that may have an organic basis. Certainly, it is wise to have a thorough physical exam to rule out organic problems that can cause emotional or mental upset (see Chapter 8). Numerous studies have shown that up to half of the individuals who are referred to a psychotherapist have undiagnosed organic problems.* This is an important caution to bear in mind.

TYPES OF PSYCHOTROPIC DRUGS

There are nine main classes of psychotropic drugs:

Antianxiety, or Anxiolytic, Drugs

These are the so-called *minor tranquilizers*. They are sedatives for the waking hours that are prescribed for people who have excessive tension and anxiety.

Neuroleptics, or Antipsychotics

Psychosis is a disorder that impairs a person's abilities to think, remember, communicate, respond with appropriate emotions, and interpret reality without great distortion. People who have these difficulties can often be treated effectively with neuroleptic or antipsychotic drugs, also known as the *major tranquilizers*, which have specific effects on the brain's activity.

---

*See, for example, L. Small, *Neuropsychodiagnosis in Psychotherapy* (New York: Brunner/Mazel, 1980).

Sedative-Hypnotic Drugs

These drugs act as sedatives at low doses and produce a "hypnotic" action at higher doses. (The word *hypnotic* as used by pharmacologists does not refer to a hypnotic trance but means simply that a drug causes drowsiness and reduces motor activity.) In even larger doses, these drugs act as anesthetics. Antianxiety drugs, the minor tranquilizers, can be grouped with these drugs because of their sedative effect.

Antidepressants

These drugs are used primarily to treat what psychiatrists call *endogenous* depression—that is, major, incapacitating depression that is not associated with an outside event or situation. Depressions that occur after the loss of a job, the death of someone close, or some other external event are called *exogenous* depressions. They can sometimes be treated effectively with antidepressants, but drug therapy for situation-induced depression generally is less successful.

Lithium therapy is a specific treatment primarily for manic-depressive disorders. Lithium carbonate is a naturally occurring mineral salt. For manic-depressive patients—with wide swings of mood from feeling extremely energetic and emotionally high to feeling seriously depressed—lithium therapy may offer help as a mood stabilizer.

Stimulants

Caffeine and nicotine are the best known of the stimulants. In therapy, stimulants are used in the treatment of narcolepsy (individuals suddenly fall asleep for short periods of time, even when engaged in activities), some forms of epilepsy, and, paradoxically, hyperkinetic children (who are excessively active and have short attention spans and explosive irritability).

Antiepileptic Drugs

For many of the two million Americans with epilepsy, these antiseizure drugs are very helpful. Epilepsy does not tend to shorten an individual's life, but it is a severe, troubling, and often disabling condition for which drug therapy can be a blessing.

Antiparkinsonian Drugs

These drugs have helped the lives of many people who are

affected by the characteristic involuntary tremors of this disease, which can cause abnormalities in gait and trembling of the voluntary muscles.

Psychedelics

Psychedelic drugs are also called *hallucinogens*. They produce altered states of consciousness and sensory distortions. Psychedelics have no established use in psychiatry at present in the United States. Great Britain and Canada, however, have experimented with psychedelics in the treatment of alcoholics, whom they sometimes appear to help. Psychedelics have also sometimes been used for the terminally ill and in certain cases of autism.

Drugs for Headache, Migraine, and Neuralgia

Drugs for these common kinds of pain are widespread. Migraines (which may cause blurred vision, vertigo, and even temporary deafness) and cluster headaches (which cause severe pain around the eyes, tearing and reddening of the eyes, and runny nose) frequently can be treated successfully with specific drugs. Neuralgias are recurrent knifelike facial and head pains that can last for days and even months. They are difficult to treat successfully.

WHAT DRUG THERAPY IS LIKE

In this section, we'll look at some of the main emotional and mental symptoms that are often helped by means of drug therapy. Since all medications have potential side effects, we will look at these as well.

Anxiety

Excessive anxiety causes very unpleasant symptoms: dizziness or light-headedness, sweating, pounding heart, vomiting, diarrhea, shaking, muscle tension, inability to sleep. Many of these symptoms can be controlled by antianxiety drugs. All of these drugs can lead to psychological dependence when they are used regularly over periods of time that vary with the person and the medication. For this reason, they are normally used for short periods, often at the beginning of psychotherapy.

The most commonly prescribed antianxiety drugs include these (trade names):

Atarax	Paxipam
Ativan	Restoril
Centrax	Serax
Clonopin	Tranxene
Dalmane	Tybatran
Doriden	Valium
Equanil	Valmid
Librium	Xanax
Loxitane	

Although relatively small percentages of patients experience them, as with most drugs, there may be side effects, including drowsiness, impaired judgment and performance, nausea/vomiting, ataxia (loss of voluntary muscle coordination), and agitation (paradoxical restlessness).

Patients who have taken an antianxiety drug for a period of time are often instructed to reduce their dosage gradually to avoid mild, infrequently severe, withdrawal symptoms.

Antianxiety drugs can reduce agitation and produce a relative sense of calm. But, unfortunately, patients usually develop a tolerance to any antianxiety drug after three to four months, and then the drug loses its effectiveness. Antianxiety drugs are usually limited, then, to short-term treatment. Long-term recovery from the symptoms of anxiety is the task of psychotherapy: to help clients change their attitudes, behavior, or way of life.

Depression

Depression can be a seriously incapacitating emotional disorder. Depression can range from a lingering sense of sadness or grief to a feeling of utter hopelessness, guilt, despondency, uncontrollable crying, and suicidal thoughts. The following symptoms are typical: insomnia or early waking, loss of appetite and loss of interest in sex, inability to concentrate, great difficulty in making decisions, and a reduced desire and ability to assume job and family responsibilities. Though depression is called "the common cold of emotional illness," it is not to be taken lightly, since severe depression *is* life-threatening, as many suicides testify. Depression affects one out of five people during their lifetimes; more women suffer from depression than men.

The most widely prescribed antidepressants are the tricyclics. They are most effective in treating endogenous depressions; MAO inhibitors (see below) are more useful in cases of "atypical" depression, which frequently is associated with a situation the patient cannot come to terms with, such as the loss of a job or of a loved one.

Tricyclic antidepressants include these (trade names):

Avenyl	Sinequan
Elavil	Surmontil
Norpramin	Tofranil
Pamelor	Vivactil

Approximately 70 percent of patients who take tricyclics improve. Several newer drugs—the tetracyclics, dibenzoxapines, and triazolopyridenes—are similar to the tricyclics in their effects. They include these (trade names):

Asedin
Desyrel
Ludiomil

If tricyclics do not help, MAO inhibitors (*monoamine oxidase* inhibitors) are usually tried. MAO inhibitors must be used with great caution because they can interact with certain foods, beverages, or drugs to produce severe high blood pressure. Many foods and beverages are prepared by fermentation processes; e.g., cheese, anchovies, pickled herring, pastrami, olives, beer, and wine, all of which patients who take MAO inhibitors must avoid. These foods and beverages contain a chemical compound, an amine called *tyramine*, which can cause dangerously high blood pressure, a hypertensive crisis, in people taking an MAO inhibitor. Furthermore, MAO inhibitors cannot be taken with antihistamines; patients who take MAO inhibitors may be warned to avoid other drug interactions. These warnings should be taken seriously because MAO inhibitors are one of the most potentially *toxic* groups of psychoactive drugs. Yet they can make the difference between night and day for many cases of depression.

There are common side effects caused by all the antidepressants we've mentioned, including an uncomfortably dry mouth, dizziness, especially when standing up quickly, headaches, difficulty in urinating, nausea/vomiting, constipation or diarrhea, impotence or inability to ejaculate, agitation/shaking, and rapid heartbeat.

Some of these side effects can be annoying but will often diminish or disappear once the patient becomes accustomed to the medication. When side effects are not tolerable, the physician or psychiatrist will usually prescribe a different antidepressant that may have fewer, or no, side effects for a given patient.

One of the drawbacks of antidepressants is that there is a waiting period of days or weeks before physician and patient know whether a particular drug is going to help. If, after four to six weeks, an antidepressant has not reduced a patient's depression, then a second drug may be tried, and, again, there will be a delay of days or weeks before it is clear whether the medication is going to work. One needed area of research in psychopharmacology is to devise tests that will help to tell a doctor what antidepressant is most likely to be effective for the individual patient. At present, though some general guidelines exist, matching patient with an effective and tolerable medication is a process of intelligent trial and error.

Lithium has been used to treat manic depression since 1954. Lithium is absorbed quickly from the gastrointestinal tract, but it acts slowly, so it also takes time to know if it is going to be of value. Blood levels of lithium need to be checked once or twice a week during the first month, twice a month for the next month or two, and then once every one to two months.

Lithium is sometimes helpful in treating chronic simple depression, that is, depression that is not associated with periodic "highs."

Unlike most drugs used in psychiatry, lithium usually has few noticeable side effects and does not tend to produce a feeling of sedation or stimulation. When side effects occur, it is usually because the lithium level in the blood has become excessive. Side effects then can include vomiting, lack of coordination, muscular weakness, or drowsiness.

In addition to antidepressant drugs, electroconvulsive therapy (ECT) is sometimes used to treat severe depression, as it is to treat some other conditions, including schizophrenia. Although ECT is not itself a form of drug therapy, it is important to mention it here since it is one of the main *medical* treatments (as opposed to the "talk therapies" of psychotherapy) used by psychiatry today. ECT is administered after a patient has been sedated and given a general anesthetic.

The main advantage of ECT is that it acts much faster than any of the antidepressants. For a seriously suicidal patient, this can be important.

The main disadvantages of ECT are that it can cause temporary memory loss, temporary disorientation and confusion after treatment, and possible permanent changes in brain function—regarded by many psychiatrists as "subtle," i.e., fairly minor. Another discouraging finding is that depression recurs after ECT in many patients—in up to 46 percent within six months after ECT.

ECT has received "poor press." As now administered, the actual treatment is painless. It is, nevertheless, a forceful, "invasive" approach, so many psychiatrists prefer not to use it if medication can be successful. As more biochemical methods of treatment are discovered, ECT very likely will be used less and less.

Psychosis

Psychosis is the most serious and incapacitating degree of mental illness. Emotional problems with symptoms of anxiety or depression, or both together, are called *affective disorders*. People who have affective disorders make up the majority of clients seen by most psychotherapists; these clients are *not* out of touch with reality. The problems that they have—though painful and sometimes obstacles to normal living—are essentially different from the difficulties that patients with psychoses have. Though there is no unanimity about this among health care professionals, we will distinguish between these two kinds of problems by calling a psychosis a *mental illness*, as opposed to an *emotional disorder*. It is a matter not only of degree but of kind. A person who is severely depressed or extremely anxious is usually still able to communicate rationally, and distinguish what is real from what is fantasy or delusion.

Psychoses, on the other hand, are disorders that impair a person's abilities to think, remember, communicate, respond with appropriate emotions, interpret reality coherently, and behave in a reasonably "normal" way. People with psychoses often have difficulty controlling their impulses, and their moods may change quickly and radically. Psychotic individuals often believe things to be true that are not, and they may hear sounds or voices that are not there.

There are many theories about the causes of psychosis. Recently, research studies in psychiatry have shown that psychosis may be due to an excess of certain chemical substances called *neurotransmitters* (such as norepinephrine or dopamine) in the brain. Another theory is that the brain of a psychotic person may be excessively sensitive to the action of certain neurotransmitters.

The antipsychotic drugs, or neuroleptics, reduce the brain's sensitivity to one or more of these chemical substances. Some of the best-known antipsychotic drugs are these (trade names):

Compazine	Stelazine
Haldol	Thorazine
Mellaril	Trilafon
Prolixin	Vesprin

Antipsychotic drugs frequently can clear thought processes, reduce or end hallucinations, relieve agitation and anxiety, and generally help patients return to the world of reality, communicate with others, and behave in a more reasonable and stable way.

Antipsychotic drugs have many possible side effects. They may produce drowsiness, dizziness and nausea, fainting, muscle tremors, a shuffling gait, blurred vision, insomnia, sensitivity of the skin to sunlight, and other effects. Particularly disturbing side effects can often be avoided by changing to a different medication. Some people with psychotic symptoms may need to take antipsychotic medication for only a few weeks or months. Recurrent or chronic illnesses, however, may require drug treatment over a long period.

WHEN DRUG THERAPY IS APPROPRIATE

Since psychotropic drugs can be prescribed only by a physician or psychiatrist, his or her judgment will determine whether a patient's difficulties seem to lend themselves to drug therapy. In cases involving serious anxiety, depression, or psychosis, it is normal to expect drug therapy to be used, often in conjunction with psychotherapy. As we noted earlier, it is the hope of drug therapy that it will be needed only temporarily, but some chronic or periodically recurring conditions may be best treated by continued medication for a number of years. Since many of the psychotropic drugs are new, it is not known whether long-term use by some patients may ultimately affect their health adversely. Unless we decide to do without medication that can be a blessing in relieving great suffering, until long-term studies can be completed, the potential risks are there. It is a matter of weighing alternatives: on the one hand, perhaps incapacitating emotional or mental distress, and on the other, side effects that cannot be fully predicted.

THERAPY THROUGH NUTRITION

There is no question that nutritional deficiencies can influence the functioning of the brain and affect the personality. There are clear-cut cases, for example, of vitamin deficiencies that result in symptoms of psychological disturbance. The majority of these cases involve people who suffer from very evident malnutrition.

Unfortunately, the connection between nutrition and mental health is still vague; biochemists are becoming more aware of the need to take into account *individual variations*. It is not always possible to specify exactly how much of a mineral, a vitamin, or an amino acid a person requires for good health. Some people, for many different reasons, cannot effectively utilize the food they eat. Others have allergic reactions to certain foods; some allergic reactions appear to be subtle, affecting a person's moods. Still other people seem to be especially sensitive to only moderate changes in their blood sugar levels. We have a great deal in common as biological organisms. Yet our biochemistries may be finely tuned in individual ways that would require a detailed and sophisticated understanding of an immense number of interrelated factors that boggle the mind in complexity.

Psychonutrition has a long road to follow before it will be a science. So-called holistic or orthomolecular (the "right" molecule) physicians and psychiatrists attempt to take individual variations and sensitivities into account. The need to do this may be essential in many cases, but dependable and exact methods of evaluation and treatment simply do not exist as yet. Except in cases of outright malnutrition, finding connections between nutrition and emotional health is still an art.

Some orthomolecular psychiatrists appear to have been dramatically successful in helping some patients with certain mental or emotional problems. But because psychonutrition is still a borderline discipline, it is an area where controversies abound and results are often open to question.

Many physical conditions can be influenced greatly by nutrition. Among these are the metabolic disorders diabetes and hypoglycemia, both of which can affect a person's emotional life (see Chapter 8). In addition, relationships have recently been discovered between lowered blood pressure, reduced cholesterol and triglyceride levels, and a diet high in fiber. A thiamine (vitamin B_1) deficiency—which causes pellagra, a chronic disease that leads to skin lesions and gastrointestinal distress—can produce depression, mania, and paranoia. Another example is pernicious anemia, in large part due to vitamin B_{12} shortage, which can cause moodiness, difficulty in remembering and concentrating, violent behavior, depression, and hallucinations.

But the fact that many physical disorders, some of which can cause psychological disturbances, are treatable in part through nutrition does not, unfortunately, imply that emotional disorders in general can be treated by means of diet. This may be the case for some individuals for whom special diets can influence a specific biochemical imbalance. But research is just beginning to develop tests that can detect these sensitive individual variations. Once they can be identified a more difficult step has to be made: to determine how this information can be used to select an effective treatment.

Nutritionists and physicians agree that good physical and mental health depend on a combination of proper body weight, adequate exercise, good diet, and decreased stress. But beyond this, an emotionally disturbed person who seeks help through dietary therapy—for example, through megavitamin doses— should realize that he or she is really involved in *self-experimentation*. Some orthomolecular psychiatrists may be very talented in treating some of their patients. These patients are very fortunate; it is hard to avoid saying they are *lucky*. The main problem that faces this new area of psychonutrition is one of general reliability and credibility.

PART III
IMPORTANT
QUESTIONS

17
LOCATING A THERAPIST

America is overcrowded with helpers; there are so many helpful people out there, they are literally bumping into each other, and must be regulated by laws and organizations to keep them from helping so much that the average client in need of help isn't torn to shreds.

Paul G. Quinnett, *The Troubled People Book*

This chapter assumes that you have used one of the two methods described in Chapter 7, "Self-Diagnosis: Mapping Your Way to a Therapy," and have now chosen an approach to therapy that seems most promising in relation to your goals or problems and your personality. You now face the practical problem of how to locate a therapist with the professional expertise to offer you the kind of help you desire.

There are three factors that you need to take into account in order to find a suitable therapist:

1. the degree of seriousness of your problem or need
2. any financial limitations you may have
3. the resources available where you live (or how far you are willing to travel if you cannot locate the help you want in your area)

The seriousness of your problem or need may fall into one of three general categories:

Very urgent need: You are severely upset, perhaps suicidal or dangerous to others. Or, you are suffering from extreme changes of mood or personality, major depression, delusions, or hallucinations. In either of these cases, you should see a professional immediately. You or a friend or relative should contact the family physician for a referral to a *psychiatrist* or call a crisis intervention center for a referral to a psychiatrist. (Crisis intervention centers, sometimes called *suicide prevention centers* or *crisis hot lines* are listed among the emergency numbers on the inside front page of your White Pages directory; otherwise, dial 911 or operator for assistance.)

Serious personal, marital, or family problems or goals: You, you and your spouse, or members of your family need help soon but can wait for an appointment, if necessary, for a number of weeks.

Moderate need: There is no urgency. You are interested, before you consider formal therapy, in exploring some alternatives—perhaps by talking with a minister, priest, or rabbi or by trying one of the adjunctive approaches to therapy (such as therapeutic exercise, meditation, relaxation training) on its own, without individual therapy.

This chapter is intended primarily for people in the well-populated middle category, people who have serious problems or goals and are able to weigh alternatives carefully and without extreme pressure.

The seriousness of the problem and the cost of treatment go hand in hand. The range of treatment alternatives is shown in the table below.

Condition	Cost	Treatment by:
more serious	more expensive	Psychiatrists
		Psychologists
		Social work counselors
		Adjunctive therapists: biofeedback, bioenergetics, exercise, meditation, etc.
		Religious counselors
less serious	less expensive	Self-help

In general, the less serious the problem, the lower the potential cost of treatment. Also, the more serious the condition, the more advisable it is to have at least a preliminary evaluation by a psychiatrist.

Similarly, the settings within which therapy is available vary widely:

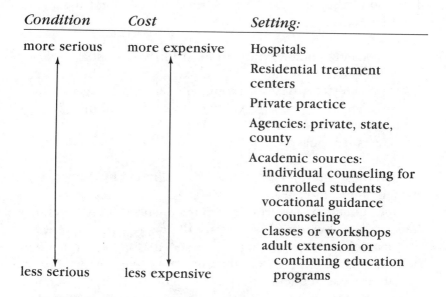

Condition	Cost	Setting:
more serious	more expensive	Hospitals
		Residential treatment centers
		Private practice
		Agencies: private, state, county
		Academic sources: individual counseling for enrolled students vocational guidance counseling classes or workshops adult extension or continuing education
less serious	less expensive	programs

FINDING A THERAPIST WITH A PARTICULAR SPECIALIZATION

During a time of increasing specialization in health care, many psychotherapists have unfortunately been attracted to eclecticism—that is, knowing a reasonable amount about a number of different forms of therapy, but resisting specialization in any one of them. For some individuals, especially people interested in wide-spectrum growth and personal development, an eclectic therapist can be very beneficial. Eclectic therapists believe that they are able to bring a wider scope of understanding to bear on a problem and a more flexible outlook. If you have fairly well-defined needs and interests, however, eclecticism makes it difficult to locate a therapist who has formal training and extensive experience specifically in treating, for example, depression, alcoholism, family conflicts, or adjustment problems. No therapist today can be an expert in the whole range of human emotional problems and in the many specialized techniques that have been developed to help.

REFERRALS

There are a number of ways of going about locating a therapist. You can start by asking for a recommendation from any of these sources:

- your family doctor, who will most likely suggest a colleague, another M.D., a psychiatrist
- your minister, priest, or rabbi, who again will suggest someone he happens to know or to have heard of
- personal friends
- referral services

All of these alternatives are, however, limited by the scope of acquaintance of the person or service you have gone to. Referral services commonly are run by groups of subscribing psychologists (or social workers), so if you call one, you will be referred to a participating psychologist (or social worker). Sometimes referral services (which usually charge nothing for their referrals, unless you request a preliminary consultation) maintain a listing of the areas of specialization of their professional members, and this information can be helpful.

If you have a specific approach to therapy in mind and want to find a therapist with strong credentials in that approach, there are two usually more promising roads to follow:

BY MAIL

First, depending on your own judgment of the seriousness of your problems or goals and the extent to which the cost of treatment is important to you, you can write for a list of therapists in your area from these organizations:

American Psychiatric Association	Canadian Psychiatric Association
1400 K St., NW	225 Lisgar St., #103
Washington, DC 20005	Ottawa, ON K2P 0C6

(for psychiatrists)

American Psychological
Association
1200 17th St., NW
Washington, DC 20036

Canadian Psychological
Association
558 King Edward Ave.
Ottawa, ON K1N 7N6

(for psychologists)

National Association of Social
Workers
7981 Eastern Ave.
Silver Spring, MA 20907

Canadian Association of Social
Workers
55 Parkdale Ave., #316
Ottawa, ON K1Y 1E5

Corporation Professionnelle
des Travailleurs Sociaux du
Quebec
5757 Decelles Ave., Ch. 335
Montreal, QC H3S 2C3

(for social work counselors)

Request a list that shows their specialties. If none is available, ask for the address of the branch office nearest you, which you then can contact for this information. Be sure to enclose a stamped, self-addressed envelope to ensure a response.

BY TELEPHONE

A second way to locate a therapist with specialization in a particular area is through careful use of your telephone directory. This may take you some time, and also some preliminary calls, but it can give you a good deal of information:

Psychiatrists

Psychiatrists are listed in the Yellow Pages under "Physicians and Surgeons." In larger metropolitan directories, you will usually find separate headings after the general listing, according to specialties. Look there for "Physicians—Psychiatrists." Many psychiatrists today will list their special focus there—for example, psychoanalysis, psychoanalytic psychotherapy (brief analysis), marriage and family therapy, hypnosis, chemical dependency treatment, child and adolescent therapy. If you want to see a psychiatrist and do not find one who indicates the specialized approach you want to try, then you will need to make some calls. Most psychiatrists' secretaries or receptionists are happy to tell you what the doctor specializes in. If the list of his or her areas of specialization is impressively and overly long, perhaps it is best to look elsewhere for a more realistic professional.

If, after locating a psychiatrist with the background you are looking for, you want to double-check his or her credentials, ask the secretary if the psychiatrist is a member of the American Psychiatric Association (or, if in Canada, the Canadian Psychiatric Association), whether he or she completed a program of study at an institute of psychotherapy or psychoanalysis, and whether he or she is board certified. (Remember, any M.D. can call himself or herself a psychiatrist, but not all have the full qualifications of a certified psychiatrist.)

Clinical Psychologists

Clinical psychologists are listed in the Yellow Pages under "Psychologists." Their specialties are often identified—e.g., marriage and family therapy, group therapy, bereavement, alcoholism, eating disorders and addiction, psychological assessment (testing), learning disorders, sexual dysfunction, depression, panic syndrome. Again, if the list below a given psychologist's name is unreasonably long, you may have come across either a genius or someone who favors advertising. Psychologists less often mention the particular approach to therapy they use, but some do; for example, behavior therapy, Gestalt, hypnosis, or "analytical approach" may be listed. Again, it will probably be necessary to make a few telephone calls.

If, after locating a psychologist with the background you are looking for, you want to double-check his or her credentials, you can frequently find a copy in your public library of the *National Register of Health Services Providers* or, in Canada, either the *Canadian Registry of Health Service Providers in Psychology* or the *International Directory of Psychologists*. They list licensed psychologists with Ph.D.s who have completed internships of supervised therapy. Psychologists will often print their state license numbers in their telephone directory listings.

Social Work Counselors

Social work counselors are listed under "Social Workers" in the Yellow Pages. Usually, their listings are less specific than those for psychiatrists and psychologists. Most commonly, you will see listings indicating "licensed MFCC" (marriage, family, and child counseling), "MSW" (master's degree in social work), "LCSW" (licensed clinical social worker), etc. State licensing numbers are often also given.

The *Register of Clinical Social Workers*, published by the National Association of Social Workers, lists members whose degrees and supervised training were in counseling; it is available in many public libraries.

Specific credentials you may also see in directory listings include the following:

Affiliation:	For therapists with specialties in:
Membership in American Psychoanalytic Association (all members are M.D.s)	
In Canada: Membership in Canadian Psychoanalytic Society	
Membership in International Psychoanalytical Society	Psychoanalysis
Membership in National Psychological Association for Psychoanalysis	
Training from Center for Studies of the Person, La Jolla, CA	Client-centered therapy
Training from Gestalt Therapy Institute of LA (or San Diego, San Francisco, New York, Boston, Chicago, Cleveland, Dallas, Miami, Hawaii, etc.)	Gestalt therapy
Training from Institute for Rational-Emotive Therapy (which maintains a register of psychotherapists who have received training in RET. Address: 45 E. 65th St., New York, NY 10021.)	Rational-emotive therapy
Training from the Institute for Reality Therapy (in LA, with branches in other cities in the U.S.)	Reality therapy

Membership in North American Society of Adlerian Psychology	Adlerian therapy
Membership in Association for the Advancement of Behavior Therapy	Behavioral psychotherapies
Membership in American Association of Marriage and Family Therapists	Marriage and family therapy
Membership in Biofeedback Society of America	Biofeedback therapy
Membership in American Society of Clinical Hypnosis In Canada: Membership in Canadian Institute of Hypnotism	Hypnosis
Membership in American Association of Sex Educators, Counselors, and Therapists	Treatment of sexual disorders

HARDER-TO-FIND THERAPIES

It can be especially difficult or confusing to locate therapists with certain orientations, either because these approaches are less widespread or because you do not know which kinds of health-care professionals make the greatest use of them.

Frequently, an effective way to locate an *existential-humanistic therapist* or *logotherapist* is through religious organizations. Call to ask for the names of ministers, priests, or rabbis with training in psychotherapy or counseling. These individuals, in turn, will often be able to put you in touch with either existential-humanistic therapists or logotherapists who may or may not be affiliated with the religious organization in question.

Emotional flooding therapists are usually found among psychologists, whose telephone directory listings will normally indicate whether they offer one of these therapies. The same is true for psychologists with experience in *direct decision therapy*.

Biofeedback therapists can be found in private practice; they will also be found at pain and stress centers (which are often run by hospitals on an outpatient basis). These offer private or publicly funded programs to help people with chronic pain or stress-related difficulties. A number of counseling agencies have begun to include biofeedback therapists on their staffs.

Biofeedback therapists in private practice, as well as pain and stress centers, are listed in telephone directories. Try looking under "Biofeedback Therapy and Training" and under "Psychologists" for those who indicate that they offer biofeedback.

Relaxation training (and sometimes also meditation) is frequently offered by biofeedback therapists (as well as by many psychologists and social workers).

Therapists who use *hypnosis* are often listed under "Hypnosis" in telephone directories. You will usually find a wide variety of educational backgrounds represented among therapists in these listings. Some are in private practice; some work for agencies. You will probably see an array of credentials advertised, perhaps ranging from therapists without degrees, to those with Ph.D.s and M.D.s. Here, especially, is an area in which to exercise consumer caution. Unfortunately, hypnotherapy is well populated by therapists who lack professionally recognized credentials. It is wise to remember that Ph.D.s can be granted in all sorts of fields—in education, theology, librarianship, etc.—as well as psychology. Some "therapists" practice with a Ph.D. after their names, yet their Ph.D.s may be in fields totally unrelated to counseling and psychotherapy. Ph.D.s who are *licensed psychologists* and who are members of the American Society of Clinical Hypnosis offer professional credibility as hypnotherapists. The certification of therapists trained in hypnosis is still unsettled in many states, where anyone can hang out a shingle. Since many licensed psychologists, psychiatrists, and some certified social workers *do* receive professional training in hypnosis, these are the professions to which it is most reliable to go for hypnotherapy.

Meditation techniques may be learned on your own (see Chapter 15), or you can seek out commercial or religious organizations that teach meditation. They are sometimes found in the Yellow Pages under "Meditation Instruction." Transcendental Meditation (TM) programs have been popular and are widespread. Yoga instructors (raja yoga rather than hatha yoga) also teach meditation.

Relatively few psychologists or social workers have actually received training in the use of *therapeutic exercise*, since this area is relatively new and its proponents are still small in number. However, most psychologists and many social workers are aware of the exercise programs advocated by Kostrubala and Glasser (see Chapter 15) and can help you plan intelligently.

ABOUT THE COST OF TREATMENT

Most health insurance plans offer at least partial coverage for psychotherapy and counseling. Consult your policy to find out what providers (psychiatrists, psychologists, or social workers) you may go to for covered treatment and for how long. (If you have special concerns about confidentiality in connection with treatment under an insurance plan, see Chapter 19.)

As we noted earlier, it is possible to obtain treatment from many psychiatrists, clinical psychologists, and social work counselors at reduced cost, if you have definite financial limitations (see Chapter 4).

Many clinical psychologists and social workers indicate in their directory listings in the Yellow Pages if fees are set on the basis of a sliding scale—on the basis, that is, of ability to pay. It is worth a telephone call to find out. Many public and some private counseling agencies also set fees in this way. Reduced fees from psychiatrists are more likely through agencies that offer psychiatric care than from psychiatrists in private practice. For public agencies, look in the White Pages under the name of your county; then look for the heading "Mental Health Services" or "County Mental Health," or the equivalent. You will frequently find one or more mental health centers or clinics listed. In the Yellow Pages, look under "Clinics" for a listing of private and sometimes also public clinics. It is usually clear from their descriptions whether they offer psychotherapy or counseling or only treatment for physical illness or injury.

Again, it may be worthwhile to mention that the costs of *group therapy*, whether through a clinical psychologist or a social work counselor, may be expected to be substantially less than the costs of individual therapy. (On the appropriateness of group therapy, see Chapter 13.)

ONCE YOU HAVE LOCATED A THERAPIST

If you believe you have found a therapist whose background, fees, and location meet your needs, I recommend that, when you telephone for an appointment, you ask for an *initial consultation*. This will make it clear, in the therapist's mind and your own, that your appointment is for a trial session. (The fee is normally the same as for a regular appointment, but check on this.)

When you go to this first session, it is very tempting to launch into what is troubling you. If you can hold yourself back in order to ask a few preliminary questions about the therapist's background, experience, approach, and a likely duration of treatment—in other words, encourage the therapist to talk to you a little bit about himself or herself—you will get a better idea of the *person* behind the professional title. This will help you decide whether you want to continue with future sessions. However, it may take several weeks, or even months, for you to *know* that the relationship will in fact benefit you.

18
SHOULD YOU BE HOSPITALIZED?

There are two main reasons for psychiatric hospitalization:

1. *You would be better off away from home.* Many things can play a role here. Perhaps there is too much family conflict at home, too much emotional strain, for you to improve. Or, your family may simply not be calm enough to handle the crisis. Or, perhaps you have too many strong and upsetting associations at home—e.g., if your spouse has just died or your daughter just committed suicide at home. Or, you may just have too little privacy at home; you feel forced to maintain a stiff upper lip in front of children, your spouse, or other family members, but you simply can do this no longer.

2. *Your condition may be too serious to be treated appropriately on an outpatient basis.* If you are no longer in touch with reality, are unable to communicate coherently, are hallucinating or have delusions, you cannot be relied on to take care of yourself. If you are psychotic, your behavior may hurt others or yourself. If you are suffering from a major, incapacitating depression, you may become suicidal. Finally, if you are unable to control an addiction to drugs or alcohol, inpatient care is more likely to be effective.

You may, of course, have reasons to *resist* hospitalization. Most likely, your resistance will be based on fear—of the unknown, of the later stigma of having been hospitalized for a psychiatric condition, or of the *inner* stigma: that you must have been terribly ill (or "weak") to justify hospitalization. Furthermore, if you have been hospitalized before, you may recall that the hospital's supportive environment encouraged you to feel dependent on it and to resist returning to normal living, and you may fear falling prey to this again.

All of these are good reasons to proceed cautiously. Only the first fear can be reasoned with in an objective way, by understanding what psychiatric hospitalization is really like, something this chapter will help you to do. Certainly, the other fears also may have some basis.

Discrimination *does* still exist against former psychiatric hospital patients. They may find it difficult, for example, to enter military service or serve in an important political capacity.

The inner stigma can be even more damaging, if you are a highly self-blaming person. If you are going to hold hospitalization as yet another black mark against yourself, then you may want to avoid hospitalization unless it means you are withholding treatment from yourself that really is essential to your well-being.

If you have been hospitalized before for psychiatric care, the last reason is very likely the most important one for you to weigh carefully. In the light of your past dependency needs, you must decide whether the problems you now face are serious enough to motivate you to walk into a situation that in the past you found difficult to leave.

Most hospital admissions for psychiatric conditions today are *voluntary*. Usually, either your own judgment leads you to accept hospitalization, or you are persuaded by family, friends, family doctor, minister, or psychiatrist that doing so is in your own best interest. Involuntary hospitalization is legally difficult and occurs primarily in cases in which, over a period of time, there is evidence that a person's behavior is not responsible, that he cannot take care of himself, or that he may injure himself or others.

WHAT HOSPITALIZATION IS LIKE

Several kinds of hospitalization are available to individuals who are emotionally troubled:

- private or public hospitals in which there are special floors or sections for psychiatric patients
- hospitals that treat only psychiatric problems
- inpatient programs that specialize in stress management or the treatment of depression, alcoholism, drug abuse, and other problems

Typically, fifteen to twenty-five patients of both sexes will reside in a hospital unit. Often a ward is divided, with men living on one side and women on the other. In private and many public hospitals, private and semiprivate rooms are available, depending on your ability to pay or your insurance coverage.

Frequently, patients dress in everyday clothes rather than in hospital gowns and pajamas. There is usually a common dining area where patients can eat at tables seating two to four people. Day rooms are common—large areas with comfortable chairs and couches, a television, stereo, books, and games.

If you were admitted to a hospital unit specializing in psychiatric care, you would probably see a psychologist or psychiatrist two or three times a week in individual sessions. It is likely, since your condition was serious enough to warrant hospitalization, that you will receive medication during at least part of your stay (see Chapter 16).

If you are a voluntary admission, you will be asked to sign consent forms for treatment that is recommended to you. You *do* have a right to refuse treatment you do not want.

A complete physical examination is routinely required to rule out underlying physical disorders. You may also be asked to take some written psychological tests, most being of the multiple-choice variety.

Group sessions in hospitals are common. In forming groups, attempts are made to choose people in ways that will be mutually beneficial. In part, these periods "in group" help to offset feelings of being alone in a strange environment.

Activities are planned to combat monotony. They may, for example, include arts and crafts, sports, dancing, and day trips to museums or the movies.

Staff members with whom you would have the most personal contact are members of the psychiatric nursing staff. Often, when former patients are asked who helped them while in the hospital, instead of mentioning the therapist, they name a member of the nursing staff. Psychiatric nurses have received special training in psychiatry and often are a major source of human warmth and caring.

Depending on your progress, you may be encouraged to return home during the day, or overnight, or for a weekend. As it becomes clear that you are improving, these periods may be lengthened to see how you handle the transition from the hospital, before being discharged.

Although hospitals expect patients to choose to remain until they are discharged, few hospitals actively confine voluntary psychiatric patients to prevent them from leaving early—and then generally only in cases judged to be very serious. The only restrictions and rules you would likely encounter are those of any hospital: to respect the rights of others, to be considerate, to refrain from taking drugs unless they are prescribed, to smoke only in smoking areas, and to maintain socially acceptable behavior.

Inpatient hospital programs specializing in stress management, depression, eating disorders, and so on, are normally intended for one- to two-week stays. Residential treatment centers for problems requiring longer treatment—e.g., drug and alcohol rehabilitation programs—are less formal than hospitals. Often, residential treatment centers are located in the country and may consist of a cluster of cottagelike buildings. The program is usually under the direction of a psychiatrist.

Hospital care and residential treatment are very expensive. Most health insurance programs cover most of the costs of inpatient psychiatric hospitalization, for several weeks or months. Public psychiatric hospitals must be relied on by most people for longer stays, unless they bear the costs of private hospital treatment themselves. Physical conditions at state psychiatric hospitals have in general improved in recent years but still tend to fall short of private facilities, for lack of adequate public funding.

LEAVING

Probably the most difficult experience if you are hospitalized for a psychiatric condition is *leaving*, not entering, the hospital. There is frequently a sense of relief and comfort that comes once you have made the decision to enter a hospital. You have a "legitimate" reason for leaving your normal responsibilities; you may feel "rescued" from family or work situations you could no longer cope with. Once you have begun to feel more at home in the hospital setting, you begin to relax, to participate in activities with less restraint or reluctance. Then, as you improve, thanks in great part to the concentrated attention and care you are receiving, you realize that you must begin to think of reentering life "outside."

Returning to your familiar life can be frightening. It is usual to wonder whether it will, perhaps again, prove to be too much of a strain. Leaving the hospital frequently means returning home or going back to work, to shoulder the same burdens again, trying to pick up where you left off.

Hospitalization is often a positive, reassuring experience. Patients become aware that others do care and that, if life becomes especially stressful, there *are* sources of professional help and encouragement available to fall back on. Most hospitals encourage former patients to maintain contact through follow-up services of some kind. Leaving the hospital is made easier for many people, for example, knowing that the psychologist or psychiatrist is still there and that they will be seen on an outpatient basis. To help former hospital patients ease back into more normal lives, groups that were formed in the hospital sometimes will also continue to meet on an outpatient basis for a time.

The decision to be hospitalized is difficult for anyone. Hospital care may help turn your life around and put you back on your feet. Or it can, if you are your own worst critic, give you another burden to carry. It is important to try not to block potentially helpful treatment with excessive pride and to try to listen to people who care about you. If they are in favor of the decision, their convictions should be considered. If your doctor or minister agrees, this adds weight to their advice. Once you have listened, try to make your decision your own, not anyone else's.

19
CONFIDENTIALITY
Your Privacy

THE NEGATIVE LABEL OF EMOTIONAL ILLNESS

Society has attached an undeniable stigma to so-called emotional or mental illness. The public is afraid of conditions that are not concrete and physical and are less easily understood. Emotional or mental difficulties seem more "hidden" and mysterious. The body is *tangible*, and we feel we have more control over it. Setting a broken leg, having your appendix removed, even open-heart surgery—they are not difficult for the public to grasp.

However, depression, anxiety, intolerance to stress, disorientation, unsettling fears, unusual behavior—these are much less readily understood by nonspecialists. There is a tendency for many people to judge rather harshly what they do not comprehend. When many individuals who are ignorant of psychology hear of someone in emotional distress, the inclination is often to condemn. Condemnation is frequently an expression of fear—fear of what is not understood.

During the last two to three decades, society has gradually become more psychologically aware and more intelligent about nonphysical problems. And yet, the stigma of emotional or mental illness has still not been erased. It will take time.

As a result, many people who are in serious emotional distress hesitate to go to a therapist. They are afraid of the negative label that others may apply to them, if information about them ever "got out."

Sometimes this is a justifiable worry. Some employers are bigoted and may discriminate against employees with known emotional problems (even though this is blatantly illegal). And some families, in which there is little psychological understanding and much fear, may withdraw from a family member who lets it be known that he or she is in emotional distress.

On the other hand, most people like to feel that they have a certain degree of compassion and openness—even those who are judgmental! If you are willing to face ignorant attitudes head-on, unflinchingly (and this can take a great deal of courage), you will frequently gain the respect of others through your honesty. They will perceive your unwillingness to judge yourself negatively and may even come to admire the strength and determination you have to improve your life.

If you are in emotional distress, you may have to face a dilemma: whether it is *prudent* to try to conceal your difficulties from people because you believe that some of them may judge you harshly and critically if they find out you are in therapy or whether it is likely that they would understand, and perhaps even sympathize, if you were able to be open and had the courage and self-confidence to help educate others on a psychological level. Unfortunately, people in real emotional distress don't have the energy, the courage, or the self-confidence to fight social battles! It therefore usually seems to be a great deal easier to try to keep your own affairs *private*. But this is not always simple to do.

THE CONFIDENTIALITY OF PSYCHOTHERAPY

Confidentiality as it relates to counseling and psychotherapy is not a straightforward thing; much that has to do with confidentiality is still unsettled. In reality, there are as yet few laws that actually protect personal privacy.

There are two central questions relating to confidentiality that I want to raise here. The first is a question only you can answer. I will try to discuss some of the answers to the second.

HOW IMPORTANT IS CONFIDENTIALITY TO YOU?

Only you can answer this. It may be reassuring to know that, usually, the safeguards observed by therapists are sufficient to protect the personal affairs of clients. And seldom does any real or lasting harm come to a client if information about him or her *is* released.

Many individuals, when they are trapped in a prison of self-concern and self-involvement, are prone to exaggerate or magnify the ultimate significance of being "discovered" in therapy, believing that a release of information about them will be potentially explosive and damaging. Individuals who are emotionally very upset are inclined to focus on threatening aspects of therapy.

We have already looked at some of the ways that a heightened sensitivity to maintain secrecy about your problems can lead to self-imprisonment, to blocks that stand in the way of positive change (see Chapter 1). Most of the information you may want kept secret is not really as damaging as you first may be inclined to think. Much depends on how *you* respond to information that might be released about you. Let's look at an example.

A little more than a year ago, George Malcolm became seriously depressed. He was forced to resign from his job, and then he received disability income for ten months. During this time he entered therapy. His experience helped him to understand a number of important things about himself that he had ignored in the past. He discovered that he had felt very unsatisfied in his previous job; he had buried his frustrations and had suppressed the anger he felt at being trapped in a situation he disliked. It was a situation he felt he had no control over because of his concern for his and his family's financial security. He was also worried about his mother, who would probably have to be admitted to a nursing home in the near future. Her situation was an added reason for George's financial worry.

He also came to realize that his marriage was suffering because of his insistence that his wife not work. She, on the other hand, felt overcontrolled by her husband: she felt that he stood in the way of her personal growth.

As a result of his increased awareness, George came to see that losing his former job was really a blessing in disguise. His marriage began to improve when George's depression for the first time put him in a *dependent* position; he needed his wife's emotional support, and she, in turn, began to see him as a *person*, with weaknesses of his own, and not as she had idealized him.

George's depression allowed him to understand and appreciate his wife's previously frustrated sense of initiative. He now encouraged her to do what she had long wanted to do, to develop a career.

Because George received disability during his depression, his insurance company had information about him on file. When George was interviewed for a new job a year after he became depressed, he was asked at the interview if he had been ill during the preceding year, when he had not worked.

George decided to be truthful and said that he had become depressed and that as a result of the experience had learned much about himself. In particular, he had learned what kind of work really interested him and gave him a sense of satisfaction. Although it had been a difficult period, George said that he felt he had gained a great deal from the experience.

George's prospective employer was impressed by George's honesty and evident sincerity. George got the job—in large part because of the attitude he took toward his depression.

WHAT LAWS PROTECT CONFIDENTIALITY?

To what extent is your privacy protected? What situations legally justify your therapist to release information about you?

These questions do not always have clear-cut answers. There may or may not be laws in your state to protect the confidentiality of psychotherapy. The legal status of therapy is still ambiguous in many states. Even in those where laws have been passed, legal protection is not reliable unless your therapist is willing to face a jail sentence if need be to maintain the confidence you have entrusted in him. If you feel a situation is likely to arise that would put legal pressure on your therapist to release information about you (for example, in a child-custody hearing), you should ask your therapist what his commitments to confidentiality are.

"Leaks"

More frequently, confidentiality is broken due to informality rather than due to an intentional release of information. For example, if you are referred to another therapist or to a physician, the chances are that information about you will be shared by your original therapist with the new therapist or doctor. You can ask your therapist *not* to release information in this way, but if you do, the care you receive as a result of the referral cannot benefit from your first therapist's understanding of you. On the other hand, if you do permit your file to be shared with a new therapist or doctor, you will probably not yet be in a position to know what his or her own policies about confidentiality are.

There is a second way that information about you may be released. Often, therapists discuss information about their clients with colleagues in an effort to provide better help for them. It is often to your definite advantage to have other therapists share their assessments and ideas with your therapist. But if you ask your therapist to refrain from discussing your case with professional colleagues, he will very likely agree to cooperate with you.

Another informal way that information about you may be disclosed has to do with those people who may have access to your therapist's files. The therapist's secretary, the therapist's professional colleagues, and perhaps certain internists or researchers may routinely have access to patient files. As a result, some information about you may be given out over the telephone to individuals you are involved with. There is no malice or intent to harm clients in this; it is usually a matter of a degree of informality (which is certainly not defensible, but this is not a perfect world, and people are not always as careful as they might be).

If you believe you have special reasons to be concerned about protecting the confidentiality of your relationship with your therapist, it will help him or her to know this, and special precautions can be taken to protect your file from access by others.

Accidental or inadvertent breaks of confidentiality sometimes can also occur. For example, billings may be mailed to your address and then be opened by a spouse, child, or parent whom you may not have wanted told that you were in therapy.

Here is another example: If you enter group therapy, other members of the group are not professionally bound by rules governing confidentiality. Because they are not counseling professionals themselves, they will be less attentive to matters involving confidentiality—although most group therapists try, when a group is first formed, to get group members to agree not to disclose privileged information outside of sessions.

Exceptions

Beyond these kinds of possible breaks of confidentiality that are due to inattention, informality, and access of information about you by others, there are a number of legal exceptions to confidentiality.

Examination by court order is one. If a judge orders you to be examined by a psychiatrist or psychologist, his findings will be transmitted to the court and so be made public.

If a client reveals his intention and decision to commit a crime, a therapist is legally required to report this to authorities. If a patient plans to commit homicide, therapists are required by law to take whatever action is necessary to prevent the murder. In California, in addition to warning the police of the homicidal intentions of a client, therapists must also take steps to warn the intended victim, if this is possible.

If a patient is seriously suicidal—that is, he has decided on a means to take his life, has decided when to do this, and cannot be persuaded to hold off while in therapy—the therapist is legally bound to take whatever action may be necessary to prevent the patient's suicide, including the disclosure of pertinent information to public officials.

Similarly, in cases of child abuse or neglect, the law requires that a client's confidential relationship with his therapist be set to one side in order to provide adequate protection and care for the child.

THREATS TO PRIVACY FROM
HEALTH INSURANCE COMPANIES

There is one other way that privacy can be invaded, and for many people it is little known and more significant than the breaks of confidentiality we have already discussed. It comes about as a result of recently formed *data banks* that are maintained and continuously updated by insurance companies. Information about insurance claims and payments not only are kept on file by individual insurance companies, but a number of national data banks have been established to provide insurance companies with information about the health histories of individuals.

For example, if you file a health insurance application or a claim for benefits with many insurance companies, they often will run a check on your health history through a national computerized clearinghouse that maintains insurance information. This information includes data about previous insurance claims you may have made. Insurance companies believe that they have a right to data of this kind, since the information protects them from having to pay for health care costs that come about due to "preexisting conditions," which most insurance policies limit or exclude. Too, if you have suffered from poor health in the past, and were covered by insurance, there are probably data about your health history on file in such a national computerized clearinghouse; by accessing information about you, an insurance company is able to form a judgment as to whether you are an excessive risk.

Like any information about you that has been compiled and is furnished without your consent, these data about your health history—maintained by agencies that service insurance companies—are subject to possible abuse. Information on file can and is used to protect the interests of subscribing insurance companies; your own interests may not be served in the process. Not only might you be denied future insurance benefits, but the information maintained about you is subject to whatever use the insurance clearinghouse believes is appropriate.

As yet, laws to secure a real measure of personal privacy have not been passed. This has been one of the goals of organizations like the American Civil Liberties Union.

There is a second insurance-related issue that has to do with confidentiality. If you have group health insurance through your employer, it will be necessary for your therapist to complete reports about you in order for you to receive benefits under your insurance plan. (I am assuming here that your insurance offers coverage for counseling, psychotherapy, or psychiatry.) The reports filed by your therapist with the group health insurance company are sometimes filed *through your employer*, and sometimes employers require their group health companies to provide *them* with information about health care supplied to their employees. In either way, the fact that you are in therapy and the general reasons for your need for therapy can come to the attention of your employer.

If your employer is a large company or organization, such information will probably be filed in your employer's business or insurance office and laid to rest; it will probably not come to the attention of individuals you actually deal with in your work. But it may. In a smaller company, there is a greater risk.

If you are really concerned about this possibility, ask your insurance officer how health claims are handled and whether health information is requested by your employer from the insurance company.

If you are then still concerned and feel that you need to avoid potential complications at work, you may prefer to see a therapist on your own *and refrain from using your employer's insurance coverage.* If you see a therapist in private practice, your decision to pay your own bill may be expensive for you. If finances are a problem, bear in mind that you can frequently locate competent help through county, state, or private counseling agencies. If you go to an agency, remember that you will almost certainly be asked whether you have insurance coverage. If you admit that you do, you will have defeated your purpose in going to an agency on your own to protect your privacy. It is, after all, your right to obtain treatment that *you* elect to pay for.

MAGNIFYING YOUR NEED FOR SECRECY

After reviewing these ways in which confidentiality may be broken—by accident or sometimes excessive informality, by legal requirements, or by what to many of us constitutes an invasion of personal privacy by insurance companies—you may wonder to what extent information that you disclose in therapy really *is* protected.

In fact, very seldom are any of the *details* of therapy ever divulged to others without a client's advance consent. Most of us do not need to be worried by legal exceptions to confidentiality: most of us are not actually homicidal (though we may feel very angry at times!); most of us are not determined to take our lives (though we may at times feel very disheartened); most of us are not concerned that a court will order us to be examined by a psychiatrist.

I have tried to give a realistic picture of confidentiality in therapy. Your identity may inadvertently be disclosed by a billing that goes astray, by a secretary's excessive informality over the telephone, by a fellow group member's inclination to talk too much outside of the group. If you decide to make use of insurance coverage, there are possible consequences you ought to be aware of.

I have tried to underline the fact that most people who enter therapy blow out of proportion the real significance of these possible, but comparatively infrequent, "leaks."

Karl A. Menninger, a renowned and original contributor to psychiatry, quotes one of his patients who shared her intelligent reflections with him:

"When I look back upon the many months I pondered as to how I might get here without anyone knowing, and the devious routes I considered and actually took to accomplish this, only to realize that some of the symptoms from which I suffer are respectable enough to be acknowledged anywhere and valid enough to explain my coming here, it all seems so utterly ridiculous. I looked furtively out of the corner of my eye at the people I met here, expecting them to betray their shame or their queerness, only to discover that I often could not distinguish the patients from the physicians, or from other visitors. I suppose it is such a commonplace experience to you that you cannot realize how startling that is to a naive layman, like myself, even one who thinks he has read a little and laid aside some of the provincialism and prejudice which to some extent blind us all. I see how there is something emotional in it; if the patient feels only depressed or guilty or confused, then one looks upon his consulting the psychiatrist as a disgraceful recourse; but if some of the symptoms take form in one of the bodily organs, all the shame vanishes. There is no sense to it, but that's how it is. I have written a dozen letters to tell people where I am, the very people from whom in the past six months I have tried to conceal my need of this."*

DON'T LET EXAGGERATED WORRIES HOLD YOU BACK

When you stop for a moment to consider how widespread personal problems are—20 percent of Americans have serious emotional difficulties—isn't there something silly, ridiculous, and, frequently, self-defeating in being overly concerned about

---

*Karl A. Menninger, *Man Against Himself* (New York: Harcourt, Brace and Company, 1938), pp. 455-456.

keeping others from knowing that, for a time, you were depressed, anxious, unsatisfied, and frustrated to the point that you *decided* to do something about these unhappy feelings?

To be sure, discretion is sometimes prudent. An employer, your family, or some of your friends may be so provincial or bigoted as to think that counseling is close to a misdemeanor. Ignorant or uninformed people do tend to judge hastily and to condemn. But often, if you do have the endurance, many of them are also willing to change their minds when they have the opportunity to understand a little bit about what they fear.

You cannot live for the approval of others. If you believe therapy may help you improve your life, don't allow yourself to be held back by exaggerated worries.

It usually *is* possible to keep confidential the fact that you have entered therapy when there are especially compelling reasons to exercise foresight and caution. *Explain* your concerns to your therapist; he or she can then make every effort to help you.

20
DOES THERAPY WORK?

Whether or not therapy works is a question that has hounded psychotherapists for more than thirty years, since evaluative studies began to cast doubts on its effectiveness. Since then, several hundred studies of the effectiveness of psychotherapy have been made. Some of them appear to show that psychotherapy is highly successful, and many have pointed to evidence that psychotherapy is no more effective than no treatment at all.

The ambiguity about this issue has been very troublesome to therapists and tends not to be openly discussed with clients, for obvious reasons.

Why reports about psychotherapy's effectiveness have been so contradictory and ambiguous has never been made clear. But understanding the reasons behind these opposing claims will give us a basis for optimism.

CLAIMS AGAINST THE EFFECTIVENESS OF PSYCHOTHERAPY

If people who are emotionally troubled "get well" through psychotherapy in about the same length of time as those who are not given any treatment at all, we would be inclined to say that psychotherapy didn't help. Several studies have shown that the majority of people with "neurotic disorders" improve spontaneously, on the average, in one to two years.* When people with similar problems *are* treated with psychotherapy, the outcome is virtually the same: the spontaneous remission rate for all practical purposes is the same as the rate of success due to therapy. Psychotherapy doesn't seem to make a difference. We'll call this the *spontaneous remission criticism* and will come back to it in a moment.

Most studies of the effectiveness of psychotherapy make use of "placebo treatments": a group of emotionally troubled individuals is treated with one of the major approaches to psychotherapy by well-trained therapists, and another group of similarly troubled people is treated by untrained "therapists" who offer their clients a "therapy" that is simply *made up* but is carefully presented so as to be believable. And, again, it turns out that clients treated with the legitimate therapy improve, but not significantly more than those in the placebo group. We'll call this the *placebo criticism* and will come back to it, too, in a moment.

A few studies have shown that psychotherapy can actually be *injurious* to clients. A disorder *brought about by* medical treatment is called an *iatrogenic disturbance. Iatrogenesis* is the Greek word for "brought about by doctors." If the iatrogenesis criticism is valid, then therapy may be not only ineffective but sometimes actually *harmful.***

Together, these three criticisms have made therapists feel very defensive—and rightly so. If fictitious treatment by a mock therapist works as well as treatment provided by a man or woman who has trained long and hard for a Ph.D. or M.D., wouldn't *you* feel ill at ease—perhaps very much ill at ease!— charging your clients $75 to $100 an hour for your time for a service that is no better than none at all and may even cause your clients to get worse?

These are not trumped-up charges against psychotherapy that we can afford to ignore. Therapists don't like to confront them. Here are some of the results of research studies:

---

*S. Rachman, *The Effects of Psychotherapy* (New York: Pergamon Press, 1971), p. 18.

**See, for example, Thomas J. Nardi, "Psychotherapy: Cui Bono?," in Jusuf Hariman, ed., *Does Psychotherapy Really Help People?* (Springfield, IL: Charles C. Thomas, 1984), pp. 154-164.

. . . [A]s compared with spontaneous remission, there is no good evidence to suggest that psychotherapy and psychoanalysis have effects that are in any way superior.*

. . .[M]ost of the verbal psychotherapies have an effect size that is only marginally greater than the effect size for . . . a "placebo treatment."**

Most writers . . . agree that the therapeutic claims made for psychotherapy range from the abysmally low to the astonishingly high and, furthermore, they would tend to agree that on the average psychotherapy appears to produce approximately the same amount of improvement as can be observed in patients who have not received this type of treatment.***

. . . [U]sing placebo treatment as a proper control (which it undoubtedly is), we find that the alleged effectiveness of psychodynamic therapy [i.e., psychoanalysis] vanishes almost completely.†

There is still no acceptable evidence to support the view that psychoanalytic treatment is effective.††

. . . [T]here is no relationship between duration of therapy and effectiveness of therapy.†††

Psychotherapy of any kind applies techniques that are based on certain theories, and these theories demand not only that there should be correlation between success and length of treatment, but also that the training and experience of the therapist should be extremely important. To find that neither of these corollaries is in fact borne out must be an absolute death blow to any claims to have demonstrated the effectiveness of psychotherapy.§

The pessimism produced by these conclusions was summed up recently by Hans J. Eysenck, professor at the Institute of Psychiatry in London:

---

*Hans J. Eysenck, "The Battle over Therapeutic Effectiveness," in J. Hariman, ed., *Does Psychotherapy Really Help People?*, p. 59.
**Edward Erwin, "Is Psychotherapy More Effective Than a Placebo?," in *Does Psychotherapy Really Help People?*, p. 39.
***Rachman, *The Effects of Psychotherapy*, p. 84.
†Eysenck, "The Battle over Therapeutic Effectiveness," p. 56.
††Rachman, *The Effects of Psychotherapy*, p. 63.
†††Eysenck, "The Battle over Therapeutic Effectiveness," p. 57.
§*Ibid.*

I have always felt that it is completely unethical to subject neurotic patients to a treatment the efficacy of which has not been proven, and indeed, the efficacy of which is very much in doubt—so much so that there is no good evidence for it, in spite of hundreds of studies devoted to the question. Patients are asked to spend money and time they can ill afford, and subject themselves to a gruelling experience, to no good purpose at all; this surely cannot be right. At least there should be a statutory warning to the effect that the treatment they are proposing to enter has never been shown to be effective, is very lengthy and costly, and may indeed do harm to the patient.*

WHY PESSIMISM IS UNFOUNDED

I hold all contemporary psychiatric approaches—all "mental-health" methods—as basically flawed because they all search for solutions along medical-technical lines. But solutions for what? For life! But life is not a problem to be solved. Life is something to be lived, as intelligently, as competently, as well as we can, day in and day out. Life is something we must endure. There is no solution for it.**

We must grab the bull by the horns. Thousands upon thousands of people continue to enter psychotherapy. How long would any service last if it failed to serve the needs of its market? It is tempting to suppose that something constructive, at least sometimes, happens as a result of psychotherapy to justify the time, expense, and faith of clients. Or is their faith really misplaced?

One of the most outspoken critics of psychotherapy is psychiatrist Thomas Szasz. His views are an unlikely source for a defense of psychotherapy, but its defense, oddly enough, can be found there.

Szasz argues that psychology has been influenced by the disease model that dominates medicine. Medicine bases its conception of treatment on the fact that there are diseases (or

---

*Eysenck, "The Battle over Therapeutic Effectiveness," in *Does Psychotherapy Really Help People?*, p. 59.
**Thomas Szasz, interviewed in Jonathan Miller, *States of Mind* (New York: Pantheon Books, 1983), p. 290.

injuries) that can be helped by means of drugs or surgery. Illnesses and injuries are *treatable conditions*. Treatment is applied from outside by the physician, and the condition, when the treatment is effective, improves.

But psychology goes a step too far when it claims that people who become emotionally helpless, hopeless, lonely, or agitated are actually *sick*. Szasz claims that they are *not* sick; they *are* helpless, hopeless, lonely, or agitated. These are not "illnesses" but, rather, some of the tragic conditions of life. They are *problems of living*. For Szasz—and for therapists like Viktor Frankl and Alfred Adler—psychological problems resemble "moral problems" much more than they do "physical diseases." They involve discouragement, loss of morale, loss of moral courage. They are *states of demoralization*.

Now, demoralization is not a *treatable condition*—not, certainly, in the medical sense. You cannot apply treatment from without and expect that the patient will get better. The situation is much more complex than this. The patient—let's shift at this point to calling him or her the *client*—is much more actively involved in the process of psychotherapy than is a *patient* in medicine. A woman who contracts pneumonia can be cured with antibiotics while she lies in bed watching television or sleeping. But an emotionally troubled woman—who has had a succession of unhappy marriages, who has lost job after job, whose personality is offensive to others, who has a low sense of self-worth, and who has lost a sense of meaning and direction in life—cannot be cured while she lies in bed and is treated with appropriate medication. "Effective treatment" just isn't possible; too much is up to the client herself.

Basically, this is why studies of the effectiveness of psychotherapy have generally led to discouraging results. Most psychological conditions (there are exceptions, as we will see) are not, at least at present, *treatable in the medical sense*. To combat them requires of the client a great deal of his or her own effort and even exertion. They require self-discipline, moral courage, faith in oneself—all the things emotional distress tends to undermine. No approach to psychotherapy can itself be medically effective in treating conditions like these. Somehow, the client must reach a point where he can lift himself by the bootstraps. He can be *encouraged* by the therapist, he can be *reasoned with*, he can be *manipulated in strategic therapeutic ways*, the therapist can *exhort* him to be rational, but the focus always comes back to the client. Is *he* or *she* motivated to *learn* how to change? Is he or she an "effective learner" — that is, a "good student"?

The hundreds of attempts to evaluate the effectiveness of approaches to psychotherapy have, incredibly, left out this essential reference to the clients themselves: What kind of people are they? What encourages *them*? What can act as a source for their motivation, for the strength they have lost?

Ironically, the answer to these questions also lies unwittingly in the hands of psychotherapy's harshest critics.

The worst blow to fall on the shoulders of psychotherapists was dealt by placebo studies. Experiments were designed that would *convince* a group of emotionally troubled clients that taking a pink pill (in reality, a sugar-filled placebo) would reduce their symptoms. In fact, their symptoms were, in general, reduced, and often by as much as treatment in formal psychotherapy. This fact has been interpreted by most therapists to mean that psychotherapy must therefore have been ineffective. If a pink and useless pill could equal the effects of therapy, then therapy was equally useless.

But this involved a huge oversight and a mistake in logic. The therapy *did* work, *as did* the placebo. But why?

The placebo effect has become increasingly interesting to psychological as well as medical researchers. Apparently, a client's or patient's strong *belief* in the therapeutic value of a process sometimes has a measurable influence on his future health. The way belief can act in this way is not necessarily mysterious or mystical. If we are prepared to see emotional difficulties in terms of demoralization, then belief in therapeutic effectiveness is the most clear-cut counterbalancing force. Strong belief of this kind may be enough — *if* the client really wishes to change and *if* the therapist and the approach to therapy together can inspire the client's confidence in his own ability to regain control of his life — to help the client begin to lift himself by the bootstraps. Just what the necessary ingredients are to make this possible is not yet definitely known. Some approaches to therapy, however, seem to be more successful than others in inspiring confidence in clients with certain personality traits and with certain goals or problems. The best evidence for this comes from clients themselves, whose evaluations of their own experiences in therapy we will look at in a moment.

The second blow that fell on psychotherapy came from the spontaneous remission critics. Again, studies demonstrated certain facts:

- How long it takes for spontaneous remission to occur depends greatly on what sorts of emotional difficulties clients have. People with depressive or anxiety reactions tend, for example, to have spontaneous remissions faster than persons with obsessive-compulsive or hypochondriacal symptoms.
- The percentages of clients who do experience spontaneous remissions are related to the period of time a study uses as a basis. (The follow-up periods of different studies vary a great deal, from months to many years. As one researcher commented, "It is doubtful whether life can guarantee five years of stability to any person."*)
- Spontaneous remissions frequently happen to clients whose lives improve because of fortunate events, such as an improved position at work, successful marriages and personal relationships, and periods during which pressing problems become fewer and life more stable.

Given these facts, spontaneous remission critics argued that, since many troubled individuals will get better anyway, *without psychotherapy*, we cannot know that psychotherapy caused any beneficial effects.

Again, poor logic. It is like saying that since certain bone fractures will eventually heal themselves in correct alignment, without being set in a cast, we cannot know for these cases that a cast had any beneficial effects. Well, for many people, a suitable psychotherapy serves much the same function as a cast does for a broken bone: it supports, lessens vulnerability, reduces pain, and makes life a little more comfortable until natural healing can take place. Again, whom do we ask to determine whether this is the case? We must ask the person with the fractured arm whether the cast made him more comfortable.

---

*Eisenbud, quoted in H. H. Mosak, "Problems in the Definition and Measurement of Success in Psychotherapy," in Werner Wolff and Joseph A. Precker, eds., *Success in Psychotherapy* (New York: Grune & Stratton, 1952), p. 13.

HOW PSYCHOTHERAPY CAN BE INJURIOUS TO YOUR HEALTH

Is there substantial evidence that psychotherapists sometimes harm, as well as benefit, their clients? I think that there definitely is and that this has been fairly well demonstrated.*

Even love can harm, and psychotherapy is no exception. Ellis identifies some of the main ways psychotherapists can make clients worse:**

- Therapists can encourage clients to be dependent on them. Directly or indirectly a therapist can convey to a client, "You cannot get along without me," "You will probably need to spend at least two more years in therapy," etc.
- Therapists can overemphasize the significance of the client's past experience to the point that they persuade the client to feel unjustifiably weighed down and controlled by past events and circumstances.
- Therapists can become so hooked on the importance of modeling positive personal qualities (warmth, positive regard, congruence, empathy) for a client that they will not provide any active-directive leadership during a time when the client is floundering and needs strong recommendations.
- Therapists may place too much importance on the role of insight. The search for insight can be never-ending. It is useful only to some clients; for others, insight is irrelevant to helping them change.
- Many therapists feel that therapy gives clients a chance to vent their feelings. But catharsis by itself is not enough to replace destructive patterns of behavior and thinking with constructive ones.
- Therapists can rely excessively on distracting the client from issues that trouble him; e.g., relaxation training, meditation, or therapeutic exercise can help clients break out of a cycle of self-preoccupation. Self-absorption

---

*Albert Ellis, "Must Most Psychotherapists Remain as Incompetent as They Now Are?," in J. Hariman, ed., *Does Psychotherapy Really Help People?*, p. 240.
**Ibid., pp. 24-36.

perpetuates emotional suffering; distractions can therefore be invaluable. But if a client's underlying self-defeating attitudes are not confronted, distraction alone will not be enough to bring about lasting change.
- Therapists can rely too heavily on getting clients to "think positively." Positive thinking can undermine a client's already shaky confidence if he fails to achieve the goals that positive thinking led him to expect.

These are undeniable shortcomings of therapy. They can reduce the effectiveness of therapy, or negate its constructive effects, or even cause clients to accept the therapist's belief that their condition is worse than they thought and so persuade them to feel, and to be, even more troubled.

It is important to be aware of these signs of what Ellis rightly calls incompetence in therapists. It is also important to realize that psychotherapy is not unique in having to deal with professional incompetence. Physicians can and do fall victim to many of the same excesses: needlessly alarming patients, misdiagnosing their conditions, and sometimes treating them in ways that lead to a general worsening of their health. Iatrogenesis exists in medicine as well as in psychotherapy.

Until the day when the world is a perfect place, we simply have to take *caveat emptor* to heart—let the buyer beware. A Ph.D. in clinical psychology, certification in marriage and family counseling, or an M.D. with specialization in psychiatry unfortunately does not guarantee against human fallibility and lack of wisdom.

WHEN PSYCHOTHERAPY IS SUCCESSFUL

It might be argued, then, that the worth of psychotherapy to the consumer (the patient) does not depend on its being superior to a placebo. Whether it is or is not superior is a theoretical question of interest to theoreticians; in judging the practical worth of psychotherapy, what matters is consumer satisfaction. Judged by the latter criterion, psychotherapy is indeed worthwhile.*

---

*Edward Erwin, "Is Psychotherapy More Effective Than a Placebo?," in J. Hariman, ed., *Does Psychotherapy Really Help People?*, p. 48.

There is a world of difference between popularity and effectiveness. Is psychotherapy only popular and simply ineffective?

All approaches to therapy have a built-in expectation that positive change will result. This belief implicitly is communicated to clients, and it can provide them with a sense of hope that replaces the helpless and demoralized state that has motivated them to seek therapy.

This happens in several ways. For example, paying attention to a person increases his morale and self-esteem. This is called the *Hawthorne effect*. "Anyone who has been in therapy can appreciate the gratification that comes from having a competent professional give undivided attention for an hour."* Also, the expectation on the part of a therapist that positive results will follow itself can influence a client's attitudes and his belief that he will get better, that emotional suffering will lessen and end.

The strength of a client's *belief* that he *can* change, that he *can* improve, is the major single force in psychotherapy. The client has to feel that his belief is *warranted*. Many factors play a role here: the client's education level and the respect he may feel toward the therapist's training and experience; the intangibles of therapy—the therapist's integrity, authenticity or convincingness, the client's sense that he is understood, that the therapist cares, that the therapist himself has learned how to cope with living and can communicate this, etc. Psychotherapy can be successful when this sense of *promise* is present in therapy sessions.

CLIENTS LOOK BACK

I know myself better than any doctor can.

Ovid

If most emotional difficulties are not illnesses at all but problems of living, and if problems of living cannot be treated medically, then the hundreds of evaluative studies of therapeutic effectiveness have been looking for something that simply is not there: an objective standard against which to judge therapeutic

---

*James O. Prochaska, *Systems of Psychotherapy: A Transtheoretical Analysis* (Homewood, IL: The Dorsey Press, 1979), p. 5.

success. It makes very little sense to speak of standards in connection with problems of living that come about from demoralization. The only standard we can reasonably appeal to is the subjective judgment of clients themselves, who have experienced periods in therapy.

> [Therapy] is a purely individual affair and can be measured only in terms of its meaning to the person, child, or adult, of its value, not for happiness, not for virtue, not for social adjustment but for growth and development in terms of a purely individual norm. *

A few representative and specific evaluations of their experiences in psychotherapy by former clients follow. They are included here not as proof of the effectiveness of psychotherapy, because proof in this area is not possible, but rather as illustrations of different ways people believe themselves to have been helped: * *

> After being in therapy, I have learned to accept myself more easily and believe that many of the people whose opinions about me matter to me also accept me for what I am. I have come to realize that what I have in my life, in the way of my marriage, my children, my work is what I have decided to settle with. It is easier and more satisfying for me to do this than always to be fighting the present and straining for things I haven't got.

> I still have problems with my own self-confidence. I accept some volunteer work at my church, in spite of these feelings of self-doubt, believing that I really am mentally capable and feeling that I can, in time, and with patience, overcome my feelings of inadequacy.

---

*J. Taft, *The Dynamics of Therapy in a Controlled Relationship* (New York: Macmillan, 1933), quoted in H. H. Mosak, "Problems in the Definition and Measurement of Success in Psychotherapy," in Wolff and Precker, eds., *Success in Psychotherapy*, p. 7.

* *Most evaluative studies of psychotherapy have attempted in some way to take into account the judgment of clients. One study in particular, however, has made clients' evaluations of their experiences in therapy its main focus, in fact, for a book-length treatment. That is Hans H. Strupp, Ronald E. Fox, and Ken Lessler, *Patients View Their Psychotherapy* (Baltimore: Johns Hopkins Press, 1969). Some of the patient evaluations included here are based on transcripts from the Strupp-Fox-Lessler study; they have been paraphrased and condensed for use here.

I now love my daughter without qualifications. I have much less hostility toward my mother. I'm much less afraid now to feel unpleasant emotions and feel less guilt than I did. I'm not afraid to stand up for myself and say what I feel.

I feel more patient now with myself and with others. I lose my temper much less often. I enjoy life much more, feel more content and happy over small things. I'm much more aware now of the feelings of others.

I didn't like being around people. Now I actually can enjoy their company. Even parties do not make me nervous like they used to. I am less inclined to condemn others when they are not like me, and I find myself offering suggestions and advice less frequently.

The greatest change that therapy has brought me has been to help me get my confidence again. I have gone through periods of grief three times since I left therapy, when members of my family have died. I do not feel I could have maintained a sense of balance during these times if I had not had the experience of therapy. I feel I am better able to trust my judgment now and can cope with living more effectively.

I feel better about myself, though I do often still feel a sense of guilt. My problems [having to do with a strong father who has condemned the client because of her style of living and has cut off relations with her] are still with me, but I feel that I have learned to face life more squarely and head-on without so much fear. I'm sure that therapy was the most important part of this change.

I feel much more able to relate to my fussy and neurotic parents. Their dark moods and bitterness don't plunge me into the dumps like they used to. Now, when I do get depressed, instead of just wanting to give up, I ask myself what it is that has depressed me, and often I can reason my way out of the negative state I'm in. I can cope with responsibilities much better now. I have fewer doubts now about my abilities.

I feel more inner calm and can cope with daily problems more easily. I have learned that it doesn't pay for me to be a perfectionist about everything. I still admire my desire for perfection in some things that are really important to me, but I no longer fuss with doing a perfect job, for example, patching the trash can.

I've accepted myself as a homosexual, and am happy at work, and feel productive. I am less anxious in relationships with others now. Although I still feel negative judgment from my family, I no longer have suicidal thoughts. I realize that I should live in a way that is true to myself and that others may differ, but I'm OK myself.

I sometimes will give myself a treat, something I never used to do. I will buy myself something that maybe is a little bit frivolous, but I think of this as my own therapy. I feel better about myself and deny myself less. I was almost a stoical nun before. Now I care more about myself. I used to think that spending money to have my hair done was silly and a waste of money. Now I think that if it makes me feel good about myself, and I want to treat myself to it, why not?

I used to analyze everything to the point that I didn't enjoy much and was always asking myself, like the bumper-sticker, am I having fun yet? Now, I just let some things be. It doesn't pay for me to question everything all the time. Now, when I don't like a person, I just accept this. I don't feel guilty because I couldn't see their better side, and I don't feel hostile just because for me the person isn't more likable.

WHAT MAKES PSYCHOTHERAPY SUCCESSFUL

▶ *It is not so much the teacher who teaches but the student who learns.* ◀

Whether or not the client gets value for fee paid to a psychotherapist depends largely on the client.

Don Diespecker in
Does Psychotherapy Really Help People?

Psychotherapy is much more like education than it is like medicine. In education, certain students—no more or less intelligent than others—will nevertheless be more successful. They have well-known characteristics: they are interested in what the experience of education can offer them, and they work hard and regularly.

Very much the same thing holds true in psychotherapy: some clients simply get more from therapy than others. Why? In part it has to do with how well matched a client and the approach of the therapist are. In part it is the amount of confidence the client comes to feel toward the therapist as a person. Beyond these, the qualities of a successful client are very similar to those of a successful student.

Specifically, clients who have successful experiences in therapy tend to share these characteristics:

- While in therapy, they are motivated to change: They feel considerable internal pressure to do something to resolve their problems. They come to feel a sense of initiative and determination. They come to believe in the process of therapy and feel it can be of help to them.
- They are self-disciplined. They keep appointments regularly, they attempt to implement the therapist's recommendations, and they are less incapacitated by their difficulties than other clients with similar problems.
- They have a level of emotional maturity that is high enough to withstand some of the painful feelings or frustrations they encounter in therapy.
- Frequently they come to *enjoy* therapy.

Obviously, a great deal does depend on the therapist. And yet, while a good student can learn much in spite of a poor teacher, a poor student learns little from an excellent teacher. Successful therapy depends primarily on the client.

Other factors can affect your ability to succeed in therapy, but these are factors over which you have no control:

- whether you have the emotional support and sympathy of an understanding and tolerant spouse or family
- whether you have had a long history of emotional problems in connection with work and interpersonal relations (deeply ingrained habits are harder to break)
- whether precipitating factors brought about your present difficulties or they just appeared "out of the blue"
- how long you have had your present problem
- what the problem is: whether it is purely emotional or it has affected your capacity to think coherently and realistically
- whether there have been fortunate or unfortunate events in your life before and during therapy

What the future holds in store for you after therapy relies greatly on many of these same factors and on many of the personality qualities that helped you, or hindered you, as a client in therapy (see Chapter 21).

SO, DOES PSYCHOTHERAPY WORK?

Yes, for certain clients and under certain circumstances. The main changes that psychotherapies aim for are either to eliminate destructive habits of thought, attitude, or behavior or to establish new, constructive habits. Neither one can be accomplished by means of a medically effective treatment that is applied to the patient until a cure occurs.

A few emotional problems fall under the heading of psychiatric disorders and result from physical causes. They include, for example, epilepsy, drug addiction, and Alzheimer's disease. But these conditions are in the minority; most emotional "disorders" have not been traced to underlying physical causes. There are several currently competing hypotheses relating to possible biochemical bases of schizophrenia, mania, depression, and anxiety disorders. As time goes by and medical research progresses, more emotional conditions will very likely be tied to underlying physical problems.

Until that time, however, they remain medically uncurable conditions. At present, the possibility of overcoming them depends heavily on clients themselves, their ability to find an approach to therapy that is appropriate for their personality and their goals or problems, and their good fortune in locating a therapist who is able to help them to summon the faith, energy, determination, and courage necessary to overcome their sense of demoralization.

21
LIFE AFTER THERAPY

Theoretically, psychotherapy is never-ending, since emotional growth can go on as long as one lives.

Lewis R. Wolberg,
The Technique of Psychotherapy

It can be difficult to know when to terminate therapy: difficult for you, the client, and sometimes also difficult for the therapist. Some periods in therapy do not lead to a successful outcome. You may become dissatisfied with the process of therapy or with the therapist. Or, the therapist may become disappointed in your willingness to work and to change. An impasse may be reached where it seems no progress can be made. When this happens, it can be hard to know when to draw a line, to say: "We've tried, but we have to face the fact that we're not getting anywhere." But sometimes this has to be said, and then you may decide to look elsewhere for help.

On the other hand, when your therapy has been successful and has led to clear, constructive results, it may also be difficult to know when to stop. To most clients, what tends to be most important is *relief from symptoms*. When this is achieved, you may be tempted to terminate. But relief from troubling symptoms is not always a sign that problems have been resolved.

282

Frequently, relief from distress comes about because of *problem avoidance*. You may have structured your life in a way that circumvents, rather than faces, the things that trouble you. There are times when this is indeed the best solution. However, the tendency is for clients to associate relief with effective therapy, and often this is not the case.

The therapist, on the other hand, may have certain personal values that he wishes to satisfy before ending therapy with you: he may favor, for example, qualities of assertiveness and ambitiousness (or qualities of submissiveness and compliance), want you to develop these traits, and feel reluctant to end therapy until you have done this.

In general, the decision to terminate therapy should be made with a number of objectives in mind:

• Have your troubling symptoms disappeared or at least been reduced to a level that is tolerable?
• Have you improved your understanding of yourself so that you feel a healthy measure of self-acceptance?
• Do you now have a greater tolerance to frustration?
• Have you developed realistic life goals?
• Are you able to function relatively well in social groups?
• Are you better able to enjoy life and work?

These goals need always to be *tempered*; they all involve comparative judgments that should take into account where you started and what you have accomplished. There is no perfection here, only degrees of adjustment, compromise, and a willingness to accept yourself as a mixture of human weaknesses and strengths.

> . . . [W]e have to content ourselves with the modest objective of freedom from disturbing symptoms, the capacity to function reasonably well, and to experience a modicum of happiness in living.*

FACING RELAPSES

Some therapists believe that therapy cannot be called successful until you have had a relapse and have been able to get

---

*Lewis R. Wolberg, *The Technique of Psychotherapy*, vol. 2, p. 747.

through it on your own. Shadows of old habits linger on. They are especially likely to resurface during periods of insecurity, disappointment, and frustration. They represent a part of you— perhaps a part you would just as soon were not there, but a part of you, nonetheless, that you cannot expect to eradicate completely.

You are much better prepared to face the challenges of the future, of events that cannot be anticipated, and of uncertainties that cannot be avoided, if you do not demand a total change in yourself to the point that old reactions never recur. You are better prepared if you realize that it is likely some will return for brief visits during periods of particular stress. If and when this happens, you can render these visits less distressing and less able to throw you by using the understanding you have gained from therapy.

> You are apt to get a flurry of anxiety and a return of symptoms from time to time. Don't be upset or intimidated by this. The best way to handle yourself is first to realize that your relapse is self-limited. It will eventually come to a halt. Nothing terrible will happen to you. Second, ask yourself what has been going on. Try to figure out what created your upset, what aroused your tension. Relate this to the general patterns that you have been pursuing. . . . Old habits hold on, but they will eventually get less and less provoking.*

HOW TO CARRY ON

Therapy is a temporary crutch or a cast in which to heal, a comfort, a source for renewed faith in yourself, and an experience of learning. It cannot solve all the problems of future living, for these pose new challenges that require of us all that we readjust our goals and expectations, become more resilient and less easily troubled or broken. (The flexible bamboo is more likely to survive a storm than the mighty oak.)

Reducing an individual's rigidity is an objective of all psychotherapies. Becoming less rigid allows you to accommodate to changes and to tolerate external stress more easily. Decreased rigidity helps you adjust to new demands placed on you by your surroundings.

---

*Wolberg, *The Technique of Psychotherapy*, vol. 2, p. 754.

But there is another side to living successfully, and that is, first, the ability to recognize situations and circumstances that cause you excessive stress and, second, the willingness to leave them before it is too late. We tend to place *all* of the responsibility for adjustment to stress on ourselves, on our inner strengths. But often this is unnecessary, unreasonable, and even self-destructive. Often it is the *situation* that is not desirable or tolerable, not a "weakness" in ourselves in being unable to cope with it. It can sometimes take more strength and courage to break free from a pattern of frustration and unhappiness than to remain on, slowly wearing down your resources and growing older fast.

Much of successful living after therapy is a matter of *prevention*: of being aware when you begin to tax yourself more than you need to, when your body and mind begin to tell you that you are developing new habits of anxiety or depression or are starting to reinforce old ones. At these times, take stock of what you are doing, of how your daily living may be in conflict with your values and attitudes. Prevention here means being willing to change an undesirable situation, not just enduring it while trying to change its consequences *in you*.

This is largely a matter of knowing and respecting yourself, of *not* requiring yourself to accept conditions that you feel will lead you to grief. Therapy may help you tolerate stress more easily, but this is one-sided if you do not also learn to protect yourself from stress that is excessive. (Even bamboos can be broken.)

Therapy is an opportunity for you to learn how to cope better with the problems of living. You learn that you can face the demands of life successfully in these ways:

- through belief in yourself and through strength of will
- by diminishing your preoccupation with yourself and developing interests outside yourself
- by understanding your reactions and accepting them rather than fighting yourself
- by living in the present
- by taking yourself less seriously, by developing a sense of humor and perspective

Having learned these things, you then simply do the best you can within the limitations of life.

PART IV
APPENDIXES

APPENDIX A:
Agencies and Organizations That Can Help (United States and Canada)

PART I: UNITED STATES

SELF-HELP ORGANIZATIONS

For General Information

Self-help groups exist for many different kinds of problems. They are listed in many communities by local branches of the Self-Help Clearinghouse. If a branch is not listed in your telephone directory and you would like a listing of self-help groups in your area, contact:

National Self-Help Clearinghouse
25 W. 43rd St.
New York, NY 10036
(212) 840-1259

A fact sheet on self-help groups prepared by the National Institute of Mental Health is available at no charge from:

Consumer Information Center
Department 609K
Pueblo, CO 81009

Also, you may wish to contact:

National Self-Help Resource Center
1729-31 Connecticut Ave., NW
Washington, DC 20009
(202) 387-0194

For a detailed guide to self-help groups, consult *HELP: A Working Guide to Self-Help Groups*, by Alan Gartner and Frank Riessman (New York: New Viewpoints/Vision Books, 1980).

For Specific Problems

For alcoholics:
Alcoholics Anonymous World Services
PO Box 459, Grand Central Station
New York, NY 10163
(212) 686-1100

For families of alcoholics:
Al-Anon Family Group Headquarters
1 Park Ave.
New York, NY 10016
(212) 683-1771

For individuals with emotional problems:
Emotions Anonymous International
1595 Selby Ave.
St. Paul, MN 55104
(612) 647-9712

Neurotics Anonymous
3636 16th St., NW
Washington, DC 20005
(202) 628-4379

For individuals who have been treated for emotional or mental difficulties:
Recovery, Inc.
802 N. Dearborn St.
Chicago, IL 60603
(312) 337-5661

National Alliance for the Mentally Ill
1901 N. Fort Myer Dr.
Ste. 500
Arlington, VA 22209
(703) 524-7600

Autism:
National Society for Autistic Children
Information & Referral Service
1234 Massachusetts Ave., NW
Washington, DC 20005
(202) 783-0125

Epilepsy:
Epilepsy Foundation of America
4351 Garden City Dr.
Landover, MD 20785
(301) 459-3700

Learning disorders:
Council for Exceptional Children
1920 Association Dr.
Reston, VA 22091
(703) 620-3660

For families who have children with behavior problems:
Families Anonymous
PO Box 528
Van Nuys, CA 91426
(818) 989-7841

For single parents with children:
Parents Without Partners International
7910 Woodmont Ave.
Washington, DC 20014
(301) 654-8850

For parents of abused children:
Parents Anonymous
7120 Franklin Ave.
Los Angeles, CA 90046
(213) 876-9642

For pathological gamblers:
Gamblers Anonymous
PO Box 17173
Los Angeles, CA 90017
(213) 386-8789

For families of pathological gamblers:
Gam-Anon
PO Box 4549
Downey, CA 90241
(213) 469-2751

For individuals with phobias:
TERRAP
1010 Doyle St.
Menlo Park, CA 94025
(415) 329-1233

For obesity:
Overeaters Anonymous
2190 W. 190th St.
Torrance, CA 90504
(213) 320-7941

Weight Watchers International
800 Community Dr.
Manhasset, NY 11030
(516) 627-9200

For narcotics addicts:
Narcotics Anonymous
8061 Vineland Ave.
Sun Valley, CA 91352
(213) 768-6203

National Association on Drug Abuse Problems
160 N. Franklin
Hempstead, NY 11550
(516) 481-0220

PROFESSIONAL ASSOCIATIONS

American Academy of Psychoanalysis
30 E. 40th St.
New York, NY 10016
(212) 679-4105

American Association for Marriage and Family Therapy
1717 K St., NW
Suite 407
Washington, DC 20006
(202) 429-1825

American Association of Sex Educators, Counselors
and Therapists
11 Dupont Circle, NW
Suite 220
Washington, DC 20036
(202) 462-1171

American Psychiatric Association
1400 K St., NW
Washington, DC 20005
(202) 682-6000

American Psychological Association
1200 17th St., NW
Washington, DC 20036
(202) 955-7686

Association for Advancement of Behavioral Therapy
15 W. 36th St.
New York, NY 10011
(212) 279-7970

National Association of Social Workers
7981 Eastern Ave.
Silver Spring, MD 20907
(301) 565-0333

PART II: CANADA
SELF-HELP ORGANIZATIONS
For General Information

The Centre for Service to the Public publishes the annual *Index to Federal Programs & Services*, which contains descriptions of more than 1,100 programs and services administered by federal departments, agencies, and Crown Corporations. The Centre also operates the Canada Service Bureaus throughout Canada, which provide telephone referral services for individuals interested in locating federal agencies and programs. Contact:

Centre for Service to the Public
365 Laurier Ave., W.
Ottawa, ON K1A 065
(613) 993-6342

Also, you may wish to contact:

Department of National Health and Welfare
Social Service Programs Branch
National Welfare Grants Program, 7th fl.
Brooke Claxton Building
Tunney's Pasture
Ottawa, ON K1A 1B5
(613) 990-9563

Canadian Mental Health Association
2160 Yonge St.
Toronto, ON M4S 2Z3
(416) 484-7750

For information about community services, contact:

Voluntary Action
Department of Secretary of State
15 Eddy St., Hull
Ottawa, ON K1A 0M5
(819) 994-2255

For Specific Problems

For alcoholics:
Alcoholics Anonymous
Intergroup Office
272 Eglinton Ave., W.
Toronto, ON M4R 1B2
(416) 487-5591

ADDICS (Alcohol & Drug Dependency
  Information & Counselling Services)
818 Portage Ave., #209
Winnipeg, MB R3G 0N4
(204) 775-1233

For individuals who are mentally or physically disabled:
Disabled Peoples' International (DPI)
207-294 Portage Ave.
Winnipeg, MB R3C 1K2
(204) 942-3604

For individuals who have been treated for emotional or mental difficulties:
Mental Patients Association
2146 Yew St.
Vancouver, BC V6K 3G7
(604) 738-5177

Autism:
Autism Society Canada
Box 472, Sta. A
Scarborough, ON M1K 5C3
(416) 444-8528

Epilepsy:
Epilepsy Ontario
2160 Yonge St., 1st fl.
Toronto, ON M4S 2A9
(416) 489-2825

Learning disorders:
Canadian Association for Children
  and Adults with Learning Disabilities
323 Chapel St.
Ottawa, ON K1N 7Z2
(613) 238-5721

For families who have children with emotional and behavior problems:
Ontario Association of Children's Mental Health Centres
40 St. Clair Ave., E., #309
Toronto, ON M4T 1M9
(416) 921-2109

For single parents with children:
One Parent Families Association of Canada
2279 Yonge St., #17
Toronto, ON M4P 2C7
(416) 487-7976

For narcotics addicts:
ADDICS (Alcohol & Drug Dependency
  Information & Counseling Services)
818 Portage Ave., #209
Winnipeg, MB R3G 0N4
(204) 775-1233

PROFESSIONAL ASSOCIATIONS

Canadian Psychiatric Association
225 Lisgar St., #103
Ottawa, ON K2P 0C6
(613) 234-2815

Canadian Psychoanalytic Society
7000 Côte des Neiges Rd.
Montreal, QC H3S 2C1
(514) 738-6105

Canadian Psychological Association
558 King Edward Ave.
Ottawa, ON K1N 7N6
(613) 238-4409

Council of Provincial Associations of Psychology
558 King Edward Ave.
Ottawa, ON K1N 7N6
(613) 238-4409

Ontario Psychological Association
1407 Yonge St., #402
Toronto, ON M4T 1Y7
(416) 961-5552

Ontario Association for Marriage and Family Therapy
271 Russell Hill Rd.
Toronto, ON M4V 2T5
(416) 968-7779

Canadian Association of Social Workers
55 Parkdale Ave., #316
Ottawa, ON K1Y 1E5
(613) 728-1865

Corporation Professionnelle des Travailleurs Sociaux du Quebec
5757 Decelles Ave., Ch. 335
Montreal, QC H3S 2C3
(514) 731-2749

Canadian Guidance & Counseling Association
Faculty of Education
University of Ottawa
651 Cumberland St., Rm. 427
Ottawa, ON K1N 6N5
(613) 234-2572

APPENDIX B:
Suggestions for Further Reading

GENERAL INFORMATION

Greenberg, Bette. *How to Find Out in Psychiatry: A Guide to Sources of Mental Health Information*. New York: Pergamon Press, 1978.

Powell, Barbara, J. *A Layman's Guide to Mental Health Problems and Treatments*. Springfield, IL: Charles C. Thomas, 1981.

Russell, Bertrand. *The Conquest of Happiness*. New York: Bantam, 1968 (first published in 1930). [One of the most psychologically perceptive attempts to identify the basic ingredients for a happy life, by a philosopher who made original contributions to whatever subjects he touched.]

Strupp, Hans H. *Patients View Their Psychotherapy*. Baltimore: Johns Hopkins Press, 1969. [Evaluations by patients of their experiences in psychotherapy.]

———. *Psychotherapists in Action*. New York: Grune & Stratton, 1960. [Focuses on what the therapist actually does in the therapy relationship.]

Watson, Robert I., Jr. *Psychotherapies: A Comparative Casebook*. New York: Holt, Reinhart and Winston, 1977. [A collection of cases treated by means of different approaches to psychotherapy.]

Wheelis, Allen. *How People Change*. New York: Harper & Row, 1973. [An insightful book about the process of therapy.]

A. PSYCHOANALYSIS (CHAPTER 9)

Brenner, Charles. *An Elementary Textbook of Psychoanalysis*. New York: International Universities Press, 1973. [A world-famous introduction to analysis that has now been translated into nine languages.]

Hall, Calvin. *A Primer of Freudian Psychology*. New York: New American Library, 1954. [Perhaps the clearest and most concise summary of psychoanalytic concepts.]

Jones, Ernest. *The Life and Work of Sigmund Freud*. New York: Basic Books, 1953-57. 3 volumes. [A biography of Freud that describes his personal development and summarizes his main contributions.]

B. CLIENT-CENTERED THERAPY (CHAPTER 10)

Rogers, Carl Ronsom. *Client-Centered Therapy*. Boston: Houghton Mifflin, 1951. [A good introduction to Rogers's approach to therapy. It was his first major exposition of his theory.]

———. *On Becoming a Person: A Therapist's View of Psychotherapy*. Boston: Houghton Mifflin, 1961. [Perhaps Rogers's best-known book. It gives a very personal view of his approach.]

C. GESTALT THERAPY (CHAPTER 10)

Fagan, J., and I. L. Sheperd, eds. *Gestalt Therapy Now*. Palo Alto: Science and Behavior Books, 1970. New York: Harper and Row, 1971. [A collection of articles on Gestalt theory, technique, and applications by well-known Gestalt therapists.]

Perls, Frederick S. *Gestalt Therapy Verbatim*. Moab, UT: Real People Press, 1965. [Probably the most widely read of Perls's books illustrating the Gestalt approach.]

D. TRANSACTIONAL ANALYSIS (CHAPTER 10)

Berne, Eric. *Games People Play*. New York: Grove Press, 1964. [A simply written summary of the main concepts of TA: ego states, transactions, games, etc.]

————. *What Do You Say After You Say Hello?* New York: Grove Press, 1972. [Published after Berne's death, this is an outline of his approach to therapy, focusing on his notion of life scripts.]

E. RATIONAL-EMOTIVE THERAPY (CHAPTER 10)

Ellis, Albert. *Humanistic Psychotherapy: The Rational-Emotive Approach*. New York: McGraw-Hill, 1973. [A clear statement of the way people can choose to make, or not make, themselves emotionally disturbed.]

————, and Robert A. Harper. *A New Guide to Rational Living*. Englewood Cliffs, NJ: Prentice Hall, 1975. [One of the best-known self-help books dealing with rational-emotive therapy.]

F. EXISTENTIAL-HUMANISTIC THERAPY (CHAPTER 10)

Arbuckle, D. *Counseling and Psychotherapy: An Existential-Humanistic View*. Boston: Allyn & Bacon, 1975. [A good introduction to this approach to therapy.]

Binswanger, Ludwig. *Being-in-the-World: Selected Papers of Ludwig Binswanger*. New York: Basic Books, 1963. [A less readable book that nevertheless gives the reader a sense of how existentialism has been applied to psychotherapy.]

May, Rollo, Ernst Angel, and Henri Ellenberger, eds. *Existence*. New York: Basic Books, 1958. [A collection of essays dealing with basic topics of existential-humanistic psychotherapy.]

G. LOGOTHERAPY (CHAPTER 11)

Frankl, Victor. *Man's Search for Meaning: An Introduction to Logotherapy*. New York: Washington Square Press, 1959. [A clear and gripping description of the development of logotherapy as a result of concentration camp suffering.]

———. *The Doctor and the Soul.* New York: Knopf, 1963. [A further description of logotherapy.]

H. REALITY THERAPY (CHAPTER 11)

Glasser, William. *Reality Therapy.* New York: Harper and Row, 1965. [Glasser describes his view that, because of loneliness and feelings of inadequacy, people tend to refuse to take responsibility for fulfilling their needs for love and worth.]
See also Glasser's book, *Positive Addiction,* listed under "T. Therapeutic Exercise."

I. ADLERIAN THERAPY (CHAPTER 11)

Adler, Alfred. *Problems of Neurosis: A Book of Case-Histories.* New York: Harper Torchbooks, 1964 (first published in 1929). [These are case examples illustrating Adler's theory of neurotic development. The book contains an introduction by H. L. Ansbacher that summarizes basic Adlerian theory.]
———. *Social Interest: A Challenge to Mankind.* New York: Capricorn Books, 1964 (first published in 1929). [This is the last exposition given by Adler of his thought. It is a good and simply written summary of Adlerian psychology.]

J. BIOENERGETICS (CHAPTER 11)

Keleman, S. *Sexuality, Self and Survival.* San Francisco: Lodestar Press, 1971.
Lowen, Alexander. *The Betrayal of the Body.* New York: Collier, 1967.

K. PRIMAL THERAPY (CHAPTER 11)

Janov, Arthur. *The Anatomy of Mental Illness: The Scientific Basis of Primal Therapy.* New York: G. P. Putnam, 1971.
———. *Primal Scream.* New York: Dell, 1971.

L. IMPLOSIVE THERAPY (CHAPTER 11)

Stampfl, Thomas G., and D. Levis. *Implosive Therapy: Theory and Technique*. Morristown, NJ: General Learning Press, 1973.

M. DIRECT DECISION THERAPY (CHAPTER 11)

Greenwald, Harold. *Decision Therapy*. New York: Peter H. Wyden, 1973.

——, and Elizabeth Rich. *The Happy Person*. New York: Stein and Day, 1984. [A very readable summary of direct decision therapy.]

N. COUNTER-CONDITIONING (CHAPTER 12)
O. BEHAVIOR MODIFICATION (CHAPTER 12)
P. COGNITIVE APPROACHES TO BEHAVIOR CHANGE (CHAPTER 12)

Alberti, R. E., and M. L. Emmons. *Stand Up, Speak Out, Talk Back*. New York: Pocket Books, 1975. [On assertiveness training.]

Burns, David. *Feeling Good: The New Mood Therapy*. New York: Signet, 1980. [A good self-help account of the general cognitive approach to behavior change.]

Kanfer, F. H., and A. P. Goldstein, eds. *Helping People Change*. New York: Pergamon Press, 1975. [This large book discusses operant, cognitive change, and self-control methods. The emphasis is on how these techniques of behavior change are used in a clinical setting.]

Wolpe, Joseph. *The Practice of Behavior Therapy*. New York: Pergamon Press, 1973. [One of the major contributors to behavioral psychotherapy describes the use of techniques to encourage behavior change.]

Q. GROUP THERAPY (CHAPTER 13)

Grotjahn, Martin, Frank M. Kline, and Claude T. H. Friedman, eds. *Handbook of Group Therapy*. New York: Van Nostrand, 1983.

Helmering, Doris W. *Group Therapy: Who Needs It?* Millbrae, CA: Celestial Arts, 1976. [A good informal summary of group therapy.]

R. MARRIAGE THERAPY (CHAPTER 14)
S. FAMILY THERAPY (CHAPTER 14)

Fay, Allen. *Making Things Better by Making Them Worse.* New York: Hawthorne Books, 1978. [A variety of applications of therapeutic paradoxical strategies in marriage communication, as well as in connection with the treatment of anxiety, depression, fears, etc.]

Foley, Vincent D. *An Introduction to Family Therapy.* New York: Grune & Stratton, 1974.

Haley, Jay, ed. *Changing Families: A Family Therapy Reader.* New York: Grune & Stratton, 1971.

Watzlawick, Paul, John Weakland, and Richard Fisch. *Change: Principles of Problem Formation and Problem Resolution.* New York: Norton, 1974. [A readable and entertaining description of the tendency of family and marriage systems to resist change and a good explanation of the use of paradoxical strategies to encourage constructive change.]

T. THERAPEUTIC EXERCISE (CHAPTER 15)

Fixx, James F. *The Complete Book of Running.* New York: Random House, 1977. [See Chapter 2, "What Happens to Your Mind."]

Glasser, William. *Positive Addiction.* New York: Harper and Row, 1976. [Glasser proposes that some activities such as running and meditation are positive addictions; their practice can help a person grow emotionally stronger.]

Glover, Bob, and Jack Shepherd. *The Runner's Handbook.* New York: Viking Press, 1977. [See Chapter 15, "Stress and Tension," and Chapter 16, "Running Inside Your Head."]

Kostrubala, Thaddeus. *The Joy of Running.* Philadelphia: J. B. Lippincott, 1976. [See Chapters 6, 7, and 8 on "Psychological Effects," "Theory," and "Running and Therapy."

U. BIOFEEDBACK (CHAPTER 15)

Brown, B. B. *Stress and the Art of Biofeedback.* New York: Harper and Row, 1977. [Reviews the effectiveness of biofeedback.]

Weiss, Anne E. *Biofeedback: Fact or Fad?* New York: Franklin Watts, 1984. [A clear, informal presentation of biofeedback.]

V. RELAXATION TRAINING (CHAPTER 15)

Benson, Herbert. *The Relaxation Response.* New York: Morrow, 1975.

Jacobson, E. *Progressive Relaxation.* Chicago: University of Chicago Press, 1930. [One of the first studies to examine systematic muscle relaxation.]

W. HYPNOSIS (CHAPTER 15)

Erickson, Milton, Ernest L. Rossi, and Sheila I. Rossi. *Hypnotic Realities: The Induction of Clinical Hypnosis and Forms of Indirect Suggestion.* New York: Irvington Publishers, 1976.

Wallace, Benjamin. *Applied Hypnosis: An Overview.* Chicago: Nelson-Hall, 1979. [A general description of hypnosis.]

Wolberg, Lewis R. *Hypnosis: Is It for You?* New York: Harcourt Brace Jovanovich, 1972. [A good, general description of hypnosis and its use in the context of psychotherapy.]

X. MEDITATION (CHAPTER 15)

Carrington, Patricia. *Freedom in Meditation.* Garden City, NY: Anchor Press, 1977. [By a clinical psychologist who uses meditation with her patients, a practical and comprehensive discussion of meditation and its connection with the human problems that bring people to psychotherapy.]

Glasser, William. *Positive Addiction.* New York: Harper and Row, 1976. [See Chapter 6, "Meditation."]

LeShan, Lawrence. *How to Meditate: A Guide to Self-Discovery.* Boston: Little, Brown & Co., 1974. [An intelligent and modest practical approach to meditation.]

Y. DRUG THERAPY (CHAPTER 16)

Leavitt, Fred. *Drugs and Behavior.* New York: Wiley, 1982.

Physician's Desk Reference to Pharmaceutical Specialties and Biologicals. New Jersey: Medical Economics, Inc. [Published annually with quarterly supplements. Gives detailed information about drugs, side effects, potential risks, etc.]

Swonger, Alvin K., and Larry L. Constantine. *Drugs and Therapy: A Psychotherapist's Handbook of Psychotropic Drugs.* Boston: Little, Brown & Co., 1976.

Z. DIET THERAPY (CHAPTER 16)

Fredericks, Carlton. *Psycho-Nutrition*. New York: Grosset & Dunlap, 1976.

Watson, George. *Nutrition and Your Mind: The Psychochemical Response*. New York: Harper and Row, 1972.

ON LEGAL ISSUES IN PSYCHOTHERAPY (CHAPTER 19)

Cohen, Ronald Jay. *Legal Guidebook in Mental Health*. New York: Free Press, 1982.

Gutheil, Thomas G., and Paul S. Appelbaum. *Clinical Handbook of Psychiatry and the Law*. New York: McGraw-Hill, 1982.

Hofling, Charles K., ed. *Law and Ethics in the Practice of Psychiatry*. New York: Brunner/Mazel, 1981.

ON THE EFFECTIVENESS OF PSYCHOTHERAPY (CHAPTER 20)

Eysenck, Hans J. "The Battle over Therapeutic Effectiveness," in Jusuf Hariman, ed., *Does Psychotherapy Really Help People?* Springfield, IL: Charles C. Thomas, 1984, pp. 52-61.

——. *The Effects of Psychotherapy*. New York: Inter-Science Press, 1966.

Hariman, Jusuf, ed. *Does Psychotherapy Really Help People?* Springfield, IL: Charles C. Thomas, 1984. [A collection of evaluative articles about psychotherapy.]

——. *The Therapeutic Efficacy of the Major Psychotherapeutic Techniques*. Springfield, IL: Charles C. Thomas, 1982. [A collection of papers about the therapeutic effectiveness of a variety of approaches to psychotherapy.]

Rachman, S., and G. T. Wilson. *The Effects of Psychological Therapy*. Oxford: Pergamon Press, 1980.

Wolff, Werner, ed. *Success in Psychotherapy*. New York: Grune & Stratton, 1952.

INDEX